THE TIGER TANKS

▼ A Tiger 2 with production turret in Budapest between 16 and 18 October 1944.

▶ The 'Stalking Tiger' unit flash of 501 Heavy Tank Battalion, the first of the heavy tank battalions to be formed, traced from a Battalion signboard in Tunis. (Lidderdale)

THE TIGER TANKS

PETER GUDGIN

Arms and Armour

Arms and Armour Press
A Cassell Imprint
Villiers House, 41-47 Strand, London WC2N 5JE.

Distributed in the USA by Sterling Publishing Co. Inc., 387 Park Avenue South, New York, NY 10016-8810.

Distributed in Australia by Capricorn Link (Australia) Pty. Ltd, P.O. Box 665, Lane Cove, New South Wales 2066, Australia.

© Peter Gudgin, 1991
All rights reserved. No part of this book may be reproduced or transmitted in any form or by any means electronic or mechanical including photocopying recording or any information storage and retrieval system without permission in writing from the Publisher.

British Library Cataloguing in Publication Data
Gudgin, Peter
The Tiger tanks.
1. Germany. Tanks (Armoured vehicles), history
I. Title
358.183
ISBN 0-85368-929-6

Designed and edited by DAG Publications Ltd. Designed by David Gibbons; edited by Michael Boxall; layout by Anthony A. Evans; typeset by Ronset Typesetters, Darwen, Lancashire; jacket illustration colour simulation by Robert A. Phasey; printed and bound in Great Britain by Courier International Ltd, Tiptree, Essex.

CONTENTS

Acknowledgements, 6

Introduction, 7

One: Background History, 12

Two: Porsche Tiger, 26
VK 3001(P) (Typ 100 – Leopard), 26
VK 4501(P) (Typ 101 – Tiger), 27
Pz Jäg Tiger (P) (Elefant, formerly Ferdinand), 32
VK 4502, 35
Maus (Typ 205), 35

Three: The Tiger 1, 37
DW 1, 37
VK 6501 (SW), 37
DW2, 38
VK 3001(H), 39
VK 3601, 41
VK 4501(H), 42
Pz Kpfw VI(H) (Tiger), Sd Kfz 181, 45

Four: Variants of the Tiger 1, 63
Pz Bef Wg Tiger, Ausf E (Sd Kfz 267 und 268), 65
Flammtiger, 65
38cm RW61 auf Stu Mrs Tiger, 65

Five: The Tiger 2 (Royal Tiger), 74
VK 4502(P), 74
VK 4503, 75
Pz Kpfw Tiger, Ausf B (Sd Kfz 182) (Königstiger), 77

Six: The Hunting Tiger (Jagdtiger), 83

Seven: Tigers in Combat, 91
1. Tiger 1, 91
   The First Tiger Action, 96; In Tunisia, 99; In Sicily, 117; On the Eastern Front, 118; In Italy, 126; In France and Germany, 128
2. Stu Mrs Tiger, 130
3. Pz Jäg Tiger (P) – Elefant, 131
4. Tiger 2, 133
   On the Eastern Front, 133; In Normandy and the Ardennes, 135
5. Hunting Tiger (Jagdtiger), 137

Postscript, 140

Source Notes, 151
Glossary, 153
Bibliography, 155
Index, 157

ACKNOWLEDGEMENTS

ALTHOUGH much of the content of this book stems from my own library, notes and photoarchive, I must gratefully acknowledge the assistance given to me by, among others, the Bovington Tank Museum, the Department of Photographs of the Imperial War Museum, the Federal German Bundesarchiv at Koblenz and the Bundesarchiv/Militärarchiv at Freiburg i. Br., the tank museum of the Kampftruppenschule II at Münster (Lager), the museum of the US Army Ordnance Center & School at Aberdeen Proving Ground, Md., the French Tank Museum at Saumur and its curator, Lieutenant-Colonel Michel Aubry, and the Directors of Thyssen Henschel at Kassel.

I am particularly grateful to: Frank Bull for many of the drawings; George Forty and David Fletcher of the Bovington Tank Museum for much help with documents and advice; Douglas Lidderdale, now of Bromley, who, as a REME major, was in charge of the team bringing the first Tiger back to the UK; Kenneth H. Powers of the US Ordnance Tank Museum, for help with photographs beyond the call of duty; Wilhem Hartmann, former Oberleutnant, Battalion Technical Officer and Commander of No 1 (Tiger) Company of s.Pz.Abt.501, for permitting me to use his excellent collection of Tiger photographs; Brigadegeneral a.D. August Seidensticker, former Commander of s.Pz.Abt.504, Brigadegeneral a.D. Hans-Georg Lueder, former Commander of s.Pz.Abt.501; and, last but not least, my wife, for her patience and excellent proof-reading.

Peter Gudgin

INTRODUCTION

THE TIGER 1 was a legend in its time, soon ousting the dreaded '88' anti-tank gun as the German weapon most feared by Allied tank crews. Although not so well-designed as the later Panther, the sheer slab-sided juggernaut size of the vehicle, together with the fact that its main armament was that same '88', was enough to impress all who saw it with the sense of its power and invincibility.

Reaction of Allied tank crews and infantry on first encountering the Tiger in action was one of wonder tinged with awe, to which I can personally testify as a member of a recently equipped Churchill tank battalion forming part of 21 Army Tank Brigade newly landed in French North Africa in March 1943. I and my fellow officers were naïvely convinced of the invincibility of the thickly armoured Churchill; even against the dreaded and legendary '88', the 8.8cm FlaK 36 anti-aircraft gun used in the anti-tank role, we felt reasonably secure. When, however, in April 1943 we detrained at the railhead at Ghardimâou in Tunisia, we were stunned to see the damage inflicted by this gun on the knocked-out Churchills of 25 Army Tank Brigade, which had preceded us to North Africa, awaiting evacuation to base workshops for scrap, cannibalization or repair. When we learned in an Intelligence briefing that this gun was now mounted on a new tank known as the Mark VI or Tiger,[1] first encountered in Tunisia earlier that year, we knew that our tanks were in for a difficult time!

My personal experience of the Tiger started on 21 April 1943, when my Churchill IV and that of a fellow troop leader were knocked out by one, together with its covering Pz Kpfw III and IV, belonging to 504 Heavy Tank Battalion. This particular Tiger was in turn put out of action by another of our tanks, but was so little damaged (the lucky telling shot had jammed the turret) that, on capture the following morning, it was found to be almost fully serviceable.[2] After being repaired and refurbished by 104 Army Tank Workshop REME, it was put on exhibition in Tunis, where it was examined by HM King George VI, the Prime Minister, Winston Churchill, and other VIPs, prior to its shipment to UK in September 1943 for detailed examination and testing.

In the meantime, I too had been evacuated to UK, in my case to convalesce, prior to joining the School of Tank Technology (STT), a wing of the Military College of Science, at Chertsey. STT not only ran year-long courses in tank technology but was also responsible for the examination of all captured AFVs

◀ An early production model Tiger 1 in the colours and markings used in Tunisia by s.Pz.Abt.501; the turret number '142' is that of the Platoon Sergeant of '4' Platoon (troop) of No. 1 Company. (Author's Collection)

▶ Middle production model Tiger 1 of 504 Heavy Tank Battalion, in Tunisia before capture on 22 April 1943; this tank belonged to the platoon commander of '3' Platoon, No. 1 Company, and carried the turret number '131'. (Author's Collection)

Introduction 7

and the subsequent publication of reports on these vehicles, with the assistance of the Department of Tank Design (DTD) and the Fighting Vehicle Proving Establishment (FVPE), Ministry of Supply establishments also located at Chertsey. Pending the commencement of my course in November 1943, I was attached to the STT staff as part of the examination team; imagine my surprise when I was joined there by the Tiger reponsible for my presence in UK. As a member of the examination team, I wrote those parts of the exhaustive report on the tank which dealt with its armament, fighting arrangements and stowage, a preliminary report being published in November 1943 and the report proper in instalments between January and September 1944.[3] Because of the influx of enemy tanks and other AFVs of later design consequent upon the Allied landings in Italy and Normandy, this report was never completed and the tank itself never re-assembled after its thorough strip examination; it sits now in the Tank Museum at Bovington.

On graduating from the School of Tank Technology I was posted to MI 10, the technical Intelligence branch of the War Office Directorate of Military Intelligence. There, from November 1944 to November 1947, I was responsible for the collation, evaluation and dissemination of all Intelligence on foreign armoured fighting vehicles; during and immediately after the war in Europe, my main concern on this desk was with German AFVs in production and under development, as well as with the producers of these vehicles and their components. Thus I was at the centre of all reports on variants of the Tiger 1, on the Tiger(P) and on the Königstiger and Jagdtiger, and had access to all the important personalities in German tank design and production for interrogation. Finally, I was responsible, in 1946–7, for writing the official War Office history of German AFV development and production from 1933 to 1945.[4] These then are my qualifications for writing this book.

Of all the combatant countries in the Second World War, Germany and the Soviet Union had the clearest appreciation of the overriding importance of firepower in the design of a tank. In all tanks designed in Germany, between the start of re-armament in the 1930s and the end of the war in Europe in 1945, firepower was accorded top priority over the other tank characteristics, mobility and protection, by those responsible for writing German tank operational requirements. This appreciation resulted in German tanks having the advantage of their enemy equivalents, as the German tank guns invariably had superior penetrative performance to those of the Allies, able to penetrate

▲ The same tank in the position in which it was knocked out by tanks of 'A' Squadron, 48 Royal Tank Regiment, on 21 April 1943; it was virtually undamaged, and was the first Tiger to fall into Allied hands in this condition. (IWM)

wagen VI (H), as the Tiger was originally called, made its premature appearance in prototype form on the Eastern Front in August 1942.

Although placing most emphasis on firepower, the German tank designers did not neglect either mobility or protection. Adequate, if not outstanding mobility was obtained by the use of cast steel skeleton dry pin tracks and an adequate number of road wheels running on them to give nominal ground pressures in the range 6 to 14 psi, combined with an engine of sufficient power to give a power-to-weight ratio of from 10 to 15 bhp/tonne.

Protection was given by rolled steel armour, initially bolted and later welded to give a box-shaped hull, to which a rectangular superstructure, overhanging the tracks on each side and carrying the turret ring, was bolted. The turret, carrying the main armament, was a welded construction of flat rolled plate, angled to give greater strength and to make penetration slightly more difficult, which rotated on the ring in the superstructure. The overhanging superstructure sides permitted the use of a turret ring of larger diameter than would have been the case had the superstructure been only as wide as the width between the tracks, as was the case with all Allied tanks produced prior to, and the majority produced during the Second World War. As the turret ring diameter dictates the maximum permitted length of recoil of the main armament, as well as the maximum length of ammunition that can be loaded, it thus also dictates the maximum calibre and muzzle velocity permissible for the main armament. This form of construction enabled the Germans consistently to up-gun their tanks and out-gun their opponents during the War.

The protection conferred by this form of construction was adequate and derived largely from the thickness of the near-vertical armoured front and side plates. Initially, it exceeded that on the Soviet BT and T-26, as well as on the British cruiser and light tanks; with the introduction of the first Tiger, it exceeded that on any tank in service in any of the Allied armies. When, however, on examination of captured Soviet T-34 tanks, the superior protection and strength afforded by sloping the armour was realized, the box form of construction was abandoned by the German and armour sloped similarly to that of the T-34 was introduced on later tanks and self-propelled anti-tank guns.

The development and production by Germany of most armaments, including tanks, had been banned by the Allies after the First World War under the terms of the Treaty of Versailles; this, however, had not stopped

their opponents' armour from ranges at which they themselves were immune to the guns of the Allied tanks.

The German belief in the supreme importance of firepower in tank design was reinforced by their examination of French and British tanks captured in the advance through France in 1940; the German General Staff was impressed by both the thickness and the quality of the cast armour on, for example, the French R35 and Char B and the British infantry tank Mark II Matilda, and emphasized, in their specifications for future tanks, the need for them to be armed with guns able to defeat the thicker armour to be expected on future British tanks.[5] The shock resulting from their encounter with the Soviet T-34 in quantity in 1941 further reinforced the German belief in bigger and better tank guns and, perforce, in bigger and heavier tanks to carry them. This policy led directly to the design and production of the Tiger tanks, about which so much has been written since the first Panzerkampf-

Introduction 9

the Germans from starting the design of tanks in the early 1920s under the guise of designing agricultural tractors, and assembling and testing the prototypes secretly in Communist Russia and neutral Sweden in the mid-1920s. If the Allies knew of this they ignored it, and thus were the foundations laid for the emergence, ten years or so later, of the German Panzer force which so brilliantly executed the *Blitzkrieg* tactics, based on the ideas of the British tank tacticians B. H. Liddell Hart and J. F. C. Fuller, used to defeat the armies of Poland, France and, initially, the USSR from 1939 until 1942.

With the coming to power of the National Socialists in Germany in 1933, German rearmament started in earnest, and the development and production of Landwirtschaftliche Schleppern (La.S.) or agricultural tractors, as their first tanks were known, started in Germany proper. The assembly of the first batch started towards the end of December 1933. The first vehicle ran on 3 February 1934, and, by the end of July 1934, further orders for a total of 150 vehicles had been placed with Henschel und Sohn GmbH of Kassel.[6] These vehicles were given the official nomenclature of 'Pz Kpfw I (Sd Kfz 101)' in the Ordnance Inventory when they were accepted into service; they were first used operationally in the Spanish Civil War.

From 1933 until the end of the war in Europe in June 1945, all German tanks on being accepted for service, were allotted an official name in the Ordnance Inventory; this took the form of 'Panzerkampfwagen' (normally abbreviated to 'Pz Kpfw' and sometimes to 'Pz Kw', and meaning 'Armoured Fighting Vehicle') followed by a Roman numeral, and a 'Sonderkraftfahrzeug Nummer' (Special Motor Vehicle Number), abbreviated to 'Sd Kfz', in the 100 series. The various models of a particular tank were distinguished by letters, starting at the beginning of the alphabet for the earliest model and progressing in alphabetical order as each succeeding one was introduced. The model was indicated by the word 'Ausführung', usually abbreviated to 'Ausf'. Thus, the entry in the Ordnance Inventory for

▼ The same tank during its detailed examination at Chertsey by the School of Tank Technology in November 1943. Note the British First Army shield and the 21 Army Tank Brigade diabolo, applied after capture when it went on display in Tunis in June of that year. (Author's Collection)

the La.S., on its being accepted for service, read: 'Panzerkampfwagen I (Sd Kfz 101) Ausf A'. The Sd Kfz numbers were allocated in bands of ten by vehicle weight class; the Pz Kpfw I was allocated the numbers from 101 to 111 while the Pz Kpfw II had numbers in the 120 series, the Pz Kpfw III in the 140 series and so on. Tank destroyers and other self-propelled guns on tank chassis were also allocated Sd Kfz numbers in the 100 series, but half-track and wheeled armoured vehicles had numbers in the 200 series.

The Pz Kpfw I and II were light tanks, lightly armed and armoured, intended basically for reconnaissance and, as they were relatively cheap and simple to produce, for training; their small size and light weight also helped to allay the suspicions of her erstwhile enemies as to Germany's intentions. They were not, however, capable of taking on the heavier tanks known by the Germans to be in service with the French, British and Soviet armies, for which purpose heavier and better-protected tanks with more powerful main armament would be required.

Development contracts were therefore placed in 1935 with the firms of MAN, Krupp and Rheinmetall Borsig for a tank in the 20-tonne weight class, and in 1936 with MAN, Rheinmetall Borsig and Daimler-Benz for one of about 15 tonnes. These were known initially as the VK 2001 or BW (Bataillonsführerwagen – battalion commander's vehicle) and the ZW (Zugführerwagen – platoon or troop commander's vehicle), respectively; on being accepted for service, the BW became the Pz Kpfw IV (Sd Kfz 161) and the ZW, the Pz Kpfw III (Sd Kfz 141). The 'VK 2001' was the first project to employ what thereafter became the standard Heereswaffenamt form of nomenclature for experimental tank projects; the 'VK' stood for 'Vollkettenfahrzeug' (fully tracked vehicle), the first two digits of the following four-digit number indicating the designed weight class in tonnes and the last two, the number of the design within that weight class. Thus, 'VK 2001' signified the first design for a 20-tonne fully tracked vehicle.

The Germans had shown great interest in pre-war British, French and Soviet development of multi-turreted heavy tanks; this interest was evidenced by their efforts to acquire by espionage details of the Vickers Independent, as a result of which the British Army officer Captain Norman Baillie-Stewart was convicted and imprisoned in the Tower of London in 1933 for passing some of this information to them.

The interest in heavy tanks on the part of the German General Staff persisted throughout the Second World War, reinforced by the detailed interest taken by Hitler both in tanks in general and in heavy tanks in particular. Hitler's influence on the development of German heavy tanks should not be under-estimated; neither should that of his favourite designer, responsible also for the design of the original Volkswagen or 'people's car', namely Dr.-Ing.h.c. Ferdinand Porsche, as will be seen from later chapters. The Tiger 1, and its successor, the Pz Kpfw Tiger Model B (Königstiger, Tiger 2 or Royal Tiger), were the heaviest tanks to see service on either side, with combat weights of 56 and 68 tonnes, respectively; the Jagdtiger, based on the Royal Tiger, was even heavier, at 72 tonnes, and was easily the heaviest self-propelled anti-tank gun in service anywhere in 1945. Even heavier tanks, with weights in excess of 150 tonnes, were being built and tested in prototype form by the Germans when the war in Europe ended in 1945; none was sufficiently developed, however, to take part in the closing engagements of the war.

All tank nomenclatures, weights and dimensions quoted in this book are taken from the original German D-Vorschriften (User Handbooks) and Heerestechnische Verordnungsblätter (HtV-Army Technical Bulletins) for the vehicles concerned, converted where necessary into imperial units. The vehicle weights quoted are combat weights, with the vehicle fully crewed and stowed with crew personal weapons and equipment, ammunition, fuel and water.

Data for design schemes and prototypes are derived from the wartime files of the Heereswaffenamt (Army Weapons Department), and, in particular, those of Waffenprüfungsamt 6 (WaPrüf 6), which had responsibility for the testing and acceptance into service of all tracked vehicles, as well as files from Krupp Gruson werk and their Department Wolfert at Egeln, and from Henschel und Sohn of Kassel. Additional prototype vehicle and production data were also derived from notes made during detailed conversations in 1945 with Ministerialrat Dipl.-Ing. (Heinrich) Ernst Kniepkamp, head of WaPrüf 6 from 1936, Dr.-Ing.habil Dipl.Ing. Erwin Aders, former Chief Designer and head of tank development for Henschel und Sohn of Kassel from 1936 to 1945, Dr. Stieler von Heydekampf, managing director of Henschel und Sohn and Professor Dr.Dipl.-Ing.h.c. Ferdinand Porsche, head of the Porsche K.G. design consultancy and wartime Chief Designer with the Steyr-Daimler-Puch tank factory Nibelungenwerk at St. Valentin, Austria.

Lastly, it has given me much pleasure to renew my former close acquaintanceship with the Tiger family in the writing of this book, some 46 years after my rude introduction to one of its first members; I hope that it will give the reader as much pleasure as it has given me.

Introduction 11

CHAPTER ONE
BACKGROUND HISTORY

BANNED by the Treaty of Versailles in 1919 from the development and manufacture of tanks and other AFVs after the First World War, Germany, between the wars and particularly after Hitler came to power, had to resort to deception and reliance on the help of countries such as 'neutral' Sweden and post-revolution Russia if she were not to lag behind the rest of the industrial world in the development of these and other weapons of war. Her real opportunity came with the signing of the secret Treaty of Rapallo between Germany and Russia in 1926, followed by the withdrawal from Germany, in January 1927, of the inspectors of the Inter-Allied Control Commission appointed to ensure Germany's compliance with the terms of the Treaty of Versailles.

The first two types of tank to be designed and tested between the wars by the Germans were prototypes only, and were assembled and tested at the Red Army tank training school at Kama near Kazan under the guise of agricultural tractors. Production of tracked tractors by Germany was permitted under the Treaty of Versailles, although it was not intended by the victors that such vehicles should be, or would need to be, protected by armour, however thin.

The first vehicle to appear, in 1926, was a 10-tonne light tank generally similar to the British Vickers Medium Mark II, designed by Rheinmetall Borsig of Berlin/Tegel and Düsseldorf and known under the cover name of 'leichter Traktor' (light tractor); the second, a larger tank euphemistically called the Grosstraktor (large tractor), appeared in three versions, all weighing about 20 tonnes, and also bore a close outward resemblance to a Vickers tank of the period, this time the 16-tonner. The Grosstraktor I was designed by Dr. Ferdinand Porsche, of whom more will be said later and who was then the chief designer for Daimler-Benz until 1928, and was built by Daimler-Benz; the Grosstraktor II was similar in appearance but mounted a 105mm gun in place of the 75mm gun of the Grosstraktor I and was built by Rheinmetall.[1] The Grosstraktor III was built by Krupp; each company produced two mild steel prototypes, all of which underwent secret testing in Kazan by the German technicians stationed there. The resemblance of these vehicles, in outward appearance at least, to Vickers tanks of the period was not surprising in view of the close association in tank design which then existed between the USSR and Vickers.

For tactical troop training in the absence of real AFVs, the Reichswehr made use of wood and canvas dummies mounted initially on push carts and later on motor cars. The sight of such vehicles caused amuse-

◄ The leichter Traktor of 1926; note the general similarity of design and layout to the Vickers Medium Tank Mark II in the next illustration. (Author's Collection)

12   One: Background History

▲ The Vickers Medium Tank Mark II of 1924, probably used as the model for the leichter Traktor. (Author's Collection).

ment in British military circles at the time, but their use reassured the Allies that Germany was not breaching the terms of the Treaty of Versailles, which was what their politicians wished to believe anyway.

Production of real tanks in Germany itself did not start until after the National Socialists came to power in 1933, although, as has been seen, various German firms such as Friedrich Krupp of Essen, Henschel und Sohn of Kassel, Maschinenfabrik Augsburg-Nürnberg (MAN) of Nuremberg, Daimler-Benz AG of Berlin/Marienfelde and others had been producing designs from 1921 onwards, in co-operation with tank designers in the Soviet Union and also with the Swedish armaments firms of Landsverk of Landskrona, and Bofors of Karlskoga. Krupp had negotiated an affiliation with both these companies with this end in view.

With the rearmament programme initiated by Hitler in 1933, a re-organization of the German army was undertaken, in the re-organized High Command (OKH – Oberkommando des Heeres), weapon development and procurement was made the responsibility of the Army Weapons Department (Heereswaffenamt, or HWA) in conjunction with Inspectorate Branch 6 (In 6) of the Amtsgruppe Kraftfahrwesen (AgK) (Directorate for Motor Vehicles) of the Allgemeine Heeresamt (AHA) or General Army Branch of the War Ministry; responsibility for tanks and other AFVs within the HWA lay with Weapons Testing Branch 6 (WaPrüf 6).[2] The head of this branch was Regierungsbaurat Dipl.-Ing.(Heinrich) Ernst Kniepkamp, a clever engineer with a good understanding of tracked and semi-tracked vehicles and with several Deutsches Reich patents in this field to his name, who had joined the Heereswaffenamt in 1928.

This office issued the competitive contracts for the design of the first light tank, known initially under the cover name of La.S.(Landwirtschaftlicher Schlepper – agricultural tractor), in early 1933; of these competing designs, that by Krupp (whose name for it was the LKA

One: Background History 13

▲ The Rheinmetall prototype of the Grosstraktor, a tank weighing some 20 tonnes which appeared some two years later than its lighter predecessor, also bore a resemblance to a Vickers tank, in this case the medium Mark III or 16-tonner. (Author's Collection)

▼ The Vickers Medium 16-tonner of 1928, which apparently served as a model for the Grosstraktor. (Author's Collection)

– Leichte Kampfwagen A, or light tank, Model A) was selected for production, as a result of which the vehicle, by whomever produced, was thereafter known within German industry as the Krupp-Traktor. The first three prototypes were ordered from Henschel, assembly of which started towards the end of December 1933; the first vehicle ran on 3 February 1934 and testing of all three had been completed by the end of July that year, by which date a first production order for 150 vehicles had been placed, again with Henschel. This first model of the La.S. became known officially as the Model A, and a second version, the Model B, was subsequently produced in the same year.[3]

The La.S, when taken into service, took the official title of Panzerkampfwagen I (Sd Kfz 101); it first saw action in the Spanish Civil War in 1936. The Pz Kpfw I weighed 5.5 tonnes in action, carried a crew of two and was armed with two 7.92mm Dreyse MG 13 machine-guns; it corresponded to the British Light Tank Mk VI, although slower and rather more reliable, which was in service in quantity at the outbreak of war in 1939.

The German Oberkommando des Heeres (OKH – Army GHQ) based their tank requirements on the theories regarding the functions, tasks and tactical employment of tanks then being propounded by the British Major-General J. F. C. Fuller and Captain B. H. Liddell Hart; thus three categories of tank, consisting of light, medium and heavy vehicles, respectively, were envisaged for the equipment of the newly emerging German Army panzer arm. These categories corresponded more or less with those employed by the French, British and Red armies, but the proposed German method of employment, in fast-moving, highly mobile formations of all arms, with close air support from dive-bombing aircraft, was very different.

The second tank to emerge under the German re-armament programme was also a light tank, the 5.5-tonne Pz Kpfw I being followed into production in 1935 by the MAN-designed La.S.100, a 10-tonne tank with a crew of three, armed with a 20mm cannon and 7.92mm machine-gun, which became the Pz Kpfw II (Sd Kfz 121) on being taken into service. Again, WaPrüf 6 had called for competitive designs in 1934 and, when the MAN design was selected for production, this production (some 3,000 vehicles) was shared between Henschel, MAN, Alkett (Altmärkischen Kettenwerk GmbH) of Berlin-Spandau and MIAG (Mühlenbau und Industrie AG) of Brunswick.[4]

In the medium category, WaPrüf 6 had called in 1936 for design proposals and prototypes for a tank in the 15-tonne weight class from Daimler-Benz, MAN and Rheinmetall Borsig. After a competitive run-off between the prototypes at Kummersdorf and Ulm proving grounds throughout 1937, the Daimler-Benz proposal was selected for production. At this time, the vehicle was known as the Zugführerwagen or ZW (Platoon Commander's Vehicle), and production of the first orders was undertaken by Henschel, MAN and Daimler-Benz. There followed a period of continuous development, in which five models of this tank, of each of which only small numbers were produced, had appeared by 1939. First used operationally in Poland in September 1939, the ZW became known in service as the Pz Kpfw III (Sd Kfz 141). Carrying a crew of five men (commander, loader and gunner in the turret, driver and hull gunner/radio operator in the hull), the Pz Kpfw III was produced in quantity until August 1943. A total of some 6,000 vehicles was produced, with a maximum monthly production of 213 being attained in 1942.[5] The Pz Kpfw III eventually ran to twelve different models, undergoing a continual up-gunning and up-armouring process during its production life; the earliest models were armed with a 37mm gun with one hull-mounted and two coaxial MG13s. Later models were up-gunned with a short 50mm gun, then a longer gun of the same calibre and finally the 75mm gun of the early Pz Kpfw IV, all with a single coaxial MG34. Weight in action was about 22 tonnes, as against the designed weight of 15 tonnes, and the 300bhp Maybach engine gave it a maximum road speed of 28mph. In addition to tanks, its chassis was used as the basis for several self-propelled assault guns (Sturmgeschütze or Stu.G).

Meanwhile, in 1935, design proposals for a 20-tonne tank had been requested by WaPrüf 6 from Krupp, MAN and Rheinmetall Borsig. This tank was known both as the Bataillonsführerwagen or BW (Battalion Commander's Vehicle) and as the VK 2001. 'VK' stood for 'Vollkettenfahrzeug' (fully-tracked vehicle) while the first two digits of '2001' indicated the projected weight class in tonnes and the last two the number of the design within that weight class. After testing of prototypes in 1937, the Krupp version was adjudged by the Heereswaffenamt to be the best and Krupp was given the first production order for the BW; production started in the same year, and the tank entered service as the Pz Kpfw IV (Sd Kfz 161). It too underwent its baptism of fire in the Polish campaign in September 1939.[6]

The Pz Kpfw IV remained in production throughout the Second World War, some 9,000 being produced in ten different models, with armament ranging from the 75mm howitzer of the earliest models up to a long-barrelled, high-velocity 75mm gun on later models. In

One: Background History   15

▲ The Neubaufahrzeug (Nb.Fz.) or Pz Kpfw V had a turret designed by Rheinmetall in which the 75mm main armament was mounted below the coaxial 37mm gun. Like earlier prototypes, it was based on a Vickers design, in this case the 31-tonne 'Independent' of 1925. (Author's Collection)

▼ This version of the Nb.Fz., known also as the Pz Kpfw VI, had a turret of Krupp design in which the 75mm and 37mm guns were mounted side-by-side. (Author's Collection)

▲ The Landwirtschaftlicher Schlepper (La.S.), also known as the leichter Kampfwagen 'A' (LKA), which later became the Pz Kpfw I in service. (Author's Collection)

▼ The Panzerkampfwagen I Model A was derived from the La.S. and was taken into German Army service in 1935. (Author's Collection)

One: Background History 17

▲ The La.S.100 was the code-name under which the Pz Kpfw II was developed; this is the MAN version, selected for production from the various competing designs as the Pz Kpfw II. (Author's Collection)

◀ This shows the Pz Kpfw II model a1, the form in which this tank first went into production; starting with the later model c, the suspension was changed to five larger diameter road wheels, independently sprung on quarter-elliptic leaf springs. (Author's Collection)

addition to being up-gunned, it was continuously up-armoured, first with additional appliqué armour in vulnerable places, then with thicker basic armour and finally with the addition of spaced hull and turret armour. Its designed weight of 20 tonnes was increased by three tonnes in its final models to 23 tonnes; in addition to its 75mm main armament, it had a ball-mounted 7.92mm MG34 in the front vertical plate and a similar MG coaxially mounted in the turret. It carried a crew of five men, consisting of commander, gunner, driver, loader and hull gunner/radio operator, and had a maximum speed on roads of 30mph. From these data,

One: Background History

it can be seen that, as far as all parameters except main armament were concerned, the Pz Kpfw IV differed little from the Pz Kpfw III; as with the Pz Kpfw III, its chassis was used as the basis for many self-propelled guns and howitzers.

With these four tanks, the German Army had vehicles which were at least the equal in reliability and firepower of anything that their probable opponents were likely to be able to field against them; while lacking in armour protection only when compared to the French Char B and R-35 and the British Infantry Tank Mk II Matilda, their speed, reliability and tactical employment more than made up for this slight deficiency. In addition, the numbers of tanks and other armoured vehicles required to equip a rapidly expanding tank force were sufficient to keep the tank and component factories fully occupied; there was little if any spare capacity for the production of heavier tanks. Partly for these reasons, comparatively little design thought or time had been devoted to the heavy tank category, although it was realized that heavier tanks might well be under development by their likely opponents in Europe.

Design of two 23-tonne tanks, again both similar in concept to a Vickers design, this time to the multi-turreted Independent, had been started in 1933 by Rheinmetall Borsig, and five prototypes had been built by Rheinmetall and Krupp; both were known by the generic title 'Neubaufahrzeuge' (Nb.Fz., meaning 'new design vehicle').[7] One was additionally known as Pz Kpfw V and the other as Pz Kpfw VI, differing only in their main armament. Neither was put into production, the five prototypes being used as training vehicles at the Putlos training area, as platforms from which Hitler made speeches and for propaganda photographs in the Norwegian campaign. One was exhibited on the German Army stand at the Berlin International Motor Show in February 1939.[8]

The German Army thus entered the war equipped with four completely different tanks, employing four different sets of components, with only five tonnes in weight separating each type from its neighbours and with weights ranging only from approximately 5 to 20 tonnes; two of these were classified as light and two as medium tanks, but the weight and size differences were not sufficient to justify the continued production of two different tanks in each category. The need to produce four completely different ranges of components and spares imposed an unnecessary burden on an economy that was to suffer increasing shortage of key materials as the war progressed. Although the two light tanks were phased out as front-line tanks comparatively early in the war, production of the Pz Kpfw III and IV continued side by side virtually throughout the war, imposing not only the burden on the economy already mentioned but also a logistic burden on the German Army's supply and repair services and a training burden on the panzer arm. As can be seen from the outline details above, there was a weight difference of about only 1 tonne between the Pz Kpfw III and IV, while their speeds and dimensions were comparable; the Pz Kpfw III even mounted the 75mm howitzer of the Pz Kpfw IV in its final version, while both used the same engine.

Later chapters will go into more detail, but this mistake was also perpetuated in the heavy tank category, both before the war with two designs of Nb.Fz., and during it, with the Pz Kpfw Panther being produced at the same time as, firstly, the Tiger 1 and, latterly, the Tiger 2. The Tiger 1 and 2 were even being produced at the same time on parallel assembly lines in the Henschel works at Kassel–Mittelfeld from December 1943 to August 1944. This basic mistake had its parallel in Britain during the war, where far too many tank types were put into production for the convenience of industry, instead of concentrating design, development and manufacturing resources on one medium (cruiser) tank and one heavy (infantry) tank at a time.

Both the German and the British war-time AFV inventories were absurdly large, particularly if the German self-propelled artillery and the British 'funnies' and special-purpose vehicles are taken into consideration. The Soviet and US armies, on the other hand, had a totally praiseworthy singleness of purpose; each concentrated production resources on only one tank in each category, each of which was capable of being up-gunned and up-armoured to cope with improvements in enemy weapons as they became known and each of which was able to serve also as the basis for both self-propelled artillery and other special-purpose AFVs.

The Germans were later in realizing their mistake than the British, who responded to the user's call for a 'Universal Tank', to undertake all tank tasks, with the Centurion, unfortunately too late for it to see action in north-west Europe. As an interim measure, to increase production of tanks in the medium weight class, the Germans in 1944 initiated design of a Pz Kpfw III/IV, incorporating components of both the Pz Kpfw III and IV; large-scale production of this hybrid vehicle was intended, but the programme was cancelled due to the deteriorating war situation before any had been completely assembled. A similar rationalization programme between the Panther and Tiger 2 was started in 1944 but never completed, again due to the deterioration of the war situation. The aim of this programme was for the Tiger 2 to incorporate as many Panther components as possible; its only result was to delay the introduction into service of the Tiger 2 by three months.

As will be seen in later chapters, not only were too many tanks of diverse types put into production by the Germans, creating logistic, training and maintenance problems for the army and a production problem for industry, but much too much design effort was tied up in a multitude of design projects which came to nothing and for which there was no realistic operational requirement. This stemmed partly from Hitler's personal interest and interference (and in this he was not alone, Churchill having had a similarly deleterious effect on design and deployment of British AFVs), which led to Dr. Ferdinand Porsche's appointment as president of the Panzer Kommission, an advisory body composed of leading engineers and industrialists, and partly to the German lack of a design and development system which would have allowed an adequate input from the tank 'users' and have given due weight to their operational requirements.

Dr. Porsche was an engineer with both a flair for, and a love of innovation, often for its own sake and at the expense of practicality. His particular hobby-horses were super-heavy tanks, electric drive, bogie tank suspensions employing a short longitudinal torsion bar as the springing medium, and air-cooled diesel tank engines. It was his innovative and inventive mind which so impressed Hitler, but it was also a weakness; in the event, none of his heavy tank designs and few of his novel ideas for tank sub-systems worked, despite the inordinate amount of time, money and manpower spent upon their development; he was replaced as president of the Panzer Kommission by Dr. Stieler von Heydekampf, the managing director of Henschel und Sohn, in December 1943.[9]

The overwhelming impression gained from study of German war-time tank design and production resources is of an all-powerful technical and procurement department, in the shape of the Heereswaffenamt, keeping industry happy with a multitude of design and development contracts which bore no relation to the panzer arm's operational requirements and which prevented designers from concentrating on more essential projects. The manufacture and testing of prototypes of these unsuccessful vehicles further dissipated the resources of both industry and the army.

This is by no means to say that each of the duplicated vehicles that entered production in each weight class was not an excellent piece of engineering, superior in most respects to its opponents in the same weight class at any given time; dissipation of resources on unnecessarily complex designs, with little regard for manufacturing costs, and on duplicated or unnecessary projects meant, however, that tank production in Germany during the war was never as high as it could, or should have been. The roll of companies forming the war-time German tank industry is remarkable for the omission of those automobile companies with real mass-production experience; apparently, the two largest producers, Ford and Opel, were excluded because of their foreign connections, and this decision cost the Germans heavily in production man/hours.[10]

With the sole exception of the two Neubaufahrzeuge heavy tank prototypes, all German tanks produced or projected during the war were of the layout which had become internationally standard after the first war; that is, a box hull of either bolted, riveted or (later) welded construction, divided by lateral bulkheads into three compartments. The forward, or driver's compartment held the driver and driving controls on the left-hand side (in the direction of travel) and the radio operator/hull machine-gunner on the right. The centre, or fighting compartment held the turret crew and ammunition, while the rear compartment housed the engine and ancillaries. The single turret was mounted, with 360° traverse, on a ball race over the central hull compartment.

All operational vehicles except for the Pz Kpfw I Model A, which had a Krupp engine, were powered by petrol engines designed by Maybach Motorenbau GmbH of Friedrichshafen, and produced by both that company and Nordbau of Berlin. The virtual Maybach monopoly also covered gearboxes, those of all operational tanks, except those of Porsche design, which had electric transmissions, having been designed and produced by their subsidiary, Zahnradfabrik (ZF), also of Friedrichshafen.

Although all German operational tanks as well as most prototypes and design schemes, employed a rear-engined layout, most had front sprocket drive to the tracks; this of course entailed the provision of a propeller shaft running forward from the engine to the gearbox, which was in the driver's compartment, the gearbox output then being led to the two sprocket final drives, one on each side of the vehicle. This layout imposed a height penalty on the vehicle, as the turret floor had to be high enough to clear the propeller shaft; this penalty was increased on those tanks, such as the Pz Kpfw III, Panther and the Henschel Tigers, which employed transverse torsion bar springing, as the propeller shaft had to run above the torsion bars.

All production and most prototype tanks employed metal springs in their suspension systems, and in most

▲ The Krupp version of the Zugführerwagen (ZW), otherwise known as the MKA (Mittlerer Kampfwagen 'A'), one of the competing prototypes of what later became the Pz Kpfw III. (Author's Collection)

▼ The Pz Kpfw III Model A was the first production version of what became one of the two standard German medium tanks of the Second World War; it differed considerably both from the ZW prototype and from later models of the Pz Kpfw III. (Author's Collection)

cases the steel road wheels were independently sprung. Exceptions to this rule, as to most other rules of German war-time tank design, were those tanks designed by Dr. Porsche; his designs, notably for the Tiger(P) and Jagdtiger, mounted the wheels in bogie pairs, each pair sprung on a short longitudinal torsion bar. The other tanks in the German inventory used quarter-elliptic leaf springs (Pz Kpfw I, Pz Kpfw II, early model Pz Kpfw IIIs and the Pz Kpfw IV) or transverse torsion bars (later Pz Kpfw IIIs, Tiger 1 and 2 and Panther). The proposed hybrid Pz Kpfw III/IV would have had volute springs, while the various other schemes on the stocks at the war's end employed helical springs, Belleville washers and longitudinal torsion bars as the springing medium.

With regard to armour arrangement and protection, the aim of the war-time German tank designer was, generally speaking, always to make the front of the tank immune at any range to its own gun, the calibre and calibre length of which were always stated first in the vehicle specification. The sides and rear were immune at the longer ranges only. Thus, with each new tank introduced, and not infrequently with new models of existing tanks, we see a continuous strengthening of the armour protection. This strengthening was obtained on the earlier tanks by face-hardening the armour; on later models, softer rolled homogeneous armour was strengthened by the addition of bolted or welded appliqué armour and, later still, of spaced plates to defeat capped shot and hollow-charge projectiles. A combination of bolted and welded construction was employed in the earlier light and medium tanks, welded superstructures being bolted to welded hulls; with the advent of thicker armour and heavy tanks, all-welded construction was used, with the thicker plates being interlocked. German tanks employed mainly homogeneous rolled plate for their armour protection; cast armour was limited to ball MG mountings, gun mantlets and other small parts; in contrast, British, US and Soviet tanks of the Second World War made very much greater use of armour castings, and of much greater size, notably for complete turrets and, in some cases, hull fronts.

It was, however, in their armament that German tanks were pre-eminent during the war; this was only to be expected in a country combining the facilities and gun-designing experience of the Krupp and Rheinmetall Borsig organizations with a clear-sighted appreciation of the overriding importance of firepower in the design of a tank. The story of the development of German tank armament from 1933 to 1945 is one of continuous increases in calibre, weight of projectile and barrel length (and, consequently, of muzzle velocity). The main armament consisted, in general, of a high-velocity anti-tank gun capable also of firing high-explosive (HE) ammunition, with a coxially-mounted 7.92mm machine-gun (MG), while an auxiliary MG was usually ball-mounted in either the superstructure front vertical plate or the hull front glacis plate. The Germans found it necessary, for all tank guns of 75mm and above with a calibre-length greater than 40 mounted in a rotating turret, to provide a muzzle brake to reduce the recoil length. All tank guns were semi-automatic in operation and all except the 128mm gun in the Jagdtiger fired fixed ammunition, in which the

◀ The first production version of the Krupp Pz Kpfw IV, the Model A, the other standard German medium tank of the Second World War; it remained in production, in several different models, throughout the war. (Author's Collection)

projectile was fixed into the cartridge case to enable both to be loaded in one operation; the cartridge case was ejected after firing by the automatic opening of the breech on recoil. All tank guns also employed electric primers for firing their ammunition rather than the mechanically operated percussion type favoured by the Allies.

Most German tank guns were provided with a variety of ammunition types, including both kinetic energy and chemical energy (hollow charge, or HEAT) armour-piercing (AP), high-explosive (HE) and smoke. The kinetic energy ammunition was of two basic types: a solid shot, usually with a penetrating cap (APC) and often additionally with a ballistic cap (APCBC), and a high-velocity composite-rigid shot (AP/CR or AP40) with a tungsten carbide penetrating core. Later tank designs additionally incorporated triple smoke grenade-launchers on each side of the turret, and some also carried single-shot anti personnel grenade-launchers on the hull roof for close-in defence against tank-hunting enemy infantry.

As would be expected of a country which had, at the time, the most advanced optical industry in the world, tank gun sighting systems in German tanks were sophisticated, giving a high standard of accuracy. The Allies were using either straight tube optical telescopes, with their attendant disadvantages, first of having an eyepiece which moved up and down as the gun was elevated or depressed and, secondly, of requiring a hole in the mantlet armour which meant that the gunner's eye was unprotected while sighting, or, in US tanks, a sighting periscope. The Soviet army employed both straight tube telescopes and periscopic sights in the T-34 medium and KV heavy tanks. The periscope was more comfortable for the gunner in that, as the gun was elevated or depressed, his head had to move only a small distance backwards or forwards instead of larger distances up and down; it also protected the gunner's eye by bending the optical path. It did, however, pose accuracy problems due to the linkage used in connecting it to the gun mounting; wear in the joints and expansion or contraction of the links due to temperature variations could both lead to loss of accuracy. The Germans chose an elegant telescope solution, in which the sight path was led through an optical and mechanical hinge by means of an arrangement of prisms; an armour plate was inserted in the hinge, to protect the gunner's eye from any fragments which might penetrate the hole in the mantlet. To compensate the additional light loss caused by the insertion of the prisms, all air/glass surfaces were 'bloomed' or coated with anti-reflection coatings. The insertion of the optical and mechanical hinge allowed the eyepiece of the telescope to remain stationary when the gun was elevated or depressed, a very great advantage to the gunner.

As has been indicated, German industry began preparation for war in the early 1930s and the design and production of tanks was shared initially between the heavy lorry, locomotive and armaments firms of Krupp, Henschel, Daimler-Benz and Rheinmetall Borsig. As production requirements increased, other heavy engineering firms such as Krupp-Grusonwerk of Magdeburg, MAN of Nuremberg, MIAG of Brunswick, VOMAG of Plauen, Deutsche Eisenwerk, Maschinenfabrik Niedersachsen–Hannover (MNH) of Hanover, Demag and Alkett of Berlin were added to the list. The incorporation into the Third Reich of Austria and Czechoslovakia added further firms such as the Steyr-Daimler-Puch Nibelungenwerke at St. Valentin in Lower Austria, and BMM (Praga) of Prague.[11] None of these firms was experienced in the mass-production methods and value engineering employed by companies such as Ford and Opel in the motor industry; excellent engineers all, they were nevertheless accustomed to small batch production of such heavy engineering products as railway locomotives, heavy trucks, luxury and racing cars, bridges and mill machinery. In some cases, such as MIAG and Alkett, new assembly factories were built, for vehicle assembly only, and which relied entirely for the supply of components on outside contractors; other longer-established and diversified manufacturers could supply many of the major components from in-house resources.

According to the British Foreign Office and Ministry of Economic Warfare report 'Economic Survey of Germany, Section K-Armaments and Munitions', published in May 1945, German annual tank production in the years 1934–9 was:

Year	Total	Average/Month
1934	500	40
1935	700	60
1936	600	50
1937	750	60
1938	1,560	130
1939	1,680	140

These figures were obviously best guesses, rounded out and based on information available at the time; as with most Allied war-time estimates of German pre-war and war-time tank production, they are somewhat overestimated, as can be seen by comparison with Dr. Stieler von Heydekampf's official Speer Ministry figures for 1939, quoted below, which did not come into Allied hands until June 1945.

One: Background History   23

To ensure the supply of components for the wide variety of armoured fighting vehicles comprising the German Ordnance Inventory to so many assembly plants necessitated an overseeing organization capable of imposing a high degree of co-ordination between materials suppliers and manufacturers, between main and sub-contractors, between designers and production engineers and between the army and industry. In addition to the Heereswaffenamt (WaPrüf 6), the Amtsgruppe Kraftfahrwesen (In 6) and the Panzer Kommission, a system of inter-locking commissions was set up within the Speer Ministry to supervise and co-ordinate industry's requirements and output; that responsible for the AFV industry was the Hauptauschuss für Panzerwagen und Zugmaschinen (Main Committee for Armoured Vehicles and Towing Vehicles), headed by a Dr. Rohland until February 1945, when he was replaced by Dr. Stieler von Heydekampf.[12] It consisted of eight sub-committees, covering:

1. AFV production.
2. AFV development.
3. Tank production.
4. Towing vehicle production.
5. Light AFV production.
6. Track production.
7. Engine production.
8. Transmission production.

A striking feature of the programme for AFV production drawn up by this committee for the period July to December 1945 is that only two turreted tanks, the Panther and Tiger 2, were included; this indicates that the waste of design and manufacturing effort caused by the proliferation of tank types evident throughout the earlier years of the war had been fully appreciated, with future effort to be concentrated on only two types, one medium and one heavy. The targets aimed at in this programme are also revealing of the change from the offensive to the defensive in the role of the German Army at this time; monthly production of 300 Panthers and 150 Tiger 2 contrasts with 2,000 self-propelled guns on the Pz Jäg 38(t) chassis, 150 Jagdpanther and 50 Jagdtiger tank destroyers.

Actual total annual production of tracked AFVs during the years of the war from 1939, with the percentage of this production devoted to tanks and to SP artillery is shown below:[13]

Year	Total of AFVs	% Tanks	% SP Guns
1939	249	100	—
1940	1,644	89	11
1941	3,804	85	15
1942	5,997	70	30
1943	12,151	49	51
1944	19,087	44	56
1945 (to June)	988 (tanks only)	100	—

◀ This is the Rheinmetall proposal for the BW or Bataillonsführerwagen; it was rejected in favour of the Krupp version, which was put into production as the Pz Kpfw IV. (Author's Collection)

The inherent complication and high standard of finish of German AFVs was similar in a way to that of the British; the relative simplicity of the US Sherman and the Soviet KV and T-34 tanks provided a stark contrast. German AFVs required more effort not only to produce them but also to maintain them; the extra effort required to produce the AFVs applied also to their spares, and an already stretched industry found it impossible to produce, within its limited capacity, both AFVs and sufficient spares at the same time. The result was that, from 1942 onwards, the German panzer troops suffered from a permanent shortage of spares. It is significant that there was no sub-committee of the Hauptauschuss für Panzerwagen und Zugmaschinen with responsibility for co-ordinating the supply of spare parts; it would seem that their importance was not fully realized either by the civil servants responsible for placing the orders and monitoring the performance of manufacturers or by Hitler and his ministers responsible for directing those civil servants.

German tank production began to be adversely affected by Allied air raids on tank assembly plants from about the middle of 1943 onwards; until that time, the industry had been only indirectly affected by raids on communication centres and rail routes. Raids on tank factories also caused damage to nearby housing and transport, with consequent effects on the morale of the workers in the factories. The Henschel works (Werk III) at Kassel–Mittelfeld, for example, the only Henschel plant involved in tank manufacture and responsible for building the Tiger 1 and some Tiger 2, sustained considerable damage in air raids in the two years prior to June 1945, necessitating much re-organization of the manufacturing facilities; when examined by a technical Intelligence team from SHAEF (Supreme HQ Allied Expeditionary Force) in April 1945, however, although badly damaged it was still capable of producing a substantial number of tanks per month, and had in fact produced 25 Tiger 2 in the previous month, as well as 40 in January and 42 in February 1945.[14]

During the last two years of the war, despite material shortages, air raid damage and the inexorable advance of the Allied armies from east, west and south, the German tank industry was engaged on design studies and manufacture of prototypes of tanks even heavier than the Tiger 2. In June 1942 Dr. Porsche had been given the order by Hitler to design and develop a tank in the 150-tonne weight class, apparently as compensation for the rejection by the HWA of the Porsche Tiger proposals; this order short-circuited the usual ordering channels, and was resented by both the army and the HWA. The latter had accordingly, in 1943, placed orders on Krupp for feasibility studies and manufacture of prototypes of a 70-tonne tank, the VK 7001, also known as Löwe (Lion) and Tiger-Maus, and on various other manufacturers for a range of six standard chassis, 'einheitsfahrgestell' vehicles, known as the 'E'-series, employing a standard range of components and ranging in weight from 5 tonnes (E-5) up to 100 tonnes (E-100). The E-series was intended for introduction into service in late 1945/46.[15]

Several prototypes of the Porsche Maus (or Typ 205) were built, turrets and armament being tested on the Krupp proving range at Meppen, where they were captured by the British in 1945. Automotive trial vehicles were tested at Böblingen and the HWA proving ground at Kummersdorf, near Berlin, where they were blown up before capture by the Russians at the end of the war. A prototype of the E-100 hull was captured by the British on the Henschel proving ground at Haustenbeck, near Sennelager and Paderborn, and shipped to UK for examination by DTD in 1945. All these projected super-heavy tanks would have been armed with a 128mm(L/55) gun with a coaxial 75mm gun.

That the German tank procurement authorities and industry could be so divorced from reality as to waste valuable resources on such projects at a time when the panzer arm was starved of spares and the war situation was manifestly worsening beggars belief; that they allowed them to proceed throughout the two years up to the war's end is incomprehensible, and an indictment of the whole German tank procurement system.

That, however, is another and a later story; this one is concerned only with the Tiger tanks and their variants, and the development projects leading up to their introduction into service. At the time with which we are concerned, late 1941, the two firms of Henschel und Sohn of Kassel and Dr.-Ing.h.c.F.Porsche, K.G., of Stuttgart-Zuffenhausen were the recipients of HWA contracts for the development of competitive proposals to meet the 45-tonne VK 4501 requirement. As we have seen, competitive proposals are fine in time of peace, when obtaining value for the tax-payers' money is a prime consideration; in war-time other considerations such as shortness of development and production time, battleworthiness, ease of production, operation and maintenance and reliability in service are of greater importance.

One: Background History 25

CHAPTER TWO
THE PORSCHE TIGER

Dr.-Ing.h.c. F. Porsche KG, of Stuttgart/ Zuffenhausen, was one of the two companies selected in May 1941 to design and build prototypes of a new 45-tonne tank to WaPrüf 6 requirement VK 4501, the requirement which was to lead directly to the Pz Kpfw Tiger.

Porsche KG had been founded as a design company by Dr. Ferdinand Porsche, who had been chief designer with Daimler-Benz until 1928 and who had subsequently been responsible for the design of the original Volkswagen (People's Car) before the Second World War. His spell with Daimler-Benz had introduced him to tank design, when he had designed the 'Grosstraktor I' for them during the period, after the signing of the Treaty of Versailles, when such work in Germany had to be carried out clandestinely or not at all. This started a personal interest in tank design which he never lost; neither did his company, which was responsible for much of the design work on the post-war Leopard and other AFVs equipping the Bundeswehr after 1956.

Porsche's work on the Volkswagen had greatly impressed Hitler. Hitler too took a great interest in the design of German tanks during the war, and many of Porsche's ideas struck a chord with him. It was thus natural that, when the German Army produced a requirement for a heavy tank, Hitler should turn to Porsche to design a tank to meet that requirement.

Porsche was, above all, an inventive innovator, often pursuing novelty for its own sake rather than practicality. His Volkswagen design was a supreme example of his innovative flair, successful because it was production-engineered for mass production; similar success, however, eluded him with tank design, as his war-time efforts were to show. This was partly due to his own relative lack of interest in the practical as compared to the theoretical and partly due to the lack of long-run mass-production experience in the German tank industry generally, and particularly in the Porsche company and the newly built Nibelungenwerke, during the war.

As Hitler's favourite designer, Porsche was almost his protégé; as a result, he was given favoured treatment, and this led to jealousy by other companies whose designs were competing with those of Porsche for production. As an example of this favoured treatment, he was made President of the Panzer Kommission in 1941, a post for which his inventive, restless but impractical mind rendered him singularly unsuitable; this was finally realized in December 1943, when he was replaced in the appointment by Dr. Stieler von Heydekampf,[1] the managing director of Henschel und Sohn, his company's rival in the VK 4501 competition.

The VK 4501 was not the first project in which Porsche KG had competed with Henschel und Sohn; they had also been competing on the VK 3001, a 30-tonne tank project in which Maschinenfabrik Augsburg-Nürnberg and Daimler-Benz were also competitors, initiated by WaPrüf 6 in 1938 and extended to include Porsche KG in 1939. The MAN and Daimler-Benz designs were later used as the basis for the Panther tank, while those of Porsche and Henschel formed the basis on which the two versions of the Pz Kpfw Tiger, the (P) and the (H), were later designed.[2]

VK 3001(P) (Typ 100 – Leopard)

Porsche's proposals for the VK 3001 were prepared under the in-house code-name of Typ 100 (Leopard); it is interesting to note that Porsche KG were the first to use a name to designate a German tank, and even more interesting that it was the name that would be given to the Bundeswehr's first post-war main battle tank of German origin, also largely designed by the Porsche consultancy. In the newly built Nibelungenwerke factory at St. Valentin, Austria, where all Porsche tanks were built, the prototypes were called the Sonderfahrzeug I (Special Vehicle No.1). It was officially known, by the Heereswaffenamt, as the VK 3001(P).

VK 3001(P) was powered by two side-by-side Typ 100 V-10 petrol engines, designed by Porsche and built by Simmering-Graz-Pauker AG of Vienna. Each gave an output of 210 metric HP and each was directly coupled to an electrical generator; cables led from the generators forward to two electric motors, one driving each track driving sprocket. Steering and speed regulation were electrical, in conjunction with a special gearbox and transformer made by the firm of Voith of Heidenheim;[3] the petrol-electric drive was very much more flexible to instal than the more conventional petrol-mechanical transmission fitted to the majority of other tanks in German and Allied service, and allowed the rear-mounted engines to drive front-mounted sprockets without the necessity for a propeller shaft running the length of the hull and the resultant increase in vehicle height.

The runnning gear comprised three pairs of twin rubber-tyred road wheels and two twin rubber-tyred return rollers per side, each pair of road wheels being sprung by a novel, patented bogie arrangement incorporating a longitudinal torsion bar. Porsche favoured the torsion spring over other metal spring types for vehicles, as was evidenced by the Volkswagen rear supension, as well as the arrangement of tank road wheels in bogie pairs; in the case of his tank suspensions, however, the selection of a longitudinal in preference to a lateral torsion bar meant that a complicated geared linkage had to be provided in the bogie unit to convert the vertical wheel movement to a longitudinal rotating movement. In addition, the torsion bar, necessarily short to allow it to be accommodated within the length of the bogie, was easily broken if large wheel movements occurred, as they were liable to do in crossing rough terrain. Again, however, the choice of longitudinal torsion bars mounted outside the vehicle hull, rather than lateral bars running transversely across and inside the hull as on conventional tanks, made for a lower vehicle silhouette, a highly desirable aim. The lateral torsion bar, however, having a greater length, allowed greater vertical wheel movement for crossing rough ground than the longitudinal bar, and with less complication.

An alternative version of the VK 3001(P) was proposed by Porsche. This was known by the Porsche designation of Typ 200, and would have employed two air-cooled V-10 diesel engines in place of the petrol engines of the Typ 100 (Leopard);[4] it was, however, never built, although the air-cooled diesel as a tank power plant was another favourite of Dr. Porsche's, to recur in later projects.

Two prototypes were built by Nibelungenwerke but were used for automotive trials only; the proposed turrets by Krupp were, however, never mounted, the prototypes carrying only weights in lieu. Either the 7.5cm K (L/24), the 24-calibre long gun mounted in the early Pz Kpfw IV models, or a 10.5cm (L/28) gun 28 calibres in length was proposed as the main armament of the VK 3001. Armour thickness ranged from 50mm at the front to 30mm at the rear; overall length of the vehicle was 6,600mm (excluding the gun), width overall was 3,200mm, height was 3,030mm, weight was 30 tonnes and it carried a crew of four, according to a Porsche KG drawing dated 26 April 1940.

The VK 3001 project was abandoned in 1941 after reasonably successful trials of the Porsche version; on the personal orders of Hitler, the 7.5cm armament for which the vehicle was originally designed was to be replaced by an 8.8cm. When this proved impossible to achieve, the project was abandoned in favour of one for a heavier tank, capable of taking the 8.8cm gun.

The only weakness shown up in the trials of the VK 3001(P) appeared to be the unreliability of the engines, but, had the project been further developed, there were undoubtedly several possible alternatives, available from other manufacturers and fully developed, which could have been substituted. The use of a new and untried design in a tank in which several other new ideas were also being tried was an example of the Porsche lack of realism or common sense; in any new vehicle, the number of new and untried components should be minimized and the maximum use made of components and sub-assemblies from which the 'bugs' have been removed. The other novel features of the VK 3001(P), however, such as the electric transmission and the suspension, appear to have come through the trials with sufficient success to convince Porsche of the soundness of his ideas and their suitability for incorporation in any future tank design project in which his organization might be involved.

VK 4501(P) (Typ 101 – Tiger)

It became involved immediately, at Hitler's behest, when, in May 1941, the Porsche organization was one of the two companies to be given design contracts for the 45-tonne VK 4501 project by the Heereswaffenamt; the other was Henschel und Sohn.[5] The need for a heavier tank than the German Army had hitherto possessed was becoming likely in view of the possible heavy tanks to be encountered in the invasion of the Soviet Union planned for the following month, as well as those believed to be on the stocks in Britain. The need for an 8.8cm gun as main armament has already been mentioned, and 45 tonnes was thought to be the minimum possible weight for a conventional turreted tank capable of mounting this calibre of gun if it was to carry frontal armour capable of defeating its own gun at all but point-blank range. At 45 tonnes, the projected tank would be half as heavy again as any with which the German Army had had experience at that time, so that a

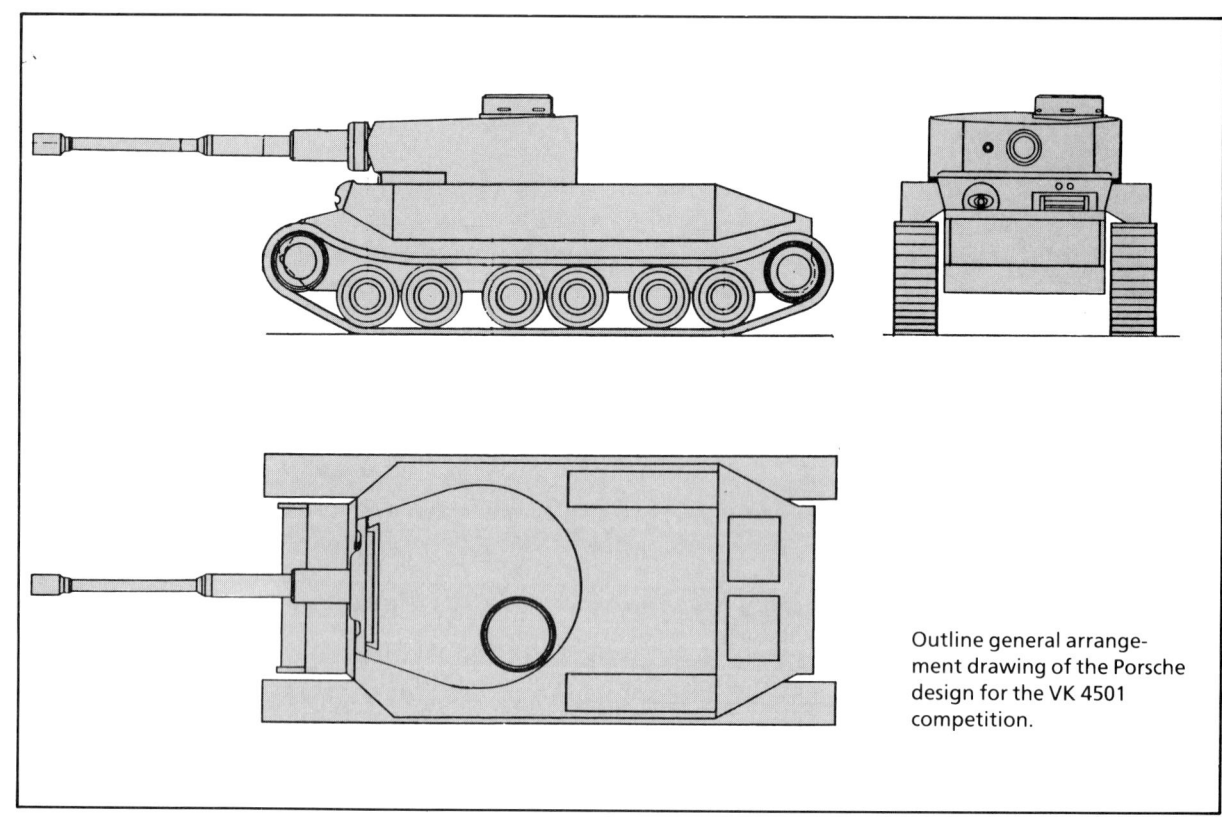

Outline general arrangement drawing of the Porsche design for the VK 4501 competition.

tank of this weight was likely to produce logistic and movement problems not hitherto met. Both contracts called for the design and completion of one prototype, the two prototypes to be demonstrated in front of Hitler at Rastenburg on his next birthday, 20 April 1942, in a competitve run-off. Porsche, meanwhile, was given special dispensation to complete the trials of the VK 3001(P) in order fully to prove the novel features of his design.

By present-day peace-time standards, when the gestation period for a new tank from feasibility study to first prototype can vary from five to ten years, the timescale imposed on the two competing design teams, with less than a year from commencement of design to demonstration of a running prototype, was breathtakingly short. With no previous experience of the design and manufacture of a tank in this weight class, Porsche had no alternative but to draw on the limited experience gained in the design and construction of the VK 3001(P), so it is not surprising to find the VK 4501(P) utilizing the same ideas for power plant, transmission and suspension as used in the earlier project.

Within the Porsche organization, the new project was known as the Typ 101, with the colloquial name 'Tiger'; it was from this unofficial naming of the project by Porsche KG that the Tiger 1 and 2 eventually taken into service derived their official names, at Hitler's behest and because the panzer users had been unofficially using the name from the start. Within the Nibelungenwerke factory the new vehicle was known as 'Sonderfahrzeug II' (Special Vehicle No.2);[6] initially, an experimental quantity of ten prototypes was foreseen.

The crucial factor affecting the basic dimensions of the new vehicle was its armament; the Porsche design was to cater for the mounting of a tank version, the 8.8cm KwK 36 (L/56), of the standard 8.8cm FlaK 36 anti-aircraft gun which had been so successful in the Middle East in the anti-tank role. Gun and turret design were in the hands of the Krupp organization; a gun of this calibre and performance required a minimum turret ring diameter of 1,850mm (72.8in), so that the vehicle width was dictated by this dimension. Because of the urgency attaching to this project, and the need for production of the selected design as soon as possible after selection, Krupp was given the order for the guns and turrets by Porsche in July 1941,[7] only two months after the design contracts for the VK 4501 had been let; the gun needed minimum redesign of cradle and recoil gear, so that production could be put in hand immediately on completion of the firing trials. Turret

▶ VK 3001(P) prototype on trials, with a weighted dummy turret in place. (Author's Collection)

▶ VK 3001(P) undergoing automotive trials, with a dummy turret weight in place of the real one. (Tank Museum)

design was done in close consultation with Porsche KG, and a preliminary production order for 90 turrets and guns was placed with Krupp before the vehicle competition had been held. A production order for a similar quantity of the VK 4501(P) was placed with Nibelungenwerke a few weeks later, on Hitler's orders and on the assumption that the Porsche design would emerge victorious from the competitive run-off.

As with the VK 3001(P), Porsche adopted petrol-electric drive for the VK 4501(P), again using his own design of air-cooled V 10 petrol engine, this time the Typ 101/1, despite the unreliability shown by his earlier similar design in the VK 3001(P). Two engines were used, again in a side-by-side configuration, each coupled via a Porsche/Siemens reduction gear to an electric generator which in turn drove a rear track sprocket via an electric motor. This combination gave a remarkably small (2.15 metres) turning circle for a vehicle of this size. The use of a rear sprocket drive in this vehicle is interesting, being almost the only example of this configuration to be found in war-time German tanks. The reason for Porsche's change from the front drive of the VK 3001(P) to rear drive for the VK 4501(P) was presumably partly to improve the weight distribution when mounting such a heavy turret forward, and partly to reduce the cable runs within the vehicle, with a consequent saving of copper.

In other respects the remainder of the Tiger(P) bore a very close resemblance to the earlier Leopard on which it was based; frontal armour thickness was upgraded to 100mm, but the hull shape was virtually unchanged, apart from the widening of the superstructure to accommodate the larger diameter turret ring. The same suspension and bogie arrangement of the road wheels was retained, together with the same number (six) of twin road wheels per side; return rollers were dispensed with, however, on the Tiger(P), the upper run of the track being returned on the top of the road wheels. An interesting feature of the running gear was the use of a toothed twin idler wheel, of the same design as the sprocket, at the front of the vehicle, presumably with the idea of reducing the risk of 'throwing' a track; another feature new to German tanks of the period was the resilient pattern of steel-tyred road wheel, a Porsche innovation which was the forerunner of similar wheels on the later Tiger 1 and Panther models, as well as the Tiger 2.

But although the overall dimensions of the Tiger(P) were little larger than those of the Leopard, and in fact the overall height was less, its weight in action was just about doubled from the 30 tonnes of the Leopard to 59 tonnes for the Tiger(P). Engine output had been increased only to 640bhp from 410bhp, so that the Tiger(P) was going to be under-powered. The track width had been increased from 600mm on the earlier vehicle to only 640mm on the Tiger(P) and the length of the track on the ground from 3,225mm to 4,175mm,[8] the increase in neither dimension being proportional to the weight increase; the vehicle weight spread over the area of track in contact with the ground gave a ground pressure of 16psi as compared to the 11.2psi of the VK 3001(P).

The design of a vehicle of this weight, which must be able to travel under its own power both on roads and across country and be transportable over land, by rail or road, and over the sea, poses problems of an order not encountered with tanks of 30 tonnes weight and less; overall width and height must not exceed the dimensions permitted by the rail loading gauge and by ship loading ramps, hatches and 'tween-decks space. Minimum tank width is dictated by the diameter of the turret ring, while minimum height is governed by both the length of gun recoil when fully depressed, the required ground clearance and the height of a standing loader. There is also, however, a relationship between the width and length of a tracked fighting vehicle if it is to have manoeuvrability and tactical mobility; too great a length of track on ground in relation to vehicle width makes a tank very difficult to steer on soft ground, while too great a width in relation to length makes it very difficult to steer a straight path on a hard surface. A ratio of length to width of approximately 1.5:1 should

◀ VK 4501(P) prototype, with turret traversed to the rear; note that the turret is identical with that on the early production model of the Tiger 1. (Tank Museum)

▶ The VK 4501(P) prototype on its rail flat, en route to the demonstration before Hitler at Rastenburg in April 1942. (Author's Collection)

not be exceeded. Finally, if a heavy vehicle is not to sink in soft ground, its track pressure on the ground should be as low as possible, and preferably not greater than 12 to 14 pounds per square inch. With a ground pressure of 16psi, the VK 4501(P) was therefore likely to become easily bogged in soft going.

By dint of working day and night shifts in the factory, assembly of the first prototype was completed on 17 April 1942.[9] Then began the task of loading the vehicle and getting it to Rastenburg by the 20th; while this exercise appears to have been an unnecessary waste of time and effort, it nevertheless acted as a spur to both competing companies without which neither prototype might have been completed to time.

A further spur had been the German Army's encounter, in July 1941, with large numbers of the Soviet T-34 medium tank; this came as a very great shock to the German Army and, by October of that year, had caused such a lowering of morale within its ranks on the Eastern Front that a special mission of tank designers (including Porsche, and Aders of Henschel) and HWA officers was sent to the Eastern Front in October 1941 at General Guderian's urgent request, to examine the captured vehicles and to see conditions at the front for themselves. Despite the mission's cordial reception by Guderian, however, the troops' hope that 'a better T-34' could result in the short term from the mission's examination of captured and knocked-out T-34s was vain, due to the time required to design a German version from scratch.[10]. The visit bore fruit in two ways, however; first, the members of the mission returned home with a better idea both of conditions at the front and of the urgency attaching to the timely completion of the VK 4501 programme and, secondly, they were able to incorporate the design principles of the T-34 into the armour layout of tanks following the VK 4501 into production, such as the Panther and the Tiger Model B.

By dint of almost superhuman efforts on the part of everybody concerned in both firms, both prototypes arrived at Rastenburg by 20 April 1942, the Porsche vehicle still having some work carried out on it on the morning of the demonstration. Owing to the lack of suitable unloading ramps there, both vehicles had to be lifted off their rail flat wagons by means of a 75-tonne steam crane; it was lucky for the Porsche team that the crane was available, as their vehicle was unable to turn through 90° under its own power and had to be lifted by the crane, turned through the requisite angle and lowered again pointing in the right direction. The Porsche prototype also suffered several fires in the engine compartment during the demonstration, and its road and cross-country performance could not therefore be fully demonstrated.[11]

The competitive demonstration was inconclusive, so further stiff and intensive comparative trials were started at the Berka military training area in May 1942; these were carried out by a combined team of military specialists, under Colonel Thomale, and technical experts under Prof.-Ing. von Eberan of the Dresden

Two: The Porsche Tiger

Technical High School.[12] The most important military requirement was for the Panzertruppen to have the finally-selected tank in their hands, in quantity, by early the following summer, at the latest. As a result of these tests, the Henschel vehicle was adjudged to be the better; this judgement was passed by Speer to Hitler, who publicly announced that it would be put into production.

The Porsche prototype had been rejected on the grounds of the complication and unreliability of its petrol-electric drive, the fragility of its suspension and the ease with which it became bogged, due to the narrowness of its tracks and its resultant high ground pressure. As an aside, Porsche's wisdom in opting for an electric transmission at a time when copper was in increasingly short supply in Germany is to be doubted; it was an example of his preference of novelty over practicality which has been already mentioned. It is of interest also to note that none of the novel design features incorporated in the VK 4501(P) was successful; the torsion bar suspension proved too fragile, due to the over-stressing of the bars in torsion by too great a vertical movement of the road wheels in rough terrain, while the petrol-electric drive was unreliable and prone to catch fire. Porsche, however, was obviously unrepentant and remained unconvinced of the inadequacy and impracticability of his ideas, for in his later design of the super-heavy tank Maus (180 tonnes), he retained the same bogie/longitudinal torsion bar suspension design, the same petrol- or diesel-electric drive and air-cooling of the power plants as he had chosen for both the VK 3001(P) and VK 4501(P).

Pz Jäg Tiger (P) (Elefant, formerly Ferdinand)

The order for 90 production Porsche VK 4501 which had already been placed with Nibelungenwerke, with first deliveries scheduled for July 1942, was amended so that they could be converted to turretless self-propelled anti-tank guns, mounting the 8.8cm PaK 43/2 (L/71) weapon. Only two were completed as tanks with turrets; the remainder were shipped as completed hulls to Alkett in Berlin/Spandau, where they were fitted with twin standard water-cooled Maybach HL120 engines in place of the Porsche-designed air-cooled Typ 101/1, together with additional appliqué armour and a heavily armoured fixed superstructure at the rear of the hull to mount the 8.8cm gun and house the gun crew. Because of the rear-mounted superstructure, the hulls had to be stripped internally to enable the engines to be mounted amidships, between the driver's and the fighting compartments. The production run at Nibelungenwerke

---

8.8cm PaK 43/2 (L/71) auf Pz Jäg Tiger (P) (Sd Kfz 184) (Elefant, früher Ferdinand)

Outline Specification

Weight in action	65 tonnes
Crew	6
Dimensions:	
Overall length incl. gun	8,140mm
Overall length excl. gun	6,800mm
Overall width	3,380mm
Overall height	2,970mm
Belly clearance	480mm
Track on ground	4,175mm
Track width	640mm
Track centres	2,680mm
Armour thicknesses:	
Turret front	200mm
Turret sides	80mm
Hull front	100mm + 100mm
Superstructure sides	80mm
Tail plate	80mm
Armament:	
Main	8.8cm PaK 43/2 (L/71)
Auxiliary	One 7.92cm MG34
Ammunition carried	55 × 8.8cm, 600 × 7.92mm
Power plant:	Twin Maybach HL120TRM
Type	V-12 water-cooled, petrol
Output	530 metric hp at 2,600rpm
Transmission	Electric
Running gear:	
No. of road wheels	6, in 3 bogie pairs, per side
Springing medium	Longitudinal torsion bar
Drive	Rear sprocket
Performance:	
Max. speed (roads)	20km/hr
Range (roads)	130km
Fording depth	1m
Step	780mm
Trench crossing	2.64m

---

started in July 1942 and ended on 8 May 1943,[13] little more than a year after the ill-fated demonstration of the Porsche Tiger to Hitler at Rastenburg; the last vehicle off the production line had the chassis number 150100, numbers having run consecutively from 150001 to include the prototypes, pre-production, production and recovery vehicles.

In its new role of heavy tank destroyer, the erstwhile VK 4501(P) was finally taken into service as the '8.8cm PaK 43/2 (L/71) auf Pz Jäg Tiger (P) (Elefant, früher Ferdinand) (Sd Kfz 184)' (8.8cm Anti-Tank Gun 43/2 on Tank Destroyer Tiger (Porsche) (Elefant, formerly

▲ Front view of the Pz Jäg Tiger (P) (Elefant, formerly Ferdinand) taken from a captured provisional handbook for the vehicle. This is an early version, without the front hull ball-mounted MG, but the illustration clearly shows the bolted-on additional hull armour. (Author's Collection)

▼ Side view of the Elefant (formerly Ferdinand); the toothed front idler is clearly shown. (Author's Collection)

Two: The Porsche Tiger 33

Ferdinand).[14] The name 'Ferdinand', by which it was first known in service, was in honour of its designer, Ferdinand Porsche. It was known within the Porsche company as the Typ 130, and it first saw service on the Eastern Front in Operation 'Citadel' near Kursk in July 1943. The 90 turrets originally ordered from Krupp for the VK 4501(P) were transferred to Henschel for mounting on the successful VK 4501(H), which became the Pz Kpfw VI (H), Ausf H1 (Sd Kfz 181) on entering service in September 1942.

Five of the Porsche Tiger chassis were converted to armoured recovery vehicles, without the additional armour of the Elefant and with a small superstructure at the rear of the vehicle, in which a ball-mounted MG 34 was fitted for close defence;[15] this vehicle does not appear to have been given an 'Sd Kfz' number.

In January 1943, Hitler ordered the building of three 'Ramm' (battering ram) Tigers on the Porsche chassis, provoked by the street fighting in Stalingrad; the battering-ram would have consisted of an armoured

▲ The Tiger (P) armoured recovery vehicle, of which only five were built. Note the MG ball mounting in the fixed turret front plate. (Tank Museum)

▼ A side view of the Tiger (P) armoured recovery vehicle. (Tank Museum)

34 *Two: The Porsche Tiger*

add-on superstructure, with a reinforced nose pointed in the fashion of the Soviet IS-3 glacis plate, and the vehicle would have towed trailers carrying fuel.[16] In the event this development was not pursued.

Porsche had continued the development of his VK 4501(P) by equipping one vehicle with an hydraulic transmission in place of the electric; the vehicle fitted with this transmission had the Porsche title of Typ 102. The transmission was supplied by Voith of Heidenheim, from whom Porsche had ordered 50 sets, of which only one was delivered. The vehicle in which this transmission was fitted was an otherwise unmodified Typ 101. A further variation was the Porsche Typ 103, in which a NITA gearbox, again provided by Voith, was fitted, together with two air-cooling blowers for the engines; neither of these two projects progressed farther than the drawing-board. Finally, Hitler asked for a Porsche Tiger mounting an 8.8cm anti-tank gun 100 calibres long to be tested; again, this project went no farther than a feasibility study.

The failure of the VK 4501(P) had in no way deterred Porsche from continuing to pursue his own ideas in further development both of this vehicle and of its heavier successors, the VK 4502 and the Maus family.

VK 4502

The VK 4502 was a Heereswaffenamt project for a heavy tank mounting the 8.8cm KwK 43 (L/71) tank gun, and was a parallel project to the VK 4503 requirement given to Henschel und Sohn, out of which developed the Pz Kpfw Tiger, Ausf B (Sd Kfz 182) otherwise known as the Tiger 2 or Königstiger. Despite the fact that the Tiger 1 produced in response to the VK 4501 project was some 11 tonnes heavier than the 45 tonnes called for in the specification, and that a tank mounting the longer and more powerful 8.8cm gun, and carrying thicker armour, would be even heavier than the Tiger 1, the HWA persisted with the notional 45-tonne weight in the project number for the new vehicle; whether this was from optimism, or an attempt to tie the designers down is not known.

The requirement was issued in late 1942 by the Heereswaffenamt and was given the Porsche in-house title of 'Typ 180'. Two schemes were produced, one with the power plant at the rear and the turret at the front of the hull, and the other with a rear-mounted turret and the power plant amidships. The hull design was based on that of the Soviet T-34, with sloped hull front and rear and sloped superstructure side plates; the armour plates were welded and interlocked. The turret also had sloping sides, but they were also bent, making production difficult; in addition the rounded turret front gave a sharp re-entrant angle below the gun centre-line, forming a conspicuous shot-trap liable to direct a striking shot into either the driver's compartment (in the case of the forward-mounted turret) or the engine compartment, in the case of the turret mounted at the rear. For some reason, an order for 50 of this design of turret was placed before the vehicle design had been approved for production. In a repeat of the situation that had earlier prevailed in the case of the Tiger (P) turrets, the Porsche vehicle design was rejected in favour of the Henschel solution, and these 50 turrets were re-directed to Henschel and fitted to their first 50 production Tiger 2s.

Porsche's proposals for the VK 4502 were similar to those already put forward for the VK 3001(P) and the VK 4501(P); again he proposed the employment of twin air-cooled engines, in the case of the Typ 180 coupled to electric generators each of which drove an electric motor at each sprocket, and in the Typ 181, coupled to hydraulic pumps and motors. The vehicle weight was estimated at about 64 tonnes and a total of 68 8.8cm rounds was to be carried, sixteen in the turret and the remainder in the hull.[17] Neither the Typ 180 nor the Typ 181 progressed beyond the scheme drawing stage; the forward turret version had been rejected on account of the excessive gun overhang and the rear-turreted scheme was turned down on account of the shortage of copper, required for the electric transmission. The Henschel proposals were again put into production and into service as the Pz Kpfw Tiger Ausf B (Sd Kfz 182) (Tiger 2 or Königstiger).

Maus (Typ 205)

With the rejection of his VK 4502 proposals, Porsche turned his full attention to his favourite project, and that of Hitler, the super-heavy (180 tonnes) barely mobile pillbox known as Maus (Mouse), or Typ 205, and previously called 'Mammut'. Although not one of the Tiger tanks, details are included here as a further illustration of Hitler's and Porsche's preoccupation with heavy tanks, and of Porsche's inability to dismount from his three-legged hobby-horse of electric transmission, air-cooled diesel engines and bogie suspension incorporating longitudinal torsion bars.

At a meeting in Berlin on 8 June 1942, Porsche had been invited by Hitler and Reichsminister Speer to start work on a project to design a tank to mount either a 12.8cm or a 15cm tank gun, with a coaxial 7.5cm gun, in a turret with 360° traverse. It was to have frontal armour 200mm thick on the hull, with 180mm on the sides, while the turret front was to be 240mm thick with 200mm-thick armour on sides and roof. Porsche wanted to design an air-cooled diesel engine specially for the vehicle, another example of his lack of practicality, but was rightly overruled by Speer on the grounds of lack of time; as a single- rather than a twin-engine installation was to be used, it was decided to use a Daimler-Benz diesel aircraft engine instead, coupled to a duplex electric generator and a redesigned electric transmission and steering system.

In the event, Daimler-Benz were unable to supply a diesel engine of the required type, so that a petrol alternative, the DB 509, had to be accepted in lieu. Initially, Porsche opted again for his bogie suspension with longitudinal torsion bar springs, and the first prototype was a larger version of his rear-turreted Typ 180. Work on building the first prototype was started by Alkett in August 1943 and the vehicle underwent automotive trials at Böblingen, near Stuttgart, from December 1943 to May 1944. The first turret, by Krupp, had been fitted by 9 June 1944 and a second prototype vehicle had meanwhile arrived at Böblingen in March of that year. Work on the project then stopped, due to the deteriorating war situation, and both prototypes were sent to the HWA Kummersdorf proving ground in October 1944, where they were both

▲ A prototype of the Porsche Typ 205 or Maus undergoing automotive trials, with a weighted dummy turret in position. Note the ladder up the vehicle side, without some form of which it would be virtually impossible for the crew to mount. (Author's Collection)

alleged to have been blown up before the proving ground was overrun by the Russians.[18]. However, recent evidence from the Curator of the Tank Museum at Bovington has confirmed seeing one 'alive and well' in a video recording of a military museum just outside Moscow.[19] Several other hulls and turrets, together with a specimen of the 12.8cm KwK 82 (L/55) main armament in a proof mounting, were found at the war's end at the Meppen proving ground of Krupp, from which it appears that at least ten prototypes were scheduled to have been built.[20]

The fact that no 'VK' project number was allocated to the Maus project by the HWA is an indication that it neither originated with the HWA nor had its approval. In fact, Kniepkamp did not approve, and thought that the vehicle would be quite unsteerable.[21] It is an indictment of the war-time German tank procurement system that a private venture project of this size, even allowing for Hitler's backing, should ever have reached the prototype stage, especially with the economy virtually on its knees and with the war's end so close.

CHAPTER THREE
THE TIGER 1

WHEN, in the spring of 1941, Henschel und Sohn were given a contract to design and build a prototype of a 45-tonne tank under the HWA project number VK 4501, they had an advantage over their Porsche rival on the project; they had previous experience of designing and building tanks with weights in excess of 30 tonnes. They had been competing with MAN and Daimler-Benz since 1937, and with Porsche since 1939, on the earlier VK 3001 project, but, since the beginning of 1937, had also been made responsible for the development of all the heaviest tank projects in Germany.

DW 1

At the end of January 1937, Baurat Kniepkamp of WaPrüf 6 first gave Henschel the task of designing a 30-tonne tank, known as the Durchbruchwagen 1 (Breakthrough Tank 1 – DW 1), to answer the VK 3001 requirement.[1] This was Henschel's first attempt at designing a tank heavier than the Pz Kpfw III and IV, and was intended ultimately to be a replacement for one of them. The resulting vehicle had a two-piece hull, bolted together, because welding of large areas of armour plate was not then practicable, with an armour basis of about 50mm and with two hatches in the belly, an escape hatch in the driver's compartment and an access hatch in the engine compartment.

The power plant was a Maybach HL120 petrol engine, with an output of 280 metric hp, and the gearbox a Maybach 'Variorex'; steering was initially intended to be by means of a three-step Cletrac clutch/brake system, but this proved faulty and had to be re-designed from scratch. The track was interesting, in that it was lubricated, and incorporated needle roller bearings for the track pins;[2] it was driven by means of a novel sprocket carrying rollers instead of teeth, the rollers of which engaged with and drove the track guide horns. This was a similar system to that used earlier on the US Christie fast tank, and later on the Soviet BT and T-34, and was possibly a legacy of the earlier German/Soviet collaboration. The running gear consisted of five twin rubber-tyred road wheels, sprung on torsion bars, and three twin rubber-tyred return rollers per side; front and rear road wheels were fitted with special shock absorbers by the firm of Boge und Sohn. One prototype hull was built, and the vehicle on test reached a maximum speed of 35km/hr. Krupp were given the task of designing the turret, to mount the 7.5cm KwK (L/24) gun of the Pz Kpfw IV, but none was built.[3]

VK 6501 (SW)

At a meeting with the HWA in April 1937, Henschel agreed to undertake the design of a 65-tonne tank,[4] known within the company as the SW (Sturmwagen or Schwerewagen – assault or heavy tank) or Pz Kpfw VII, to answer the VK 6501 requirement, and the design contract was received on 9 September 1938.[5] At the same time as work started on the VK 6501, trials of the DW 1 were halted. Doubts were expressed by the Henschel design team as to whether it would be possible to design and build a tank of this weight within the dimensional limitations imposed by the rail loading gauge; a three-piece hull design was therefore adopted in which the hull would be disassembled for travel and re-assembled at its destination, with the help of two mobile cranes, with a combined lifting capacity of 20 tonnes, specially designed by Faun of Nuremberg. The three parts of the hull were connected at the side plates with tension bolts, yokes and bolts with conical seatings; the side armour thickness was 80mm and that in front of the driver, 100mm. This method of construction made the sealing of the hull for wading more complicated; special sealing kits had to be used for this purpose and the hull re-sealed after each re-assembly.[6]

The VK 6501 was powered by a Maybach HL224 petrol engine, with an output of 600 metric hp at 3,000rpm; cooling air was drawn in through the hull sides and expelled through a slit at the rear of the vehicle. A newly developed Maybach gearbox was employed; the steering mechanism gave three radii of turn, and was specially designed for the vehicle by a team of four Henschel designers, who took a year to complete the design. The track drive was similar to that

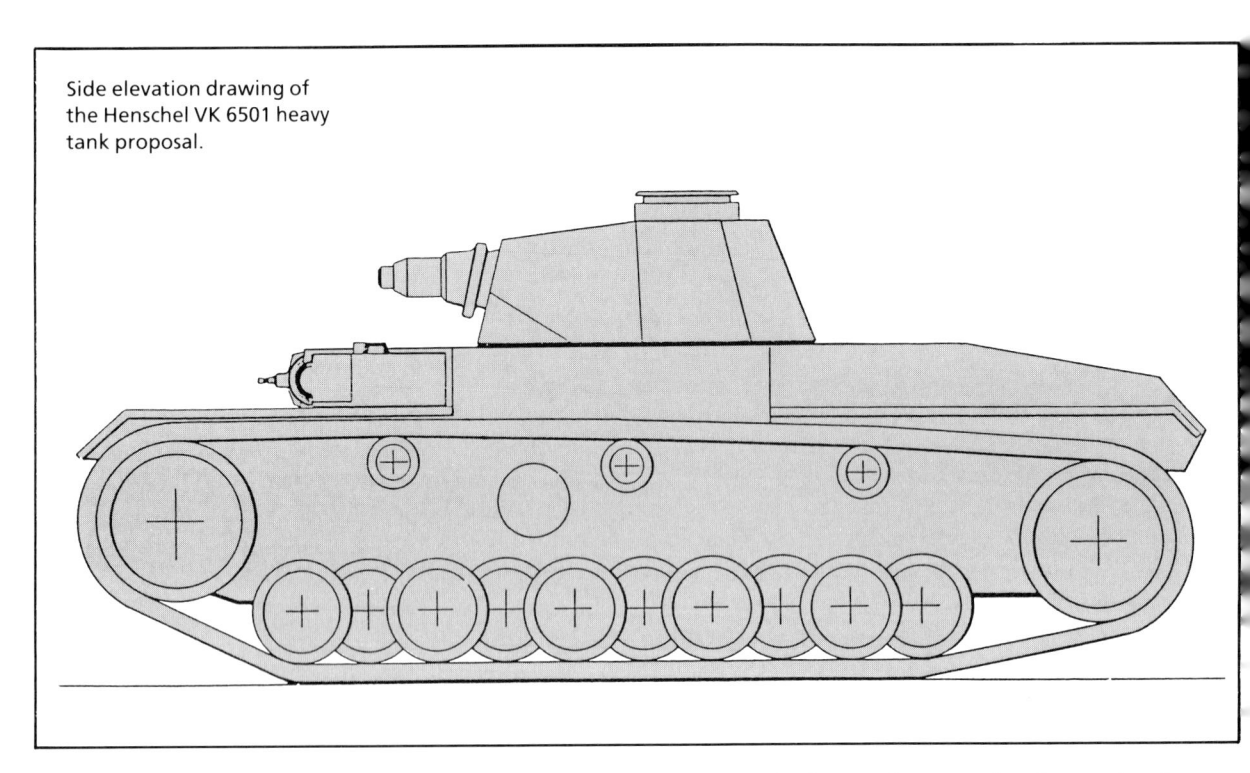

Side elevation drawing of the Henschel VK 6501 heavy tank proposal.

of the DW 1, the front sprocket rollers transmitting the drive to the tracks by means of the track link guide horns. The running gear was of novel design, consisting of ten wheel stations per side with the wheels of one station interleaved with those of its neighbours in an attempt to spread the vehicle weight evenly over the tracks. Road wheels were of small diameter and of steel, with rubber tyres, as were the return rollers, of which there were three on each side. Suspension was by means of transverse torsion bars, one to each road wheel station. The two twin sprockets and idler wheels were also provided with rubber tyres. The turret, as usual of Krupp design, resembled that of the Pz Kpfw IV (also of Krupp design) and was intended in the first instance to mount the 7.5cm KwK (L/24) gun of that vehicle. Two mild-steel prototypes of the VK 6501 were built, and trials showed that the 65-tonne vehicle, with a crew of five, was capable of a maximum road speed of 25km/hr;[7] these trials were, however, suspended, as was all work on the VK 6501, when the contract was terminated in 1940 and work started on a further development of the DW 1.[8]

DW 2

In general design, this vehicle differed little from the earlier version; the same running gear layout, torsion bar suspension and roller sprocket driving the track guide horns were retained, although minor differences involved a higher spring rate for the torsion bars, a smaller track pitch and a different steering system employing magnetic clutches and giving three radii of turn. The needle roller bearings for the track pins were retained. Again, only one prototype was built and tested, less the turret, the 30-tonne vehicle achieving the same maximum speed of 35km/hr as its predecessor. Krupp had again been asked to design the turret, but again none was built.[9]

Neither the DW 1 nor the DW 2 was further developed, although trials continued intermittently into 1941. The experience gained from their design and development was used later to good effect in the development of the VK 3001(H), the 30-tonne project in which, initially, Henschel were competing with MAN and Daimler-Benz and also, from 1939 onwards, with Porsche KG.[10] It is probable that the 'DW' nomenclature for the DW 1 and 2 was an internal Henschel code-name only, and that both these vehicles were also, in fact, part of the Heereswaffenamt VK 3001 project; certainly the Henschel prototypes of all three vehicles had a weight of 30 tonnes, a maximum speed of 35km/hr and a 7.5cm main armament, but it is difficult at this remove to establish the true facts without further access to the Heereswaffenamt (WaPrüf 6) files. The 'DW' nomenclature was in line with the 'ZW' and 'BW' names for what later became the Pz Kpfw III and IV, respectively, as well as with the 'SW' of the VK 6501 project.

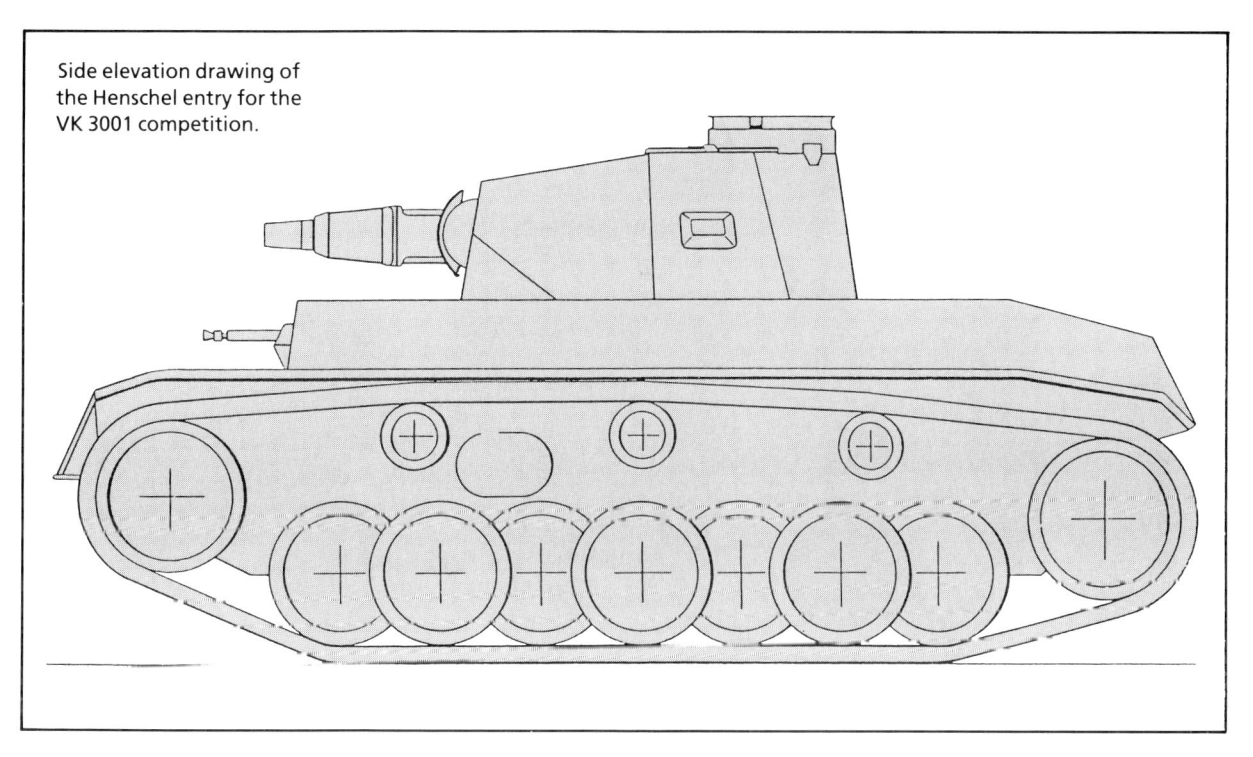

Side elevation drawing of the Henschel entry for the VK 3001 competition.

VK 3001(H)

In 1941, Henschel received a further order from WaPrüf 6 to design another vehicle in the 30-tonne weight class to meet the VK 3001 requirement. This was known as the VK 3001(H),[11] to distinguish it from those of the other competitors on the project, that of Porsche having a (P) suffix and those of MAN and Daimler-Benz an (M) and a (D), respectively.

As their starting-point, Henschel took the DW 2 as the basis for their design, but with important modifications as the result both of trials experience with the earlier vehicles and of changed WaPrüf 6 requirements. For example, welding expertise had progressed since the DW vehicles had been designed, so that the VK 3001(H) was given a one-piece welded hull, with entry hatches forward in the right and left hull side plates. The hull side profile was similar to that of the two earlier designs, with a conventionally stepped hull front; the superstructure was not extended over the tracks, but was contained between them as on the Pz Kpfw III. Frontal and rear armour thickness was 50mm, as was that of the hull sides. The roller front sprocket was abandoned in favour of the more conventional twin toothed-ring type, the teeth engaging in bosses on the ends of the track links, the lubricated track pins with needle roller bearings were replaced by a dry single-pin design of link with a single central guide horn. The twin rubber-tyred road wheels were interleaved after the fashion of those of the VK 6501; in this case, however, they were of a larger diameter, with seven wheel stations per side. There were three twin rubber-tyred return rollers per side, and the twin idler wheels were also rubber-tyred. Springing was by means of transverse torsion bars, one per wheel station.

The power plant selected was the Maybach HL116 6-cylinder water-cooled petrol engine with an output of 300 metric hp at 3,000rpm; it was cooled by two radiators and four fans behind the engine. The transmission was again the Maybach Variorex, connected to a Type L320C steering system, giving three radii of turn; brakes were those of the Pz Kpfw III. The VK 3001(H) weighed 30 tonnes, as projected, and achieved a maximum road speed of 35km/hr, as had its predecessors. Again, Krupp had been tasked to design a turret for the vehicle, again mounting the 7.5cm K (L/24) tank gun; twelve turrets were built, of which six were issued for mounting in permanent emplacements, but none was ever mounted on chassis.[12]

Four prototypes of the VK 3001(H) were produced, differing only in detail, two in March 1942 and two in October of the same year; the first two were used initially for vehicle trials and later as trials vehicles for various special devices such as dozer blades and mine ploughs at the Haustenbeck proving ground of Henschel, near Paderborn, and at the HWA Kummersdorf proving ground, near Berlin. The latter two were converted by Rheinmetall Borsig of Düsseldorf to self-

▲ The VK 3001(H) prototype hull; note the use of small interleaved road wheels, in conjunction with return rollers. (Author's Collection)

◄ One of the VK 3001(H) prototype hulls, with weights in place of the turret; this vehicle was used at the Henschel proving ground at Haustenbeck for mine plough trials. The plough can just be seen, raised at the rear of the vehicle. (Author's Collection)

Opposite page, top: One of the two prototype 128mm self-propelled guns on the VK 3001(H) chassis. The hull has been extended rearwards, as can be seen from the distance between the rear road wheel and idler wheel centres. (Author's Collection)

Three: The Tiger 1

propelled carriages for the 12.8cm K.40 (L/61) gun, in which form they were known as the Pz Sfl V (Armoured Self-propelled Mounting V).[13] Because of the great weight of the gun, the side armour of these two VK 3001(H) chassis was reduced in thickness to 30mm; the original superstructure was replaced by an open-topped construction at the rear of the vehicle, while the driver and co-driver were housed in individual compartments on either side of the gun, forward of this construction. The 12.8cm gun had originally been developed as an anti-aircraft gun by Rheinmetall and weighed seven tonnes in the self-propelled version; its mounting in the vehicle allowed a traverse of 7° to left and right, and an elevation range from −15° to +10°. In view of the total vehicle weight increase from 30 to 36 tonnes, an extra road wheel station was added to each side and the hull and track lengthened accordingly.[14]

Photographs of the completed vehicle are dated 9 March 1942;[15] this 12.8cm gun was the largest anti-tank gun taken into service during the Second World War. Both vehicles were sent to the Eastern Front, where one fell into Soviet hands in the autumn of 1943; the fate of the other is not known. One of the first two prototype VK 3001(H) chassis was found at the Henschel experimental establishment at Haustenbeck at the end of the war, where it had been used as a recovery and towing vehicle; again, it is not known what happened to the other one.

VK 3601

In the meantime, Henschel had also been brought into the VK 3601 project in May 1941 as chassis designers, again with Krupp as the designers of the turret;[16] the testing of the VK 3001(H) was therefore abandoned in order to concentrate design effort on the new project, also known as the Pz Kpfw VI, Ausf B.[17] The requirement was for a 36-tonne vehicle with frontal armour thickness of 100mm and side armour of 60mm in the hull and 80/60mm in the turret, a maximum speed of 40km/hr and armed with a 7.5cm taper-bore hyper-velocity gun Type 0725 in the turret.[18]

The Henschel vehicle was based on the design of the VK 3001(H), but with eight twin interleaved and rubber-tyred road wheels of a much larger diameter, and no return rollers, on each side. Again, the superstructure was contained within the width between the tracks, with large engine air intakes projecting over the tracks on each side of the rear engine compartment. The standard stepped hull front configuration was adopted, with the driver's and hull gunner/radio operator's positions on the left and right of the driver's compartment, respectively.

An initial order of one prototype followed by a further six experimental vehicles was envisaged, for delivery from April 1942. However, the Panzerprogramm 41 of 30 May 1941 foresaw the provision of at least 116, and probably 172, of the Pz Kpfw VI/VK 3601, with variants such as armoured command vehicles included. In the event, due to shortage of tungsten carbide, required as the penetrating core of the ammunition for the 7.5cm Type 0725 gun, Hitler ordered that no further development of this gun be undertaken;[19] as the turrets to mount it were also cancelled, four turretless prototype chassis were delivered in September 1942 for use as recovery vehicles

◀ The VK 3601 prototype on automotive running trials; note the narrow track, and the lack of return rollers in conjunction with large-diameter interleaved road wheels. (Author's Collection)

for the Tiger 1. The first prototype had been finished in March 1942 and delivered to the HWA as an experimental vehicle for WaPrüf 6 use. For use as a recovery vehicle, the chassis needed modification so that a 40-tonne capacity winch, by the firm of FAMO-Ursus, could be installed; this development, however, was not continued after 1942, on Hitler's decision that no armoured recovery vehicle would be provided for the Tiger 1;[20]

With the cancellation of the Type 0725 gun development, there remained only one other available gun with the required penetration performance (100mm at 1,500 metres' range); this was the Krupp-designed 8.8cm FlaK 36 (L/56) anti-aircraft gun. This gun in a tank turret required a turret ring diameter of 1,850mm as opposed to the 1,650mm diameter for the 7.5cm Type 0725 gun; it was not therefore possible to mount it on the VK 3601 without considerable modification to the vehicle. A development contract was therefore placed on Rheinmetall to design a turret for their 7.5cm KwK 42 (L/70) tank gun which would not necessitate the enlarging of the turret ring on the VK 3601.[21]

VK 4501(H)

In the event, time ran out for Rheinmetall and their turret was never put into production; the competitive order for Porsche and Henschel to produce 45-tonne vehicles mounting the 8.8cm KwK 36 (L/56) tank gun was placed on the two companies under the project number VK 4501 in May 1941, with the proviso by Reichsminister Speer that prototypes of each design must be available for demonstration to Hitler on his

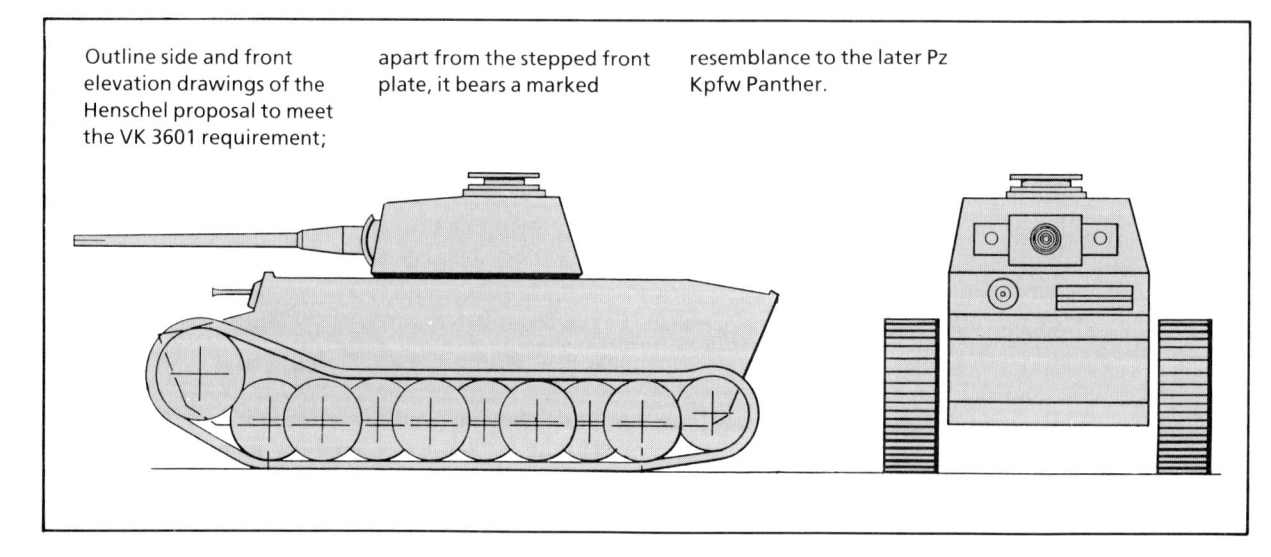

Outline side and front elevation drawings of the Henschel proposal to meet the VK 3601 requirement; apart from the stepped front plate, it bears a marked resemblance to the later Pz Kpfw Panther.

42　Three: The Tiger 1

◀ The VK 4501(H) prototype in the Henschel experimental assembly shop, probably just before the demonstration to Hitler in April 1942. Note the lack of track guards and turret rear stowage bin, as well as the pistol port in the turret side wall in place of the later escape hatch. (Author's Collection)

birthday, 20 April 1942, at his Rastenburg headquarters.[22] This exercise might appear to have been an unnecessary waste of valuable engineers' time and effort, but it undoubtedly acted as a spur to both design teams to complete their vehicles to time. Henschel decided to cover both armament options at the outset, by designing the VK 4501 (H) Model H1 to take the 8.8cm gun in the Krupp turret and the Model H2 to take the Rheinmetall turret and 7.5cm gun.[23]

It was here that Henschel benefited from their previous experience with the design of heavy tanks, and they were able to save development and design time by basing their proposals, known as the VK 4501 (H), on their earlier VK 3601; the same frontal armour of 100mm and side armour of 60mm was required on the new vehicle as on the old, but considerable modification was required on the H1 model to enable the larger diameter turret ring of the 8.8cm gun turret to be fitted. Accordingly, the hull and superstructure were redesigned, so that the superstructure projected over the greater part of the track on each side; the running gear, however, was retained unchanged, apart from the necessity of providing a wider cross-country track and an additional bolt-on wheel at alternate wheel stations to distribute the vehicle weight more evenly over the wider track and reduce the loading on the rubber tyres of the road wheels. A more powerful engine, the Maybach HL210, with an output of 650 metric hp at 3,000rpm, was fitted in conjunction with a modified Maybach Olvar gearbox, giving four reverse speeds in addition to eight forward; otherwise, the differences between the VK 3601 and the VK 4501(H) were only of detail.

According to Dr.-Ing.habil. Erwin Aders, Hen-

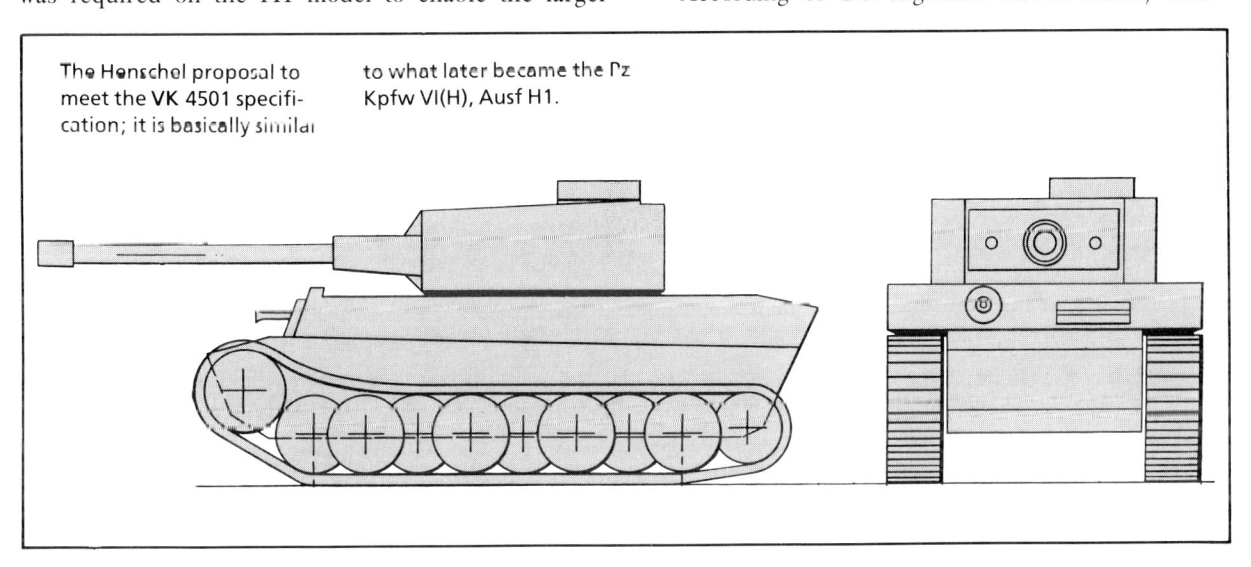

The Henschel proposal to meet the VK 4501 specification; it is basically similar to what later became the Pz Kpfw VI(H), Ausf H1.

Three: The Tiger 1   43

schel's chief designer since 1936 and responsible for the design of the Tiger 1, in conversation with the author in 1945, the building of a demonstration-ready prototype of the VK 4501(H) by mid-April 1942 meant day and night shift work virtually throughout the design and prototype-building phases. Despite the fact that the prototype would be based on an already proven design and despite Henschel's greater experience in the design and building of heavy tanks, the time-scale was incredibly short; impossibly so by today's standards. Aders in particular was a thorough, painstaking engineer who brought great practical engineering experience to the project; his direction, based on sound engineering practice and traditional methods, gave Henschel a further advantage over their rivals on the project, Porsche KG. Dr.-Ing. Ferdinand Porsche, by contrast, was an ebullient, dynamic designer with political flair, but with an impatience towards bureaucracy and established solutions to engineering problems that, eventually, would work to his and his company's disadvantage.

By the middle of 1941, the first production run of the VK 4501(H) had been fixed at 60 vehicles, to be built by Henschel at Kassel, with materials ordered for a further 100. The first production run of the VK 4501(P) was fixed at 90 tanks, to be built by Nibelungenwerke; at the same time, 50 guns and turrets were ordered from Krupp, on the assumption that the Porsche vehicle would emerge triumphant from the comparative trials in April of the following year. As both competitors would eventually use the same gun and turret, due to the cancellation of the 7.5cm Type 0725 gun, turrets and guns could be ordered with impunity; with production orders for the hull and chassis, however, it was a case of WaPrüf 6 hedging their bets at this stage.

In July 1941, a further spur to the competing design teams was provided when the German Army encountered large numbers of the hitherto unknown Soviet T-34 medium tank in action on the Eastern Front. This encounter came as a very great shock to the Germans; as a result, by October of that year, their morale had been so lowered that their commander, Colonel-General Guderian, issued an urgent request in October 1941 from his HQ in Orel for a representative team of senior HWA officers and representatives of the German tank industry to visit the Eastern Front, firstly to see the appalling conditions under which their tanks had to operate and secondly to inspect and assess the T-34 with a view to designing a German version as soon as possible. This visit took place in November 1941, the team, consisting of Colonels Kniepkamp and Fichtner of the HWA, Aders, Porsche and a representative from MAN, flying in Hitler's personal Fieseler Storch from Berlin to Orel and motoring from there to the Tula area, whence, over a period of three days, they toured the battle area, escorted by a very experienced Panzer-regiment commander.[24]

Despite the mission's cordial reception by Guderian, however, the troops' hope that 'a better T-34' could result, in the short term, from the mission's inspection of captured and knocked-out tanks was vain; the time required to design a German version from scratch was much too long. The visit bore fruit in two ways, however; first, the members of the mission returned to Germany with a very much better idea both of conditions at the front and of the urgency attaching to the completion of the VK 4501 programme, and, secondly, they were able to incorporate the design principles of the T-34 into the armour arrangement of tanks following the VK 4501 into production, such as the Panther and Tiger 2. The water obstacles found in the USSR were the cause of an additional requirement for the VK 4501; it had to be able to operate under water to a depth of 4.5 metres, a requirement which imposed further complication and delay on the design.

As has been recounted in an earlier chapter, by dint of superhuman efforts on the part of all concerned in both firms, the two VK 4501 prototypes were ready just in time for the demonstration to Hitler on 20 April 1942. While the demonstration was not conclusive in indicating the winner of the competition, it did indicate that the Henschel vehicle was likely to prove the more reliable; this was confirmed, to the surprise of Hitler, who had already ordered the production of 90 Porsche vehicles, by the subsequent exhaustive trials at Berka overseen by Colonel Thomale and Professor von Eberan.[25], as a result of which:

a. The Henschel vehicle was ordered into production.
b. The 90 Porsche vehicles already ordered were converted to self-propelled mountings for the 8.8cm PaK 43(L/71) anti-tank gun.
c. The 50 turrets ordered from Krupp for the Porsche vehicle were diverted to Henschel for mounting on their first 50 vehicles.

The most important military requirement was for the Panzertruppen to have the vehicle that was finally chosen in their hands, in quantity, by the early summer of 1943 at the latest; Hitler, with boundless optimism and in complete ignorance of the problems involved, insisted that it must be ready for action in September 1942!

Pz Kpfw VI(H) (Tiger), Sd Kfz 181

By dint of extraordinary efforts by all involved at Henschel, the first pre-production vehicle, now known as the Pz Kpfw VI(H), left Henschel's Kassel factory in August 1942; it was sent to the Panzer barracks at Fallingbostel on the Lüneburger Heide. On being taken into service, it was given the official Ordnance vocabulary title 'Pz Kpfw VI(H), Ausf H1 (Sd Kfz 181)'. By this time, its weight in action had risen from the specified 45 tonnes to a staggering 56 tonnes; this increase was largely attributable to the increase in the main armament calibre from 7.5cm to 8.8cm, and the consequent increases in turret size, turret ring diameter, superstructure width and track width, together with the additional road wheels.

Three experimental prototypes and a pre-production run of thirty tanks were followed by a succession of production orders covering a production life of two years, from August 1942 to August 1944. Despite the urgency with which prototype trials had been carried out, however, it proved impossible to have an action-ready unit of 25 tanks by 1 October 1942, as Hitler had required, due to the large number of modifications found to be essential during these trials. The 25 tanks were to have equipped the first of the two Tiger units promised to Rommel as reinforcements and due to reach his Afrika Korps in that month. Nevertheless, by 31 December 1942 a total of 83 Tigers had been completed, all in Henschel's Kassel works, and the minimum total of 145 tanks forecast to be completed by 1 May 1943 was in fact exceeded.

By May 1943, three versions of the Pz Kpfw VI(H) had made their appearance:

a. The prototypes, which did not see overseas service but were used at Fallingbostel for training the newly formed Tiger units, and for trials.
b. Early production vehicles (chassis nos. 250001 to 250100), which equipped the first two Heavy Tank Battalions (501 and 502).
c. Middle production tanks (chassis nos. 250101 to 251164), which equipped subsequently formed units and formed the bulk of production. From no. 250495 onwards, the deep-wading equipment was omitted.

As will be seen from the illustrations, and from the chart, the external differences between these versions were ones of detail only; they can, however, be useful in identifying from photographs the unit to which the tank depicted belonged.

A fourth version began to appear in 1944, in which one or more of the following modifications were incorporated:

a. The rubber-tyred road wheels were replaced by

▼ The first two prototype Tigers arrive at Fallingbostel in August 1942; note the early turrets, with two pistol ports and a Pz Kpfw III turret rear stowage bin, as well as the lack of track guards. (Hartmann)

steel-tyred resilient wheels from approximately chassis no. 250800.

b. The early 'dustbin' type of commander's cupola was replaced by the later lower version, with an AA MG mounting ring, as also used on Panther and Tiger 2, from chassis no. 250391 onwards.

c. The three smoke grenade-launchers on each side of the turret were dispensed with.

d. Stowage for five vertically stowed track links was provided externally on each turret side wall.

e. The two hull roof-mounted headlamps were replaced by a single lamp mounted on the driver's front plate.

Of a total of 1,376 Tiger 1 ordered, 1,350 were produced; chassis numbers ran in a continuous series from 250001 to 251350. Maximum production in one month was attained in April 1944, when 104 tanks came off the assembly line.[26] Three vehicles from the October 1942 production, named V1, V2 and V3, were allocated as experimental vehicles (Versuchsfahrzeuge): of these, chassis no. 250017 (V1) was sent to the Döllersheim proving ground for comparative trials against the Tiger(P); no. 250018 (V2), without its turret but fitted with a ZF electric gearbox, was also sent to Döllersheim and V3, with chassis no. 250019, was used for submersed running trials (UK-Versuche) in the Henschel diving tank at Haustenbeck/L in April 1943.[27] Two other early chassis, numbers 250003 and 250006, were used for 'firing-at' trials at Kummersdorf ranges, in comparison with a VK 4501(P) hull. Three other chassis, from the middle production series, with the chassis numbers 250363, 250366 and 250367, were also taken to Kummersdorf for comparative firing-at trials of hulls by Krupp and Dortmund Hoerder Huttenverein. Other interesting chassis numbers were 250122, the vehicle captured in Tunisia and now in the Bovington Tank Museum, 250012, also captured in Tunisia, formerly in the US Army Ordnance Corps Tank Museum at Aberdeen Proving Ground, Maryland, and now back in Germany at the military vehicle museum at Sinsheim, Baden/Wurttemberg, and 250455, which was ordered by Japan at a cost of 645,000 Reichsmarks[28] but, although invoiced in November 1943, was never sent.

Although known colloquially as the Tiger by the troops from the time of its first introduction into service, it was not until late 1943 that the Pz Kpfw VI, Ausf H, was renamed the Pz Kpfw Tiger, Ausf E by Hitler's order.[29] As the Ausf B came into service, the Ausf E also became known colloquially within units as the Tiger 1, to distinguish it from its younger brother the Ausf B, or Tiger 2.

General arrangement drawings of the mid-production model of the Tiger 1, in this case fitted with wide tracks.

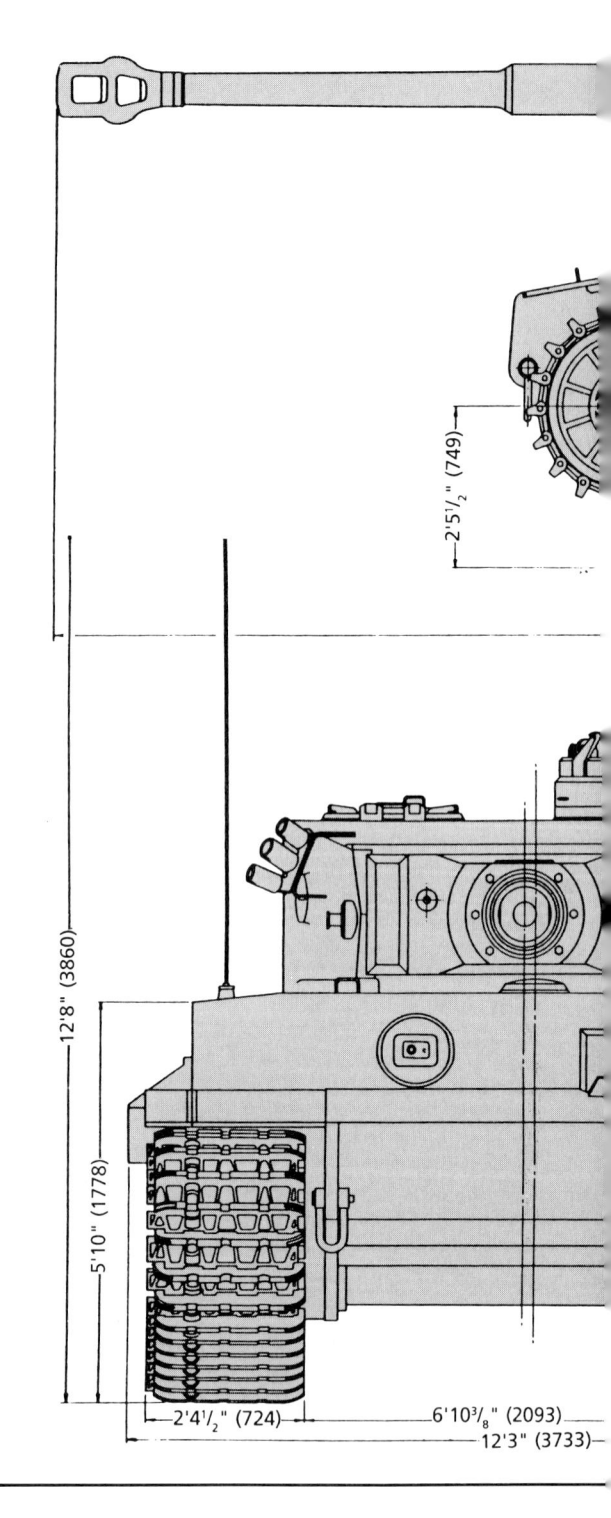

11'10 1/8" (3610)
27'9" (8464)

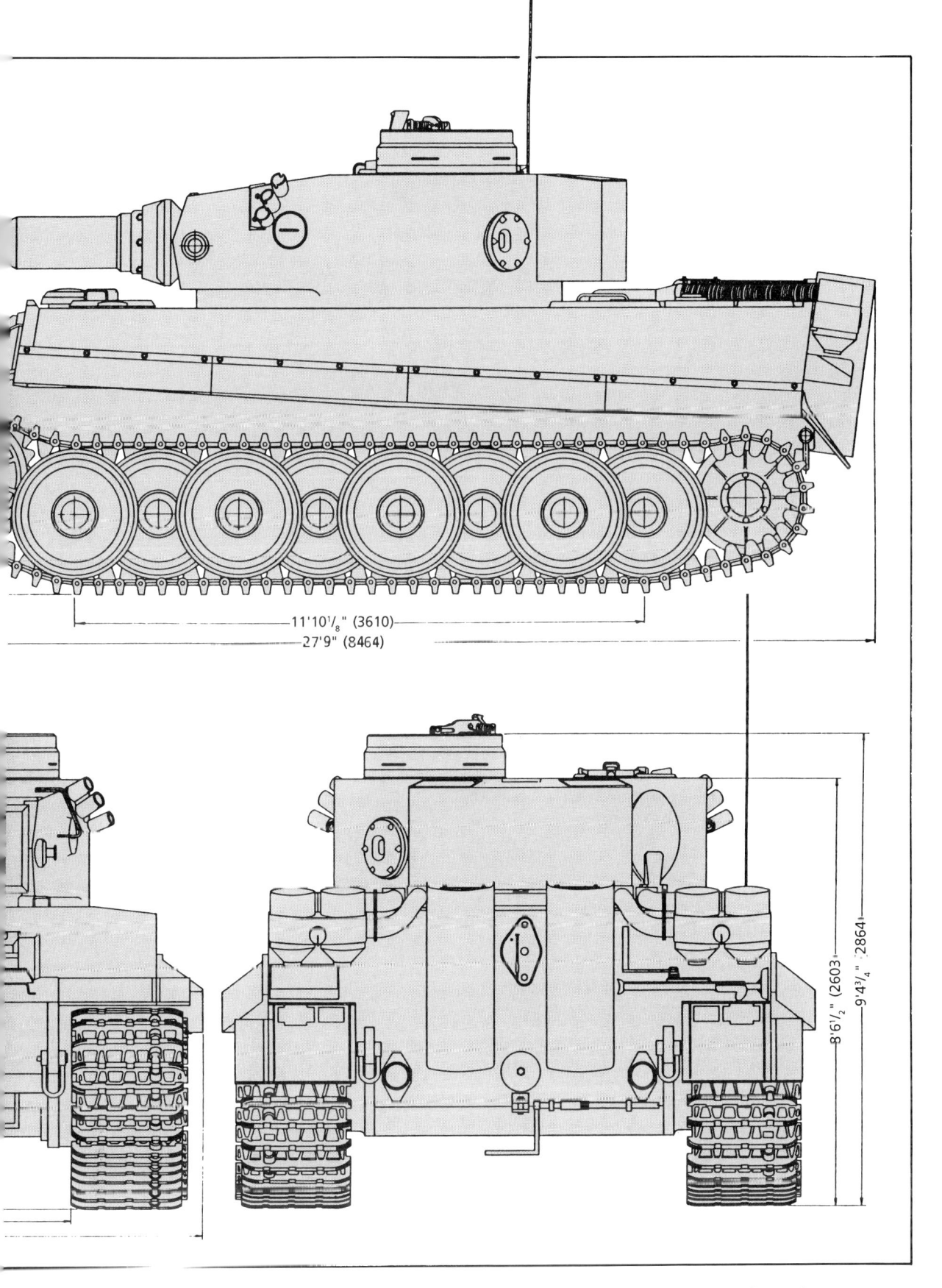

8'6 1/2" (2603)
9'4 3/4" (2864)

Three: The Tiger 1   47

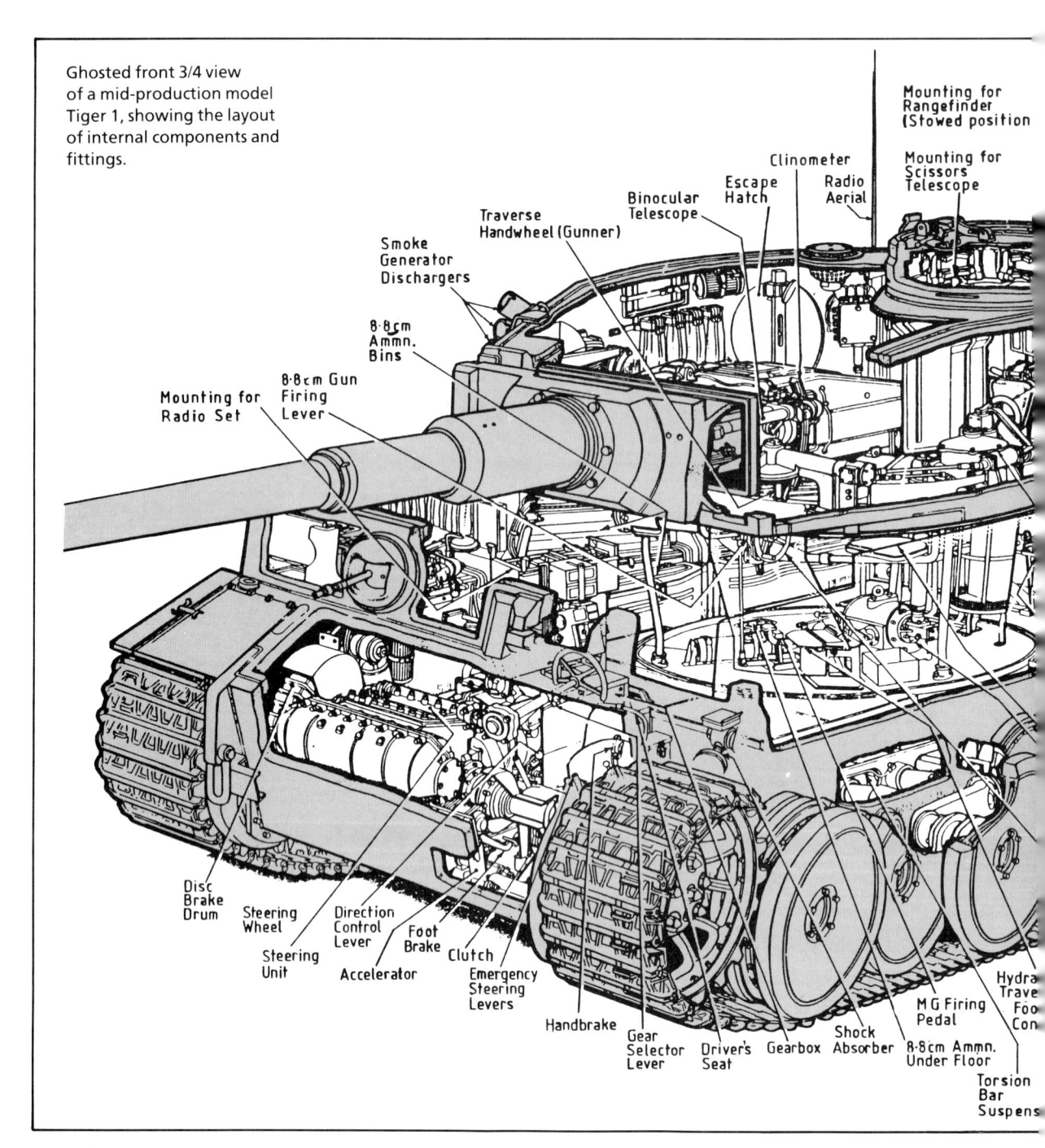

Ghosted front 3/4 view of a mid-production model Tiger 1, showing the layout of internal components and fittings.

Labels: Smoke Generator Dischargers; Traverse Handwheel (Gunner); Binocular Telescope; Escape Hatch; Clinometer; Radio Aerial; Mounting for Rangefinder (Stowed position); Mounting for Scissors Telescope; 8·8cm Ammn. Bins; 8·8cm Gun Firing Lever; Mounting for Radio Set; Disc Brake Drum; Steering Wheel; Steering Unit; Direction Control Lever; Foot Brake; Accelerator; Clutch; Emergency Steering Levers; Handbrake; Gear Selector Lever; Driver's Seat; Gearbox; Shock Absorber; 8·8cm Ammn. Under Floor; MG Firing Pedal; Hydra Trave Foo Con; Torsion Bar Suspens

Because of the large number of wide water obstacles likely to be encountered in the USSR, and inspired initially by the preparations for the projected invasion of Britain, the Tiger 1 was initially equipped for full submersion, to a depth of approximately 4.5 metres; the all-welded construction of hull and turret facilitated the task of waterproofing the vehicle, but in addition:

a. All hatches and other openings incorporated built-in rubber sealing rings.
b. The turret ring was sealed by means of a built-in inflatable tube.
c. Elaborate arrangements were made to feed air to the crew and engine via a collapsible telescopic snorkel tube erected on the rear engine deck.
d. The entire interior of the tank was sealed except for a small compartment on each side of the engine compartment, containing the radiators;

48   Three: The Tiger 1

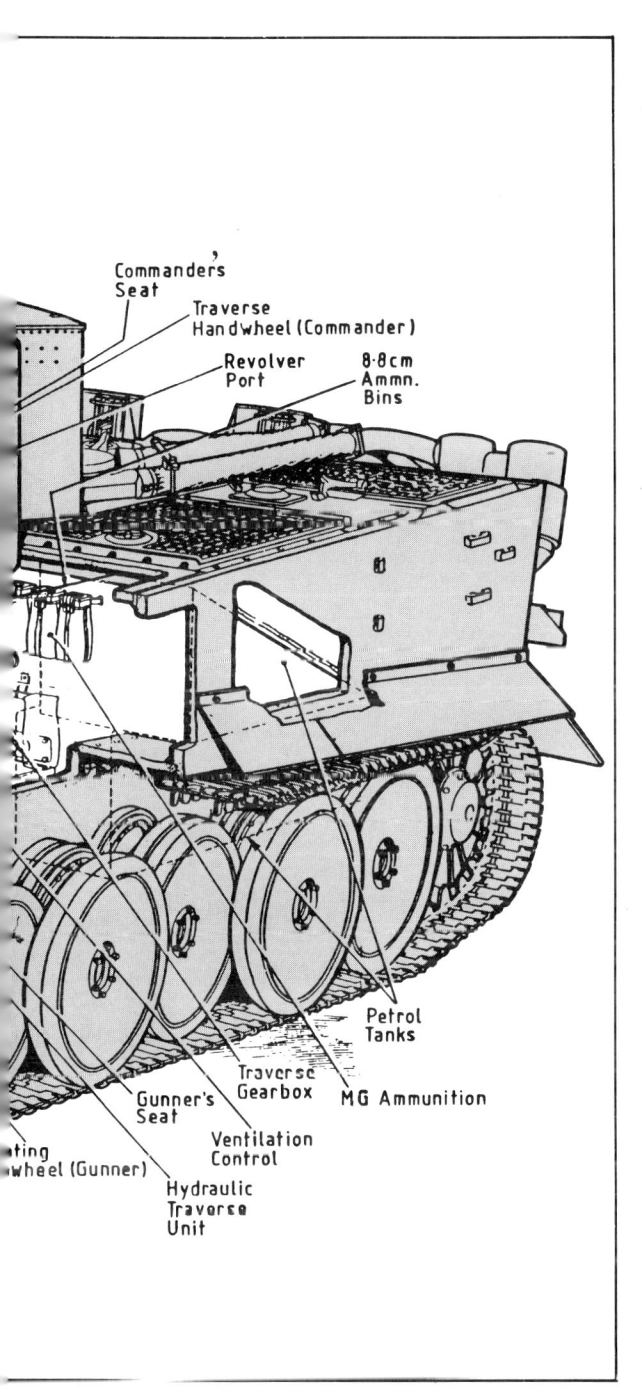

these were cooled by the water entering the compartments rather than by air.

e. The gun mantlet was sealed by means of a rubber-lined frame clamped into position, the gun by the canvas muzzle cover and a round of ammunition in the breech.

Although elaborate and expensive, these far-sighted arrangements were effective in permitting under-water travel to the designed depth; they were abandoned, from chassis no. 250495 onwards as the need for them was reduced by war conditions. Their effectiveness, however, was such as to impress all the Allied designers who, after the war, incorporated similar ideas in their post-war designs of main battle tank.

As compared with other tanks in service at the time, the Tiger 1 was outstandingly well armed and protected; it was the first German tank to carry armour of greater thickness than 50mm and mounted an outstanding gun in a fully traversing turret. As a result, it was of exceptional size and weight, factors which limited its radius of action (due to small fuel tank capacity and high petrol consumption) and its transportability by rail and road. For rail transportation, special rail flat wagons had to be built; these were the six-axled SSyms wagons of the Reichsbahn, a design still in use in Germany after the war for transporting the tanks of the Occupying Powers. In addition, the wide battle tracks, together with the outer road wheels, the track guards and the air pre-cleaners, had to be removed and replaced by narrow tracks to bring the tank width within the loading gauge limits; as each track weighed some 3 tonnes and took up considerable stowage space, this presented quite a logistic problem. The operation of changing the tracks took some 25 minutes. For road transportation, a 60-tonne capacity low-loader trailer, by the firm of Kassböhrer of Ulm, was introduced; this trailer had 48 rubber-tyred wheels.

Recovery of broken-down or bogged tanks in the field also posed a problem, in the absence of any specially designed tracked ARV; generally speaking, recovering a Tiger in the forward area entailed the use of at least one other Tiger, while in rear areas on the line of march two 18-tonne half-tracked tractors were required.

The use of heavy armour plate necessitated the employment of flat plates wherever possible, resulting in a simple box-like shape to the hull; in a departure from previous German practice, the superstructure was welded to the hull rather than bolted, while interlocking as well as step-jointing of the plates was also introduced. Similarly, the vertical sides and rear of the turret were formed from a single rolled plate in the form of a horseshoe, giving that also a simple, slab-sided appearance.

Massive cast manganese steel tracks of comparatively short pitch were driven by twin, toothed front sprockets; track tensioning was by means of an adjustable rear idler, access to the internal adjusting mechanism being through the hull rear plate. The vehicle was sprung on torsion bars, one to each wheel station,

Three: The Tiger 1 49

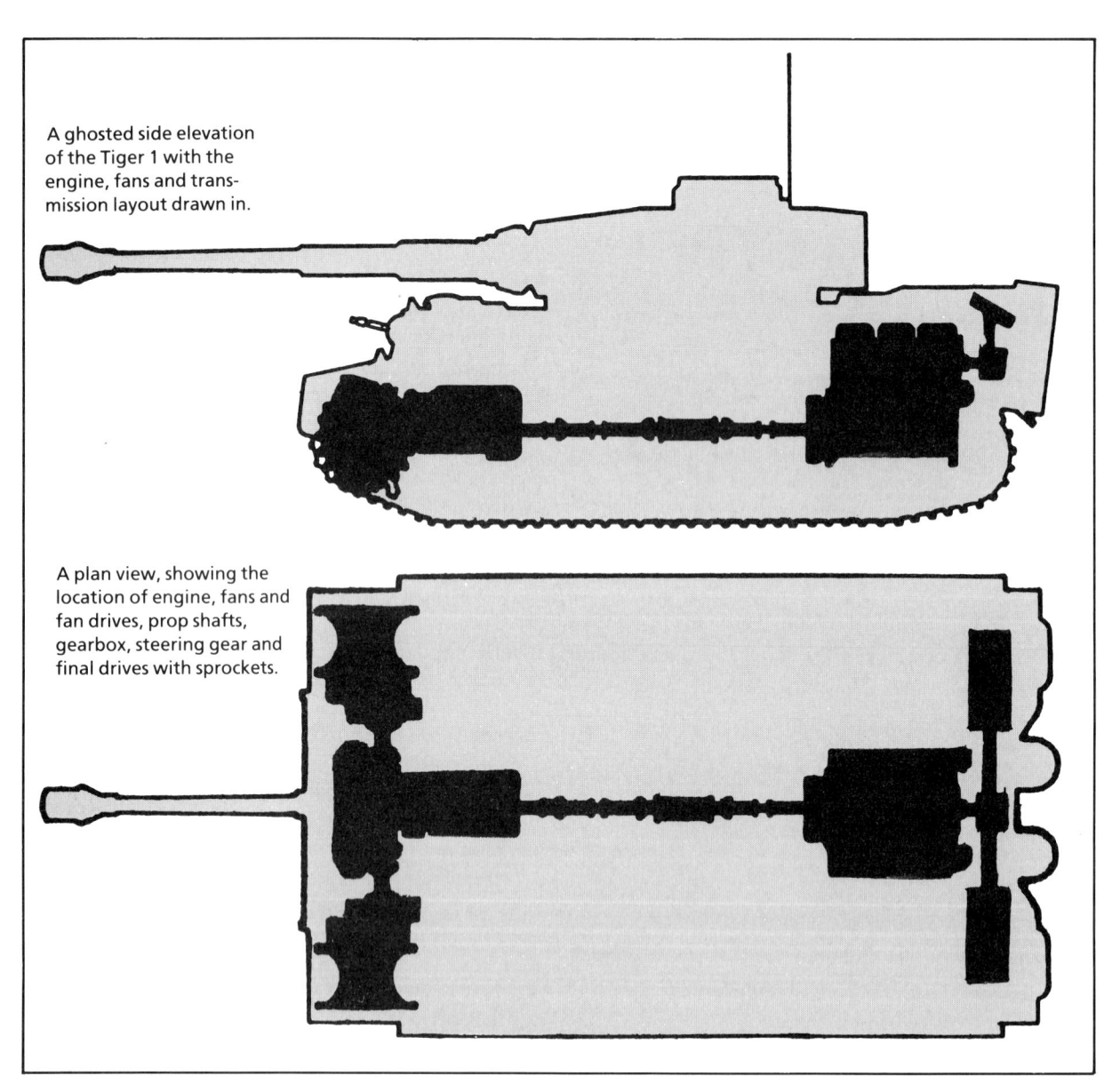

A ghosted side elevation of the Tiger 1 with the engine, fans and transmission layout drawn in.

A plan view, showing the location of engine, fans and fan drives, prop shafts, gearbox, steering gear and final drives with sprockets.

◄ Front 3/4 view of the prototype Tiger 1, fitted with narrow tracks. (Author's Collection)

► Rear 3/4 view of the same vehicle; note the lack of protection round the exhausts, as well as the Pz Kpfw III stowage bin on the rear of the turret. (Author's Collection)

▲ The first Tiger rolls off the rail flat SSyms wagon at Fallingbostel; narrow tracks are fitted and the outer road wheels removed. (Hartmann)

Three: The Tiger 1

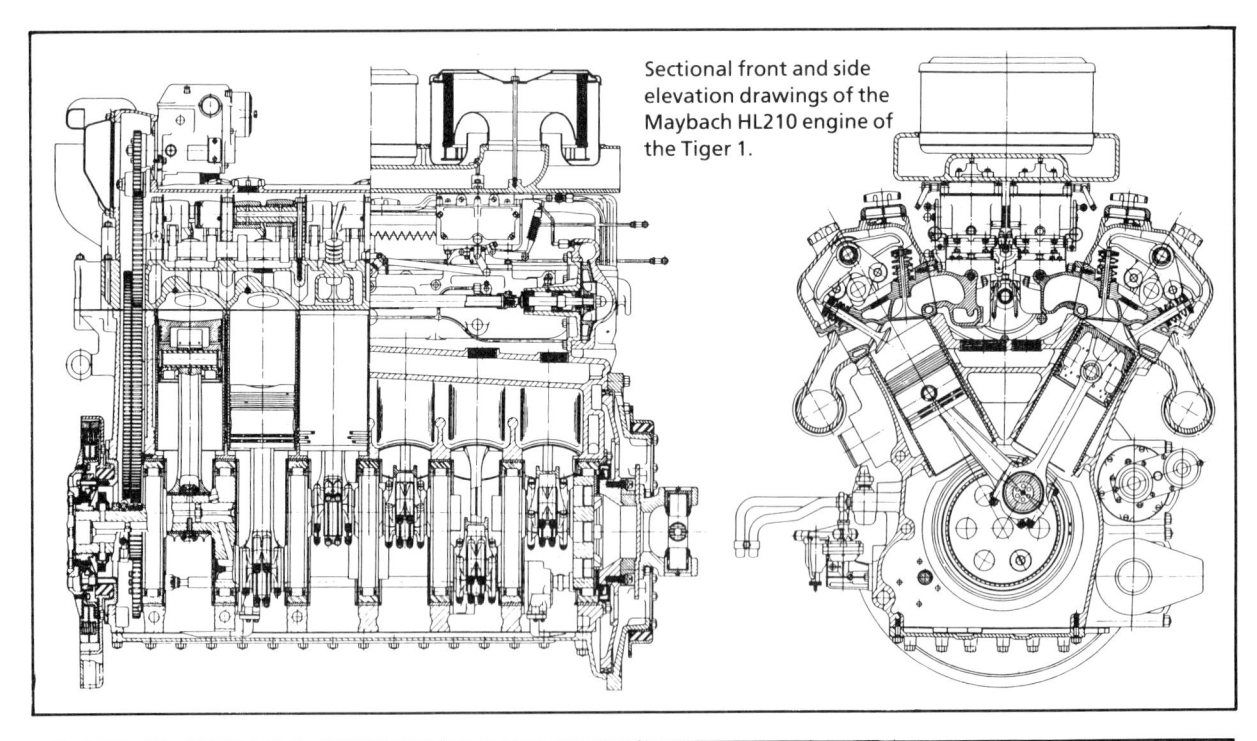

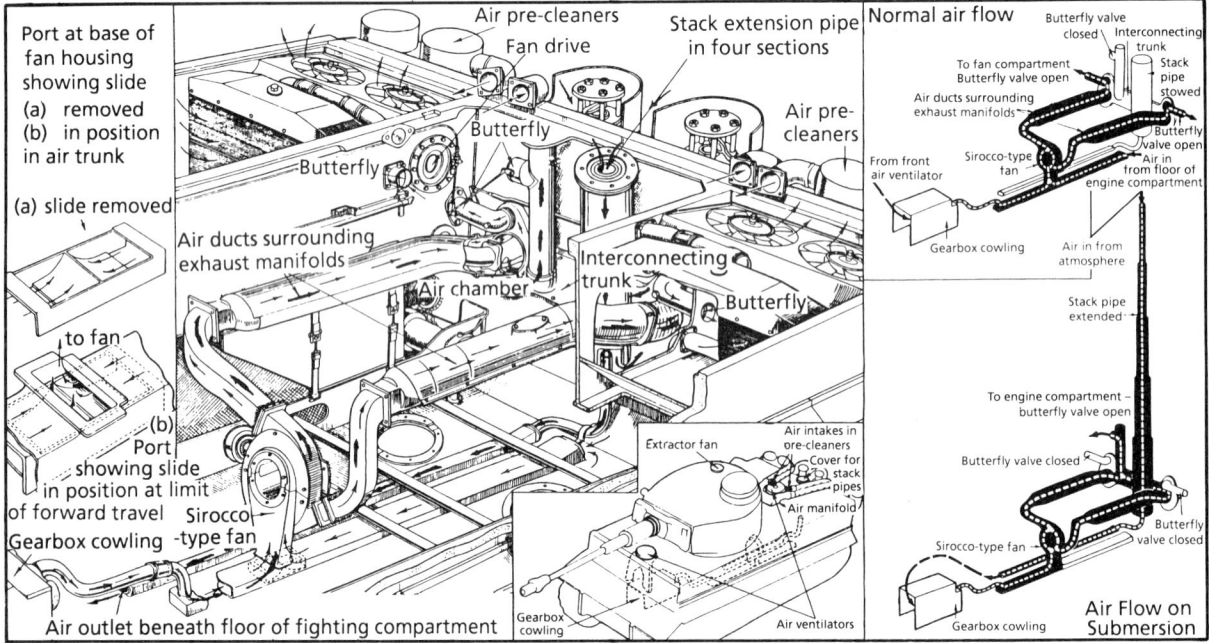

Sectional front and side elevation drawings of the Maybach HL210 engine of the Tiger 1.

mounted transversely across the belly plate. Even distribution of the vehicle weight on the tracks was achieved by the use of triple rubber-tyred road wheels, interleaved with their neighbours. In order to accommodate the sixteen torsion bars within the hull floor space, trailing suspension arms were used on one side and leading arms on the other.

The mechanical and crew layout followed normal German practice, although the elaboration and refinement in design of certain components was carried to an exceptional degree; the Maybach HL210 (or 230 in later versions) V-12 petrol engine was mounted centrally at the rear, driving forward by means of a propeller shaft beneath the turret floor to the clutch and the pre-selective Maybach Olvar gearbox accommodated forward in the driver's compartment. Bolted to the gearbox was the hydraulic steering unit, mounted transversely in the hull nose and incorporating a bevel

52 *Three: The Tiger 1*

◀ Layout of the Tiger cooling systems, showing method of adaptation to submerged travel and consequent change in air flow, indicated by the thicker black arrows.

▲ The first two Tigers are now both off the rail flats; the Pz Kpfw III rear turret bin can be clearly seen on the front vehicle. (Hartmann)

▼ An early production model Tiger 1, in this case the platoon sergeant's tank of '3' Platoon, No. 1 Company, of 501 Heavy Tank Battalion in Tunisia. Note the lack of hinged outer portions to the curved front track guards. (Hartmann)

54   *Three: The Tiger 1*

▲ Side view of a middle-production Tiger 1, in this case that of the platoon commander of '3' Platoon, No 1 Company of 504 Heavy Tank Battalion; this is the tank captured intact in April 1943 and shipped to UK for examination by STT. (Author's Collection)

◀ Rear view of an early production Tiger 1, showing the slotted exhaust guards; the prickly pear, coupled with the Feifel air pre-cleaners on the tail plate, indicate that this vehicle is in North Africa, in fact belonging to 501 Heavy Tank Battalion. (Hartmann)

◀ A late production model Tiger 1; note the steel-tyred resilient road wheels, the track links stowed on the turret side wall and the late model commander's cupola with swivelling hatch cover. (Author's Collection)

▶ The turret removed showing (top picture) the turret basket; this is a late model turret, with the episcope-fitted commander's cupola with rotating hatch cover and stowage for extra track links on the side wall. The lower picture shows the turret with mantlet, gun and interior fittings removed. (Author's Collection)

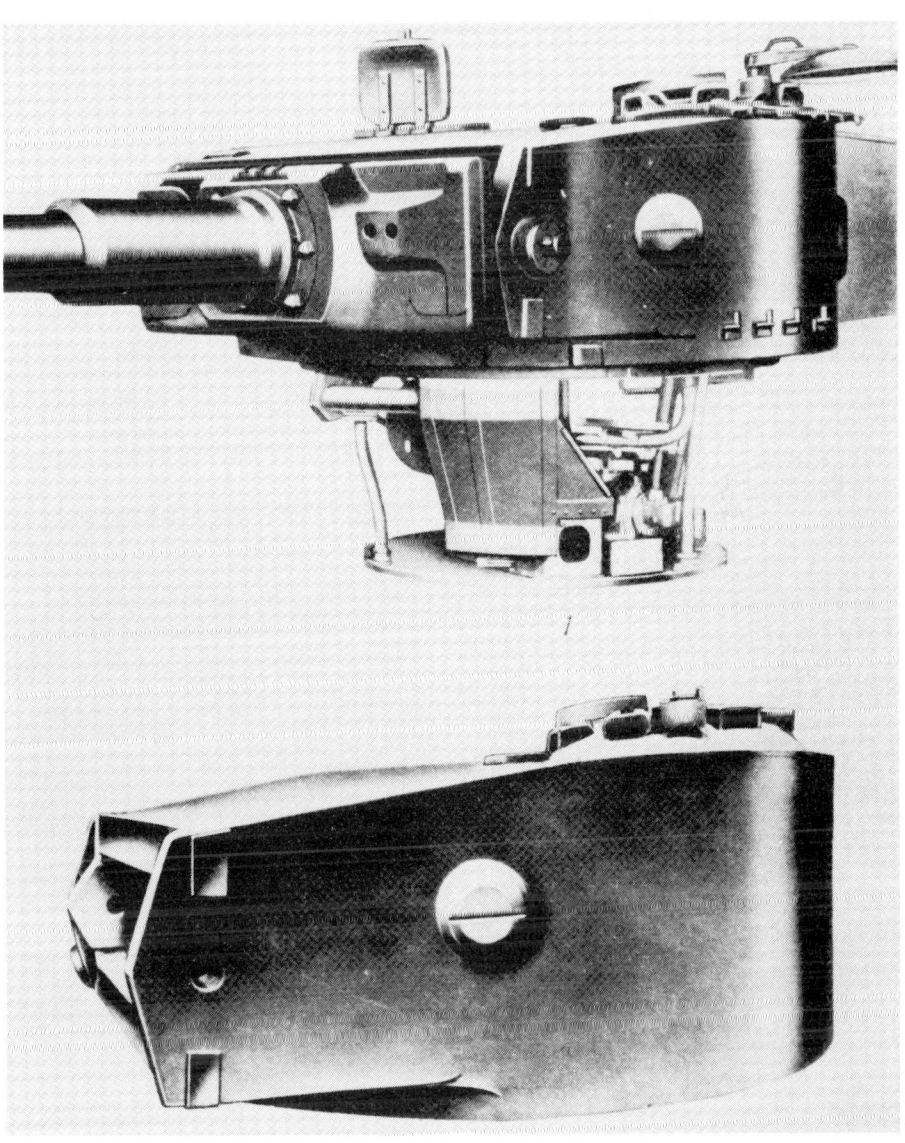

Three: The Tiger 1   55

drive to the reduction gears housed in each final drive unit. In addition to the steering levers of the normal German tank, the Tiger 1 had a steering wheel to operate the power steering; the steering levers operated steering brakes, to be used when the power steering was inoperative. The steering unit was similar in principle to the British Merritt-Brown, with the refinement of giving two radii of turn in each gear; the adoption of a fully-regenerative steering system represented a considerable departure from the simple clutch/brake system previously employed on German tanks, and was no doubt necessitated by the much greater weight of the Tiger. The transmission and steering units were extremely complicated and undoubtedly costly in man/hours to produce; however, those who drove the tank commented favourably upon the resultant lightness of control of such a heavy vehicle, so that this expenditure was probably justified.

The turret was unusually spacious but, even so, the breech of the 8.8cm gun reached nearly to the rear wall, dividing the fighting compartment in two; the gunner with his binocular, stationary-eyepiece sighting telescope, sat on the left-hand side of the gun with the commander behind him, while the loader sat facing the rear on the other side of the gun. On early and mid-production models the commander had a cupola with five vision slits; on later production models, the lower, Panther type, with an AA MG mounting ring and with seven episcopes, replaced it. The turret was provided with manual and power traverse, the latter from an hydraulic pump unit mechanically driven from a power take-off at the rear of the gearbox and mounted on the rotating turret floor. When the turret was removed for any purpose, therefore, it was necessary only to disconnect the shaft drive to the hydraulic pump; there was no need to disconnect the hydraulics. Gun elevation was manual only, by handwheel. Ready rounds for the 8.8cm gun were stowed in bins on each side of the fighting compartment; the remainder of the main armament ammunition was stowed under the turret floor and alongside the driver, in all a total of 92 rounds.

Auxiliary MG armament consisted of a coaxial 7.92mm MG 34 in the turret, a ball-mounted MG 34 in the hull front plate, and an AA MG 34 on the later model commander's cupola; in addition, a three-barrelled smoke grenade-launcher, electrically fired from within the turret, firing the 90mm smoke grenade Nb.K.39 (Smoke Candle 39), was mounted forward on each side of the turret on all except the latest model. On early and middle-production tanks, five mountings for electrically operated anti-personnel 'S'-Mine-dischargers were mounted on the hull roof, one at each corner facing outwards at 45° and one at the centre of the left-hand side; primarily intended for use against tank-hunting infantry on the Eastern Front, they were omitted from late production models.

56 Three: The Tiger 1

▶ Detail of a typical German double-baffle muzzle brake for a high-velocity gun, in this case the 88mm KwK 36 (L/56) of the Tiger 1.

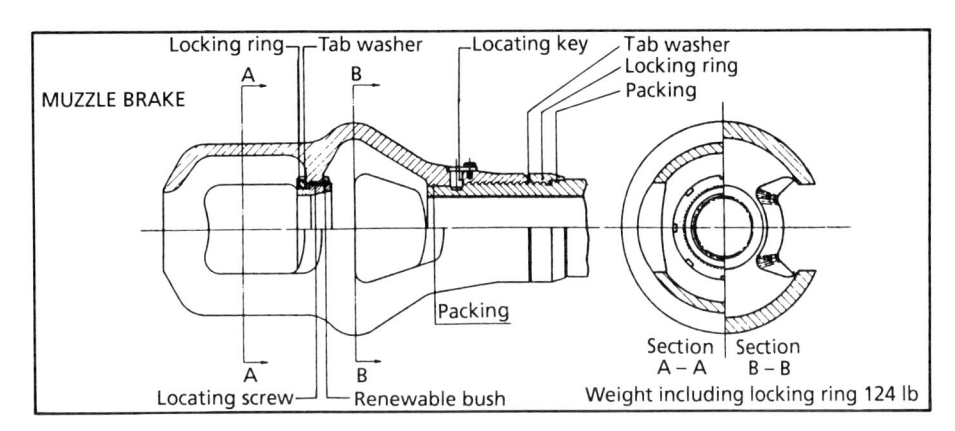

▶ Three different views of the Tiger's steering gearbox, taken from the driver's handbook for the vehicle. (Author's Collection)

◀ The VK 4501 (H) prototype vehicle with snorkel for underwater travel erected on the engine deck. (Tank Museum)

Three: The Tiger 1 57

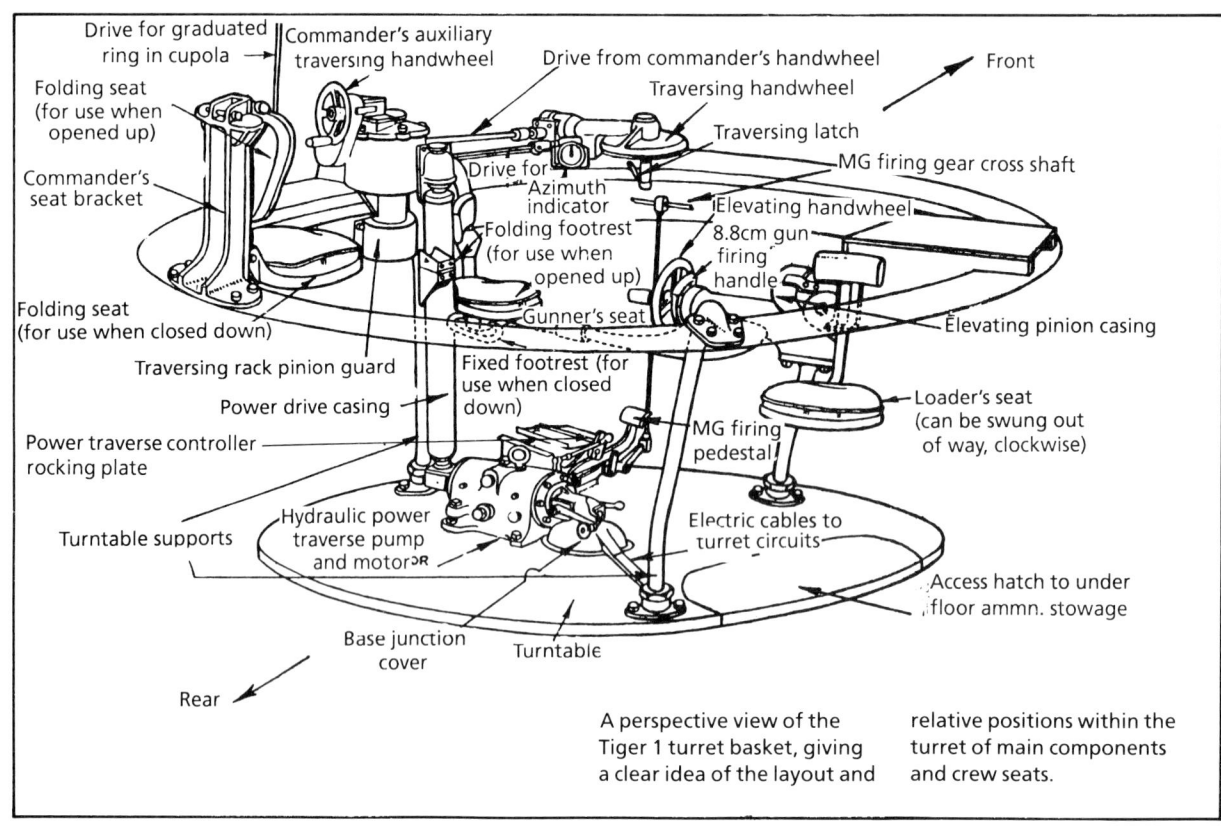

A perspective view of the Tiger 1 turret basket, giving a clear idea of the layout and relative positions within the turret of main components and crew seats.

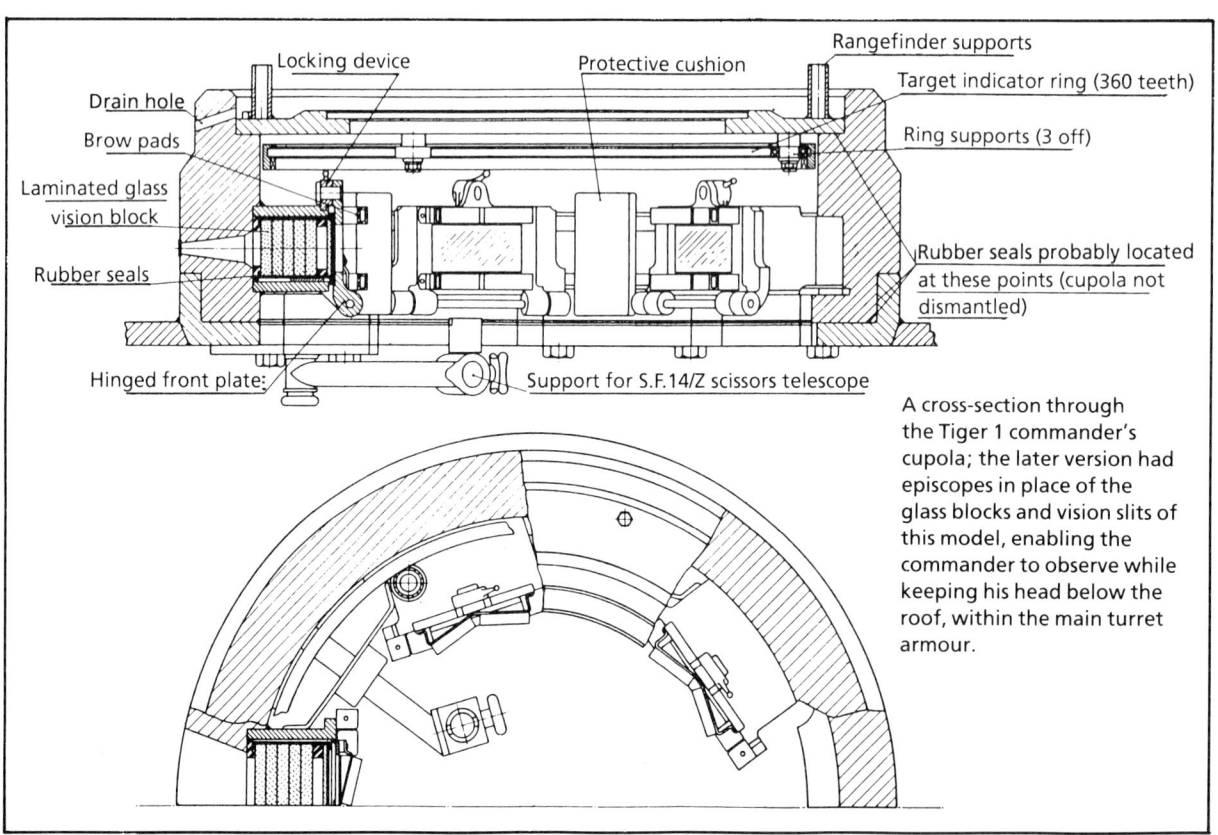

A cross-section through the Tiger 1 commander's cupola; the later version had episcopes in place of the glass blocks and vision slits of this model, enabling the commander to observe while keeping his head below the roof, within the main turret armour.

58   Three: The Tiger 1

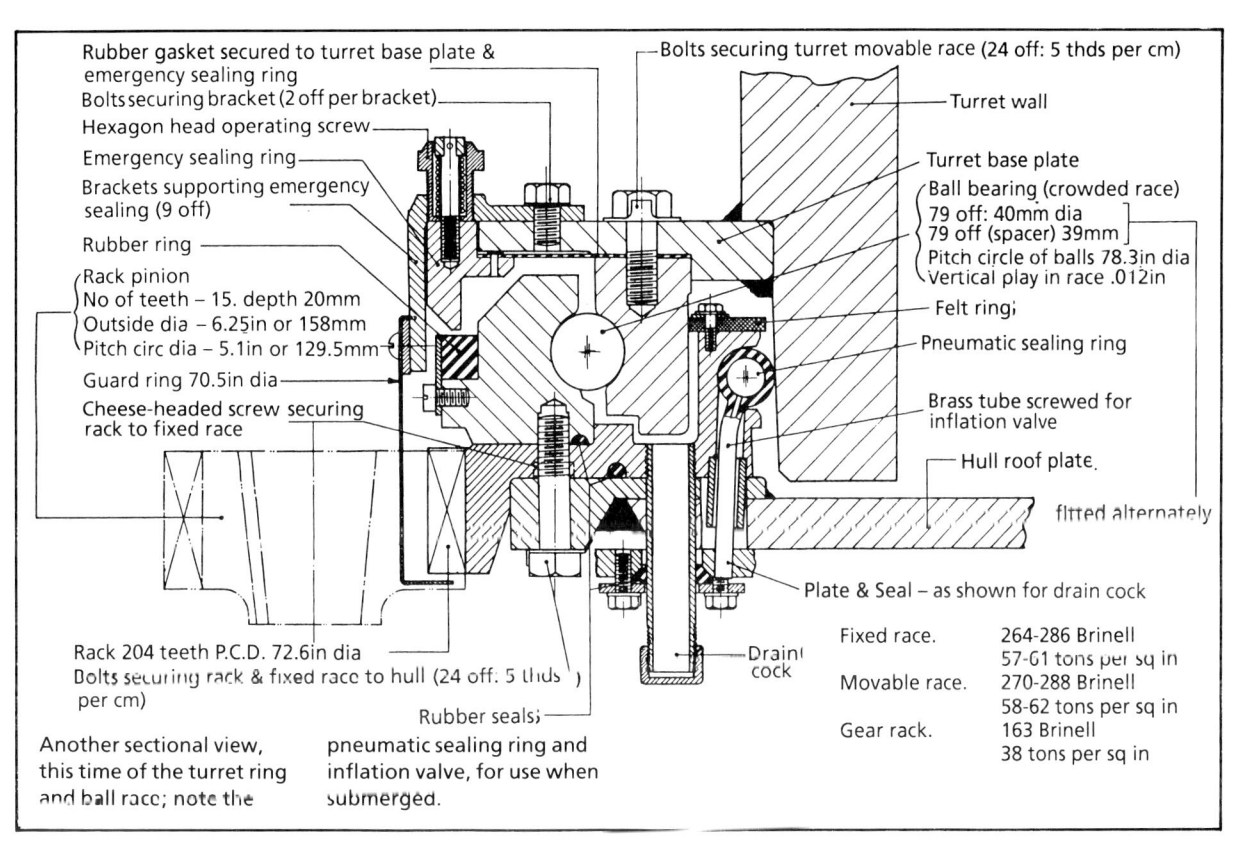

- Rubber gasket secured to turret base plate & emergency sealing ring
- Bolts securing bracket (2 off per bracket)
- Hexagon head operating screw
- Emergency sealing ring
- Brackets supporting emergency sealing (9 off)
- Rubber ring
- Rack pinion
  - No of teeth – 15. depth 20mm
  - Outside dia – 6.25in or 158mm
  - Pitch circ dia – 5.1in or 129.5mm
- Guard ring 70.5in dia
- Cheese-headed screw securing rack to fixed race
- Rack 204 teeth P.C.D. 72.6in dia
- Bolts securing rack & fixed race to hull (24 off. 5 thds per cm)
- Bolts securing turret movable race (24 off: 5 thds per cm)
- Turret wall
- Turret base plate
- Ball bearing (crowded race)
  - 79 off: 40mm dia
  - 79 off (spacer) 39mm
  - Pitch circle of balls 78.3in dia
  - Vertical play in race .012in
- Felt ring
- Pneumatic sealing ring
- Brass tube screwed for inflation valve
- Hull roof plate
- fitted alternately
- Plate & Seal – as shown for drain cock
- Drain cock
- Rubber seals

Fixed race.	264-286 Brinell	57-61 tons per sq in
Movable race.	270-288 Brinell	58-62 tons per sq in
Gear rack.	163 Brinell	38 tons per sq in

Another sectional view, this time of the turret ring and ball race; note the pneumatic sealing ring and inflation valve, for use when submerged.

▼ Recovery of a Tiger 1, showing the two Sd Kfz 9 half-tracks required to tow it. (Author's Collection)

▲ A Tiger 1 fitted with narrow transport tracks on a Reichsbahn SSyms wagon. (Author's Collection)

▼ The first Tiger (turret no. 131) to be captured in running condition by the Allies, in the position in which it was captured on 22 April 1943, near Medjez-el-Bab, Tunisia; note the step below the spare track link rack, which distinguishes this Tiger 1 from any other. (IWM)

▲ The captured Tiger '131' on display in Tunis in June 1943, with snorkel erected and Winston Churchill standing on the turret. (Author's Collection)

Pz Kpfw VI (H) Ausf H1 (Later Pz Kpfw Tiger Ausf E) (Sd Kfz 181)

Outline Specification

Weight in action	56 tonnes	Auxiliary	Three 7.92mm MG34
Crew	5		Six 90mm smoke grenade-launchers
Dimensions:			Five 'S'-mine launchers
Overall length incl. gun	8,450mm	Ammunition carried:	92 × 8.8cm, 3,920 × 7.92mm
Overall length excl. gun	6,316mm	Power plant:	Maybach HL210 or HL230
Overall width with battle tracks	3,733mm	Type	V-12 water-cooled, petrol
Overall width with narrow tracks	3,150mm	Output	650 metric hp (HL210)
Overall height	2,870mm		700 metric hp (HL230)
Belly clearance	432mm	Transmission	Maybach OLVAR with 8 forward
Track on ground	3,605mm		& 4 reverse speeds
Track width with battle tracks	725mm		
Track width with narrow tracks	520mm	Running gear:	
Track centres	2,844mm	No. of road wheels	Eight triple, Interleaved, per side
Armour thicknesses:		Springing medium	Transverse torsion bars
Turret front	100mm	Drive	Front sprocket
Turret sides	80mm	Performance:	
Hull front	100mm	Max. speed (roads)	45km/hr
Superstructure sides	80mm	Range (roads)	100km
Tail plate	80mm	Fording depth	4.5m
Armament:		Step	790mm
Main	8.8cm KwK 36 (L/56)	Trench crossing	2.3m

◀ The same Tiger after its return to the UK, undergoing examination in the STT foreign vehicle hangar at Chertsey in November 1943; note the Pz Kpfw III in the foreground. (Author's Collection)

The other Tiger 1 captured in running condition in Tunisia was an early production model, the platoon sergeant's tank of 'I' Platoon, No. 1 Company of s.Pz.Abt.501, which went to the USA for detailed examination. It is shown here in the tank park at Aberdeen Proving Ground, Md., bearing the turret number 712, which it carried when captured because the Company had come under command of 7 Panzer Regiment as its seventh Company. (APG). ◀

Pz Kpfw VI (H), Ausf H1 – Sd Kfz 181
EXTERNAL DIFFERENCES BETWEEN VERSIONS

TURRET

Pre-Production	Early Production	Middle Production
Pistol Port on R.H. Rear Side Wall as on L.H. Side		Large Circular Loading/Escape Hatch on R.H. Rear Wall
Pz Kpfw III Rear Bin (as for Porsche Tiger)	Standard Large Rectangular Bin	
No Track Link Stowage Lugs on Turret Side Walls		Lugs for Vertical Stowage of 3 Spare Track Links on R.H. Side and 5 on L.H. Side
No Episcope in Turret Roof		Episcope with Armoured Hood in Turret Roof, Forward of Loader's Hatch

HULL

Pre-Production	Early Production	Middle Production
No Side Track Guards or Track Guard Mounting Points	Removable Side Track Guards Bolted to Each Superstructure Side Plate	
No 'S'-Mine Discharger Mounting Provision on Hull Roof		Provision on Hull Roof for 5 'S'-Mine Dischargers (Mounted Only on Eastern Front Vehicles)
No R.H. Superstructure Side Plate Stowage. Track Pulling Rope on L.H. Side Plate	Several Stowage Items on R.H. Superstructure Side Plate (Some Vehicles Only)	No Stowage on R.H. Superstructure Sideplate. Track Pulling Rope on L.H. Side Plate
No Spare Track Link Stowage on Hull		Stowage Bar for 12 Spare Track Links on Lower Nose Plate
Front of Hull Lower Side Plates, Above Front Towing Shackles, Undercut		Ditto Cut Vertical
No Exhaust Pipe Shields	Exhaust Pipe Shields of Bevelled Rectangular Cross-Section, with 3 Horizontal Slits in Sides	Semi-Circular Cross-Section Exhaust Pipe Covers, without Slits
No Zimmerit Used		Zimmerit Used
Front Mudguards Angled to Follow Curve of Sprocket, Cross-Hatch Non-Slip Surface to Width of Transport Tracks Only. No Outer Folding Section to Cover X-Country Wide Tracks		Front Mudguards Straight with No Surface Pattern, Lined Up with Glacis Plate. Outer Section (to Width of Wide Track) Hinged for Rail Travel
2 Holes, for KFF-2 Driver's Periscope, Above Driver's Visor		Holes for KFF-2, Above Driver's Visor, Filled In
2 Headlamps, Mounted on Front of Hull Roof, One Each Side	2 Headlamps Mounted on Brackets on L.H. & R.H. Sides of Superstructure Front Plate	Provision for 2 Headlamps Mounted on Front of Hull Roof
No Stowage on Front Glacis Plate		Shovel Stowed on Front Glacis Plate

CHAPTER FOUR
VARIANTS OF THE TIGER 1

FOR LOGISTIC and training reasons, it was, and still is, normal practice for variants of a standard tank to be designed and introduced into those units equipped with that tank. Such variants can consist of command tanks, armoured recovery vehicles, bridge-laying tanks, assault vehicles and others, too numerous to mention, such as those equipping the British 79th Armoured Division (Hobo's 'Funnies') in the Second World War.

The German Army was no exception. Command tanks and self-propelled guns of all types were based on the Pz Kpfw I, II, III and IV chassis; the Pz Kpfw III was also used as the basis for assault guns, flame-thrower tanks, artillery armoured OP tanks, armoured recovery vehicles, armoured bridge-layers, and armoured ammunition carriers, while the Pz Kpfw IV was additionally used in large numbers as an anti-aircraft tank in several different forms, an armoured infantry assault bridge and an amphibious tracked ferry. The Pz Kpfw Panther was built also in ARV, armoured OP and command tank versions, as well as a highly effective tank destroyer.

The Tiger 1, however, was an exception to this rule, partly because of the urgency attaching to the production of as many gun tanks as possible and partly because of the worsening war situation, with increasing shortages of materials, after its introduction. An armoured recovery vehicle based on its chassis was really required, as the tank was too heavy to be recoverable by ARVs based on either the Pz Kpfw III or IV, and the only other means readily available within Tiger units was to use either one or more gun tanks and their tow-ropes or two, and in soft going three, unarmoured 18-tonne half-track heavy tractors (s Zgkw 18 tonne) Sd Kfz 9, with their 2.8-tonne capacity winches. The lack of armoured protection on these vehicles made recovery

▼ Side view of a Tiger 1 ARV captured in Italy. It was a one-off unit modification, effected by removing the armament from a late production gun tank turret and mounting a primitive winch on the rear of the turret. (Tank Museum)

▲ Front 3/4 view of the Tiger ARV turret, showing the plate bolted over the hole in the mantlet after removal of the main armament. (Tank Museum)

▼ Rear view of the Tiger 1 ARV turret, showing the winch. (Tank Museum)

in the forward area by this means a dangerous business, but Hitler, as has been seen, had vetoed the development of an ARV based on the Tiger 1. The only recovery vehicle based on the Tiger 1 ever seen, by the Western Allies at least, was a unit field conversion of a standard gun tank, found in Italy in June 1944; in this vehicle the 8.8cm main armament had been removed, the mantlet retained and the opening in its centre covered by a circular plate with a hole in the centre for the muzzle of an MG. A winch and derrick were mounted on the turret.[1]

Command vehicles were another matter, however; it was obviously necessary that command tanks in Tiger units should be as indistinguishable as possible from normal gun tanks, to prevent their being singled out for attack and to simplify unit repair and maintenance as well as training. Whereas earlier command tanks, based on the Pz Kpfw III, had been provided with dummy main armament, to give more room inside for radios and map boards, this was not necessary on the much more roomy Tiger 1; a standard gun tank was converted to the command role by reducing the main armament ammunition stowage capacity from 92 to 66 rounds, removing the coaxial MG34 and, in the space thus made available, mounting an additional long-range radio set. Some 84 Tiger 1s were so converted,[2] known as 'Panzerbefehlswagen Tiger, Ausf E.' (Pz Bef Wg Tiger, Ausf E – Armoured Command Vehicle Tiger, Model E); apart from the additional 'star' radio aerial, they were externally identical with the Tiger 1 gun tank. The Tiger 1 commander's vehicles were allocated the Sd Kfz numbers 267 and 268, which had earlier been allocated to the Pz Kpfw III commanders' tanks; the latter had, by this time, become obsolete so that it had become convenient to re-allocate these numbers to the Tiger 1 series.[3]

Pz Bef Wg Tiger, Ausf E (Sd Kfz 267 und 268)

Two versions of command tank were introduced; the first, for Heavy Tank Company (s.Pz.Kp.) commanders, was known as the Sd Kfz 268, carried a crew of five (commander, radio officer/gunner, radio operator 1/loader, radio operator 2/hull gunner and driver), and was fitted with the following radio equipment:

a. Fu 5 radio, for communications within the company.
b. Fu 7 radio, for communications back to battalion HQ.
c. Bordsprechanlage B (internal communication set Type B).

The second version, known as the Sd Kfz 267, was for Heavy Tank Battalion (s.Pz.Abt.) commanders; it was similarly crewed and equipped, except that the Fu 7 was replaced by the longer-range Fu 8 radio for rearward communication from battalion HQ to regiment or higher formation headquarters.[4]

Flammtiger

It had been planned to introduce a flame-throwing version of the Tiger 1 in 1945. The original plan had involved removing the turret of a normal Tiger 1, roofing over the turret ring and mounting the flame-thrower in the roof. This idea was abandoned, however, when it was realized that such a modification would make the flame thrower tank stand out from its gun tank fellows, enabling it easily to be singled out for attack.

The final plan was to take a normal turreted Tiger and to mount the flame-thrower in the hull ball mounting in place of the MG; the weapon would have had a range of 120m – 140m and a fuel capacity of 300 litres. None of these weapons fell into the hands of the Western Allies at the end of the war, and it is not known whether or not any were actually produced.

38cm RW61 auf Stu Mrs Tiger

The only other variant of the Pz Kpfw Tiger Ausf E to enter service was a 38cm rocket assault mortar based on a turretless Tiger 1 chassis, known as the '38cm Raketenwerfer 61 auf Sturmmörser Tiger' (38cm Rocket Launcher 61 on Assault Mortar Tiger), abbreviated to '38cm RW61 auf Stu Mrs Tiger'; as far as is known, no Sd Kfz number was allocated to this vehicle.

The project arose out of a requirement, stated by Hitler in August 1943, to mount the naval 38cm launcher, Gerät 562, on the Tiger 1; he set a planning production target for the vehicle of ten Sturmmörser per month, and a mild steel prototype was demonstrated to him at the Arys troop training area in October 1943. In April 1944, in view of the limited manufacturing resources then available, the total production requirement was reduced, and the manufacture of twelve launchers, mountings and armoured superstructures was put in hand, for mounting on repaired Tiger 1 chassis. The vehicle conversion was carried out by Alkett at their Berlin/Spandau works, and by 21 September 1944 the first seven vehicles had been completed; by the end of 1944 a total of eighteen had been converted, the process – given the urgency

Side elevation drawing by MI 10, then the technical Intelligence branch of the War Office, of the Stu Mrs Tiger mounting the 38cm RW 61.

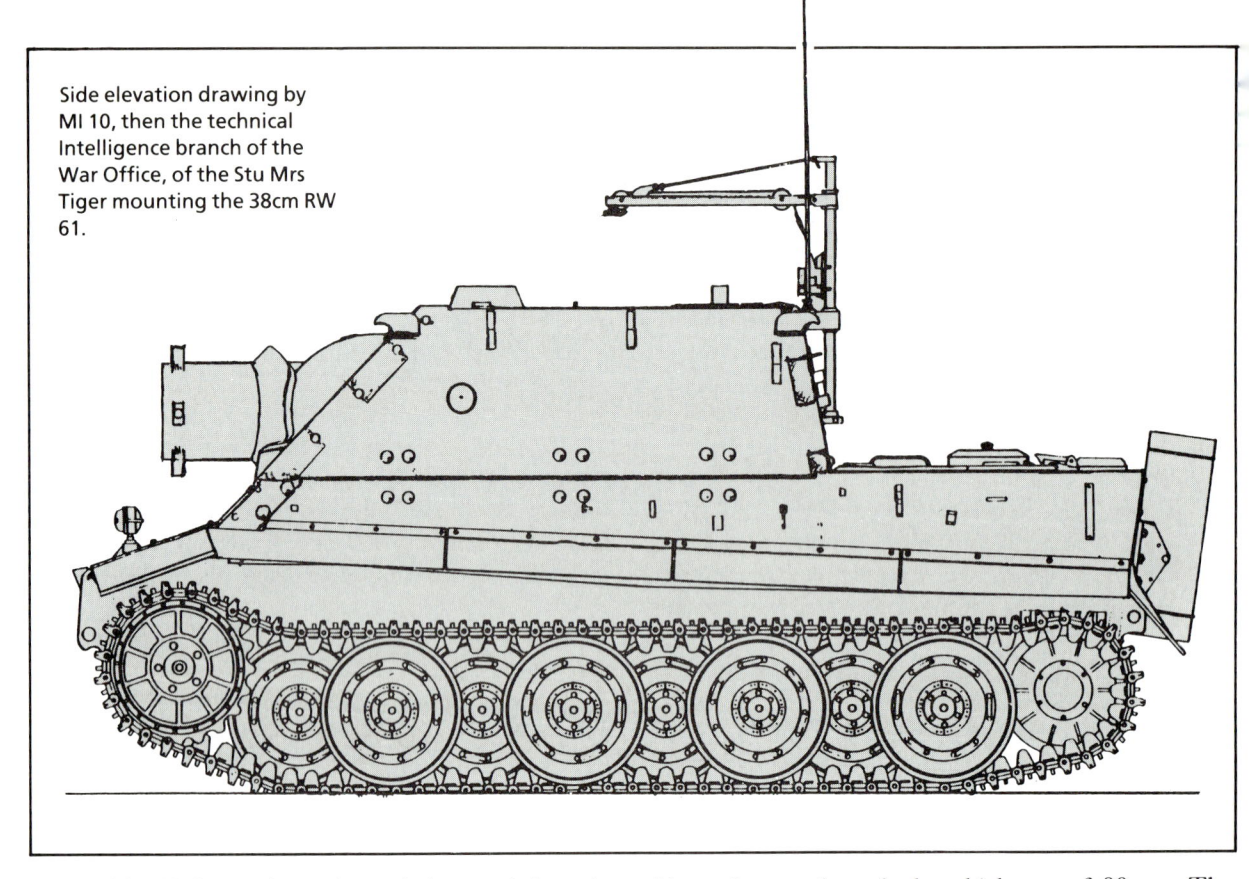

attached by Hitler to the project – being carried out in three days. Special chassis numbers, in the 0300 series, were allocated to the Sturmtigers.[5]

A monthly output of 300 rocket rounds for the 38cm launchers was envisaged; both the rocket and launcher, with a calibre length of L/5.4, had been developed for the German Navy by Rheinmetall Borsig in their Düsseldorf plant, for use in anti-submarine warfare. High-explosive (38cm R.Sprgr.4581 – 38cm High Explosive Rocket 4581) and hollow charge (HEAT) (38cm R.Hlgr 4592 – 38cm Hollow Charge Rocket 4592)[6] warheads were provided, both using the same rocket motor, the Treibsatz 4581.[7] The complete round of warhead and motor weighed some 726 pounds and was some five feet long,[8] necessitating the provision of a hand-operated crane on the rear of the superstructure for the loading of rounds into the vehicle, and a hand-operated winch running on overhead rails on the fighting compartment roof for the lifting of rounds from the stowage racks into the launcher loading tray.

The vehicle conversion consisted of the removal of the standard Tiger 1 turret and the superstructure roof forward of the engine compartment, and their replacement by a roofed, box-like superstructure/fighting compartment built of thick sloping armour plates; the front plate, sloped at 45°, was 150mm thick while the side and rear plates had a thickness of 80mm. The RW61 was ball-mounted in the superstructure front plate with a total traverse arc of 20°, made up of 10° left and 10° right, and an elevation arc of from 0° to approximately +85°. Both traverse and elevation were by hand. A folding loading tray equipped with rollers was fitted inside the fighting compartment behind the launcher; a round to be loaded was placed in the loading tray with the help of the roof-mounted winch and could be rammed into the breech only when the launcher was brought back to the horizontal. Stowage racks for twelve 38cm rounds were provided within the fighting compartment, six on each side; a thirteenth round was carried in the launcher in action. An auxiliary MG34 was also ball-mounted on the right-hand side of the superstructure front plate.

The rocket-launcher was the most interesting part of this vehicle; it was breech loaded and rifled, the rifling consist of 9 grooves with a right-hand twist to impart spin to the projectile on launching, for greater accuracy. As the projectile was rocket-propelled, some arrangement had to be made to prevent the rearward-flowing rocket exhaust gases from entering the fighting compartment, while at the same time having an outlet on firing; this was done, first, by using the initial propelling gases to actuate an obturator in the breech-

Four: Variants of the Tiger 1

▲The Sturmmörser Tiger, showing the 38cm RW61 mounted in the front plate of the fixed superstructure; note the vent holes around the muzzle. (Author's Collection)

▼Front 3/4 view of the Stu Mrs Tiger showing the complicated camouflage pattern, the resilient road wheels of a late production vehicle and the muzzle cover for the RW 61 rocket-launcher. (Author's Collection).

Four: Variants of the Tiger 1   67

block, and, secondly, by forming an expansion chamber 1½ inches deep all round the rifled liner, between the liner and the jacket, with outlet holes around the muzzle for the rocket exhaust gases to be evacuated from the closed barrel.[9]

It is believed that no more than ten of these vehicles were completed, with eight more in various stages of completion in Alkett's Berlin works at the end of the war; it had been intended that they should operate in conjunction with tracked ammunition supply vehicles, also based on the Tiger 1 chassis, carrying some 40 rounds.[10] As far as is known, only one of these extraordinary vehicles has survived; formerly in the US Army Ordnance Tank Museum at Aberdeen Proving Ground, Maryland, it has now been returned to the country of its birth, and is located in Koblenz at the Wehrtechnische Studiensammlung des Bundesamtes für Wehrtechnik und Beschaffung (BWB).

What purpose Hitler had in mind for these short-range heavy assault weapons for attacking strongly constructed emplacements, at a time when the German Army was in retreat and on the defensive on all fronts, is not clear; it is another example of his pre-occupation with size and his interference in German tank design and production, with adverse effects on both. The modified vehicle weighed some 65 tonnes in action, eleven tonnes more than the weight with which the automotive components had been designed to cope, so that it was relatively immobile; in addition, the high-explosive rocket had a maximum range of only 5,500 metres at an ambient temperature of 15°C, according to the official range table dated August 1944.

38cm RW61 auf Stu Mrs Tiger
Outline Specification

Weight in action	65 tonnes
Crew	5
Dimensions:	
Overall length	6,280mm
Overall width	3,570mm
Overall height	2,850mm
Belly clearance	432mm
Track on ground	3,605mm
Track centres	2,844mm
Armour thicknesses:	
Superstructure front	150mm
Superstructure sides	80mm
Hull	As for Tiger 1
Armament:	
Main	38cm RW61 (L/5.4)
Auxiliary	One 7.92mm MG34
Ammunition carried	13 × 38cm rounds

Other data as for Pz Kpfw Tiger, Ausf E

▼ Side view of a captured Stu Mrs Tiger, taken at the School of Tank Technology while undergoing examination. The stencil indicates that the vehicle was recovered by a US Ordnance unit, and this vehicle was subsequently shipped to the USA; it now rests in the BWB museum at Koblenz. (Tank Museum)

▲ Top view of the Stu Mrs Tiger; this clearly shows the ball mounting, giving a high maximum angle of elevation for the rocket-launcher, as well as the rocket-loading hatch in the roof. (Tank Museum)

▼ Front 3/4 view of the Stu Mrs Tiger; note the thickness of the superstructure front plate, and the ammunition-lifting crane on the superstructure rear. (Author's Collection)

Four: Variants of the Tiger 1   69

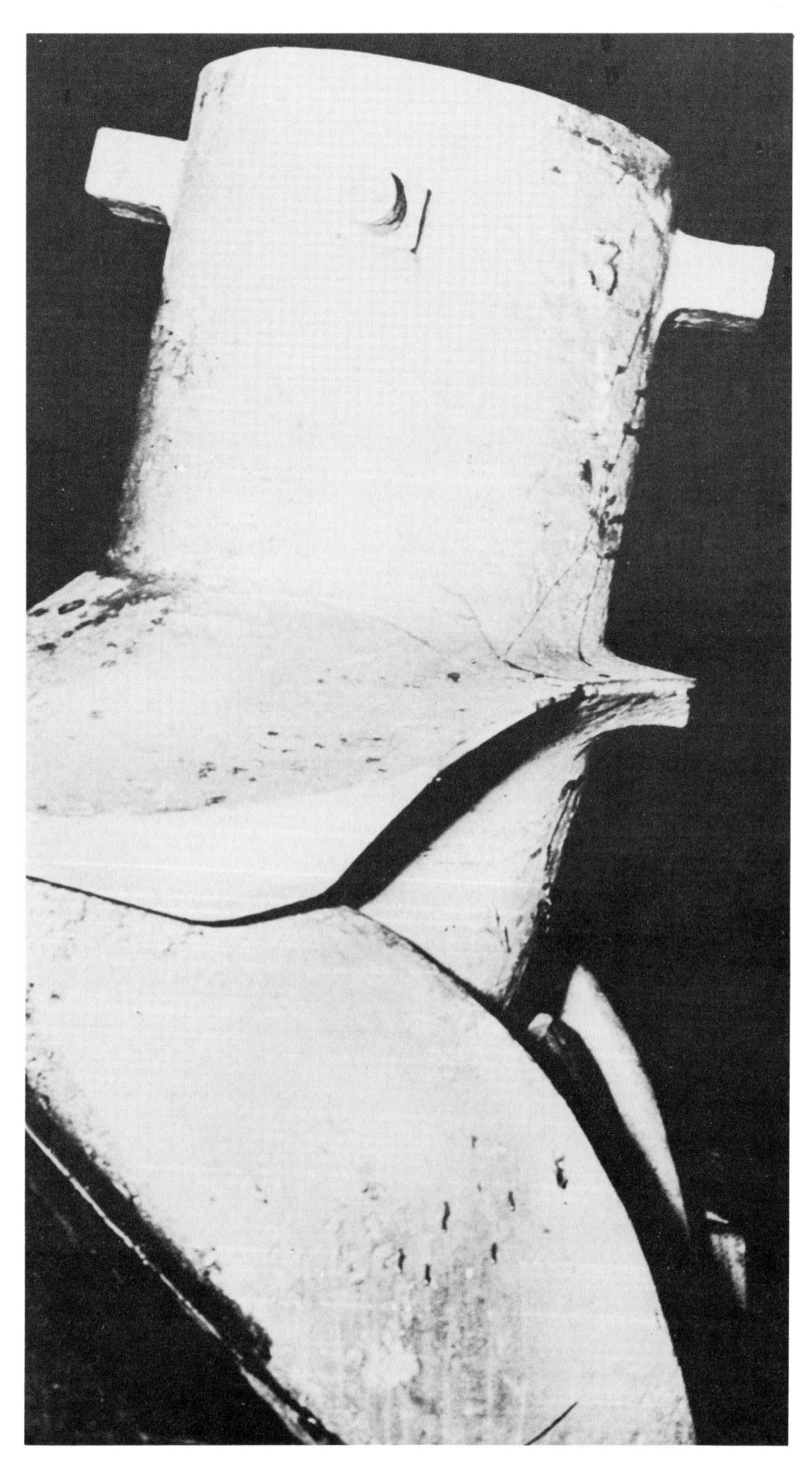

◀ Side view of the rocket-launcher at maximum elevation; note the roughcast finish of the launcher outer casing and integral mantlet. (Tank Museum)

▶ The superstructure removed from the Tiger hull; the bolt holes for attaching it to the hull are clearly visible. (Tank Museum)

▶ The Stu Mrs Tiger hull with superstructure removed, looking forward; note the driver's steering wheel at the left front, the rocket-loading rollers in the centre and the rocket-stowage racks on left and right in the fighting compartment. (Tank Museum)

70   *Four: Variants of the Tiger 1*

Four: Variants of the Tiger 1 71

Four: Variants of the Tiger 1

◄ An official German Army photograph from the vehicle instruction manual, showing the vehicle crane in use for loading a rocket into the vehicle. (Tank Museum)

► The nose fuze being inserted into the rocket prior to loading; the rocket is resting on the loading tray. This is another photograph from the user handbook for the Stu Mrs Tiger. (Tank Museum)

► A further illustration from the official German Army handbook for the Stu Mrs Tiger, this time showing a rocket in the breech of the launcher. Note the vent holes in the rocket motor base, as well as the three rockets in the stowage racks on the right of the picture. (Tank Museum)

Four: Variants of the Tiger 1   73

CHAPTER FIVE
THE TIGER 2 (ROYAL TIGER)

IN THE AUTUMN of 1942, although production of the Tiger 1 had started only in August of that year, the Heereswaffenamt placed a contract on Henschel und Sohn, under the project number VK 4503, to design a new version of the Tiger incorporating sloped plates on the lines of the MAN Panther, thicker frontal armour (150mm) and mounting the high-performance 8.8cm KwK43 (L/71) tank gun.[1] Significantly, the design of the Panther itself had been based on the hull armour layout of the Soviet T-34, as a result of the combined visit to the Eastern Front in October 1941 by senior representatives of the tank industry and the Heereswaffenamt. The same urgency was to be attached to this project as had been associated with the development of the Tiger 1, and a similarly short time-scale from design study to production was again imposed.

This time-scale was considerably lengthened, however, by a further requirement, issued by WaPrüf 6 in February 1943, that the components of the VK 4503 should be standardized as far as possible with those of the improved Panther, the Ausf F or Panther II, being designed concurrently by MAN.[2] In the event, this almost fruitless quest added several months to the development time-scale of what eventually became the Pz Kpfw Tiger, Ausf B, Tiger 2 or Königstiger (Royal Tiger).

VK 4502(P)

In the meantime, the Porsche organization had also been issued with a development contract, possibly as compensation for having lost the VK 4501 competition, for a vehicle of similar specification under the project number VK 4502. Porsche's proposals, known under the Porsche code-names of Typ 180/181 or 'Sonderfahrzeug III' (Special Vehicle III), were basically for a tank of similar, if up-rated, design to the VK 4501(P) (Typ 101), again incorporating petrol- or diesel-electric transmission and a running gear of six twin road wheels per side, sprung in bogie pairs by means of longitudinal torsion bars. The hull sides were made in three parts, the armour welded and interlocked.[3]

The Porsche proposals were in two forms: one, which was rejected due to the excessive amount of gun overhang, with a front-mounted turret and a rear engine, the other having the engine compartment central and the turret at the rear; both versions employed the same turret, in which sixteen 8.8cm rounds were stowed, for which an initial production

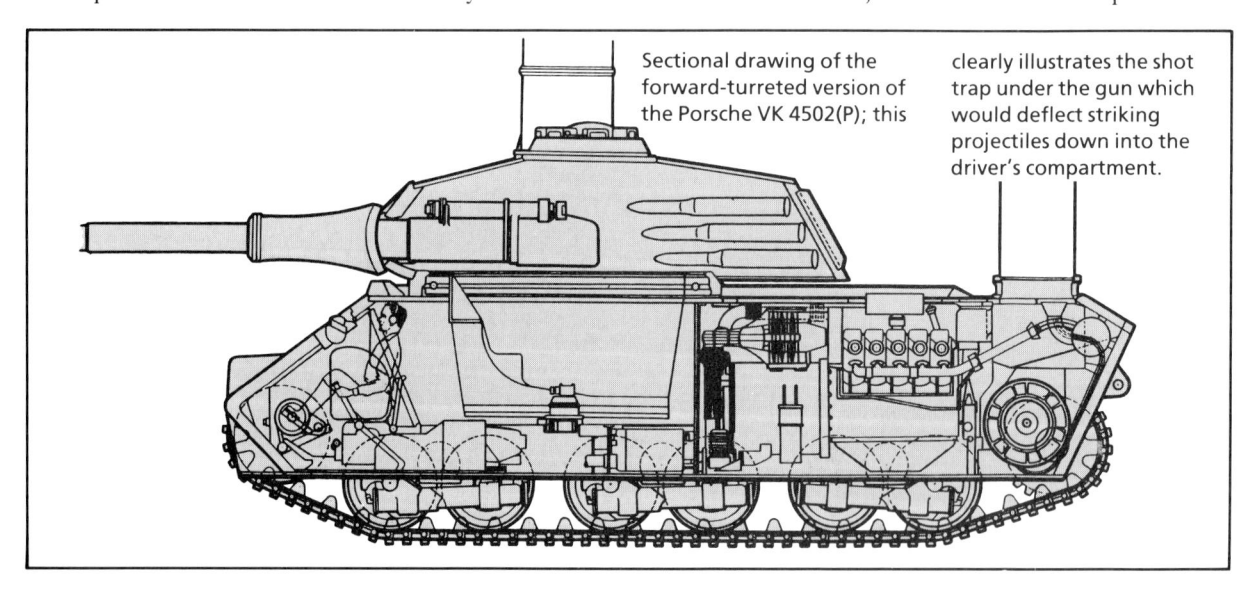

Sectional drawing of the forward-turreted version of the Porsche VK 4502(P); this clearly illustrates the shot trap under the gun which would deflect striking projectiles down into the driver's compartment.

74 *Five: The Tiger 2 (Royal Tiger)*

order of 50 was placed.[4] It was estimated that the vehicle would have had a battle weight of some 64 tonnes in either version. In the event, Porsche's proposals got no further than the drawing-board; they were rejected for the same reasons as their VK 4501(P) proposals had been, reinforced by the unreliability in service of the vehicle based upon them, the Pz Jäg Tiger(P) (Elefant). This left the HWA and Henschel free to develop the VK 4503 into the Tiger 2 and Porsche to get on with playing with his and Hitler's favourite tank project, the Typ 205 or Maus, which, in June 1942, he had been commissioned by Hitler to develop. The fifty turrets prematurely ordered from Krupp for the VK 4502(P) were diverted to Henschel,[5] for mounting on the first fifty vehicles off the production line; a similar fate, it will be remembered, had befallen the turrets prematurely ordered for the VK 4501(P), diverted to Henschel for early Tiger 1 production.

VK 4503

The Henschel proposals were for a tank with the conventional layout of the Tiger 1, with a crew of five consisting of, in the turret, commander, gunner and loader and, in the hull, driver and hull machine-gunner/radio operator. The armour layout, however, was based on that of the Panther rather than the Tiger 1, with a front glacis plate, of 150mm thickness, sloped at 50° (to the vertical), a lower nose plate of 100mm with the same slope, superstructure sides 80mm thick sloped at 25°, tail plate, also of 80mm, sloped at 30° and the belly and roof plates of 40mm, horizontal.[6] Both hull and turret were to be constructed of rolled plates, interlocked and welded.

The turret was mounted centrally, with the engine compartment at the rear and the driver's compartment, containing the gearbox and steering gear, at the front. The turret power traverse was to be driven from a

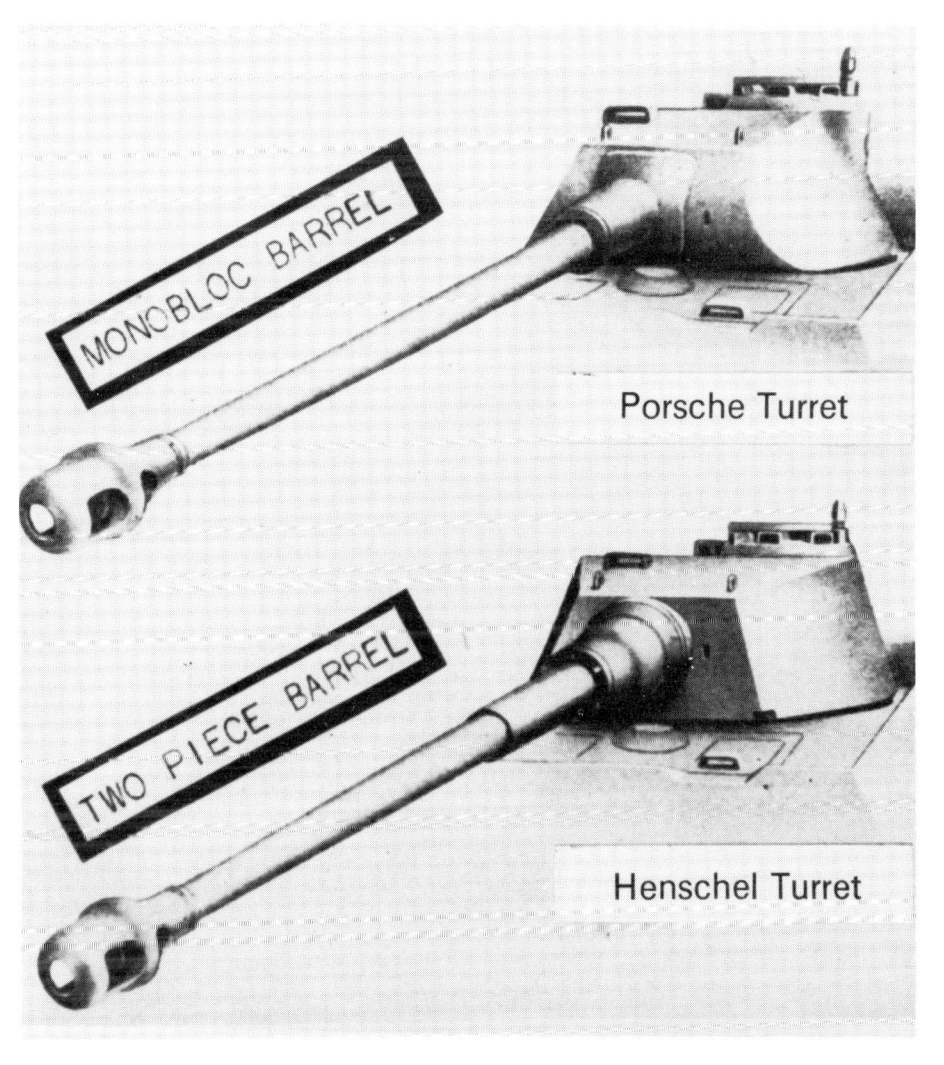

▶ Comparison between the Porsche and Henschel turrets for the Tiger 2; note that the gun in the Porsche turret has a one-piece (monobloc), and that in the Henschel turret a two-piece barrel. (Tank Museum)

Five: The Tiger 2 (Royal Tiger)

power take-off from the main propeller shaft, under the turret, as with the Tiger 1. The Porsche-designed turret had a curved front plate and side plates; this made it not only difficult and expensive to manufacture but also gave it the additional disadvantage of having a large re-entrant angle under the gun trunnion axis, which acted as a shot trap to deflect projectiles downward through the hull roof and into the driver's or engine compartments. The Henschel design, on the other hand, was more simply constructed of flat plates; the turret front plate, of 180mm thickness, was sloped at 10° and, in conjunction with the bell-shaped mantlet, eliminated the shot trap. Manufacture of the Henschel-designed turret was to be by the firm of Wegmann, also of Kassel.

Automotively, the VK 4503 was similar to the Tiger 1 and Panther, employing the Maybach HL230 engine, giving an output of 700 metric hp at 3,000rpm, in conjunction with a Maybach Olvar gearbox and a Henschel-developed steering gearbox, the L801; the running gear consisted of nine twin resilient road wheels with steel tyres, overlapping but not, as on the Tiger 1 and Panther, interleaved. Each pair of road wheels was independently sprung by a single transverse torsion bar, anchored on the opposite side of the hull; road arms were trailing on the right-hand side and leading on the left.

The 8.8cm KwK 43 (L/71) tank gun, although designed and developed by Krupp under a contract placed in November 1941, was produced mainly by the firm of Fr. Garny in Frankfurt/Main; production started in October 1942.[7] The gun and its coaxially mounted 7.92mm MG34 were mounted centrally in the turret front plate; because the length of the 8.8cm barrel made the gun muzzle-heavy, the gun trunnions, on which it pivoted in elevation, had to be placed well forward, requiring the turret to be extended to the rear, not only to accommodate its recoil but also to balance the turret. To reduce the recoil length, the gun was provided with a double baffle muzzle brake, similar to that of its predecessor, the 8.8cm KwK 36, in the Tiger 1. A rectangular hatch, incorporating a plug-type pistol port, was provided in the rear wall of the turret, for purposes of gun removal and installation. In the turret roof a smoke bomb-projector, similar to the British 2in bomb-thrower, was mounted in a rotatable mounting,

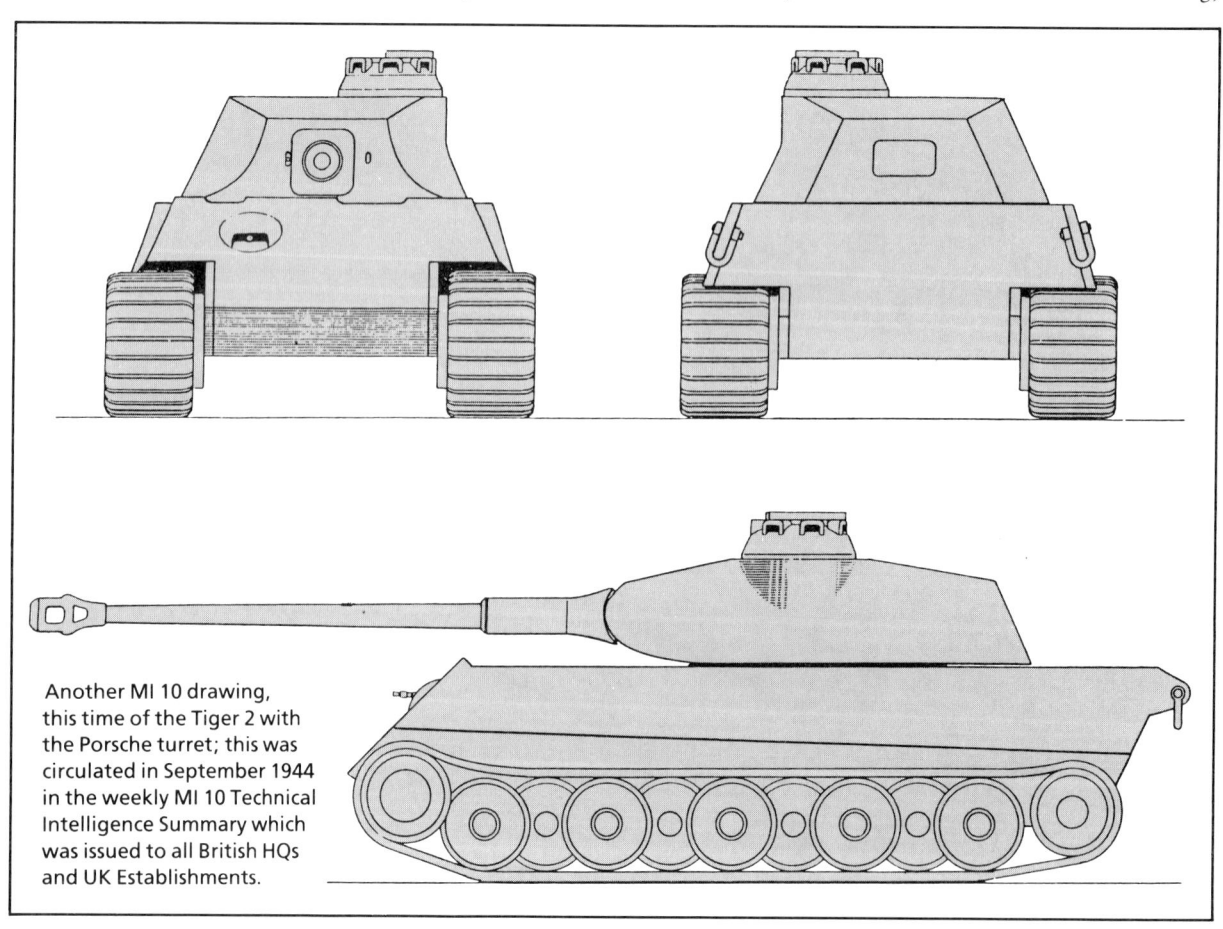

Another MI 10 drawing, this time of the Tiger 2 with the Porsche turret; this was circulated in September 1944 in the weekly MI 10 Technical Intelligence Summary which was issued to all British HQs and UK Establishments.

Five: The Tiger 2 (Royal Tiger)

permitting both loading and firing from within the turret; it could also fire anti-personnel grenades in close combat conditions.

The wooden mock-up of the Henschel vehicle was shown to Hitler in January 1943, as a result of which he gave his approval for it to be put into production.[8] A first order for three experimental vehicles was placed with Henschel, the first completed in October and the other two by December 1943. The first prototype was demonstrated to Hitler on 20 October 1943, together with the Panther and the full-size wooden mock-up of the Pz Jäg Tiger, Ausf B (Jagdtiger).[9]

Pz Kpfw Tiger, Ausf B (Sd Kfz 182) (Königstiger)

The Pz Kpfw Tiger, Ausf B, as put into production, was a virtually unchanged VK 4503. A total of 1,237 Königstiger (known as 'Royal Tiger' to the British, and, more literally, as 'King Tiger' to the Americans) was ordered from Henschel by the HWA,[10] with 950 due to have been completed by September 1945;[11] apart from the three experimental vehicles, the remaining 1,234 were ordered in four batches, of 176, 350, 379 and 329 vehicles, respectively.[12]

Production vehicles under these contracts were allocated chassis numbers running consecutively from 280001 and 281234, and started coming off the production line in January 1944, in which month three vehicles were produced. The first order was completed in August of that year, the first 50 vehicles being equipped with the Porsche turret. In August 1944 84 tanks were completed, which was the highest monthly total achieved and which coincided with the cessation of production of the Tiger 1 in the same factory. In the following month, however, the total was reduced to 73 and in October, to 26 vehicles, showing the effect of Allied air raids on both Henschel itself (on 7 October) and its suppliers. Output of Tiger 2 was further reduced to 22 vehicles the following month, but picked up to 60 in December, while, in 1945, 40, 42 and 18 vehicles were produced in January, February and March, respectively. Thus only 477 tanks of a scheduled 512 were completed by 31 March,[13] with a further eight vehicles in various stages of completion on the production line, with chassis numbers ending at 280485, when Allied troops reached the factory.[14]

To have produced even this number under the chaotic conditions caused by Allied air raids and other action, with the resulting damage to production facilities and road and rail supply routes, to say nothing of material and fuel shortages, showed considerable adaptability and ability to improvise on the part of the Henschel management. In an attempt to recoup the lag in production, Henschel had earlier sub-contracted the building of 100 Tiger 2, to have started in May 1945, to Nibelungenwerke in St. Valentin, Lower Austria;[15] the latter firm was already engaged in building the Jagdtiger, on a very slightly modified Tiger 2 chassis, so was already in possession of most of the jigs, tooling and drawings required.

Why the new version of the Tiger should have been called the Model B and the old, the Model E has never been understood; a similar lack of logic applied to the Panther, of which the first version was the Model D, the second the Model A, the third the Model G and the Panther II/neu (new), the Model F. Within Henschel, the Tiger 2 was known as the Model H3.

▼ The Tiger 2 with the Porsche turret. (Author's Collection)

Pz Kpfw Tiger, Ausf B (Sd Kfz 182) (Königstiger)

Outline Specification

Weight in action (Henschel turret)	68 tonnes
Crew	5
Dimensions:	
Overall length incl. gun	10,280mm
Overall length excl. gun	7,264mm
Overall width over tracks	3,625mm
Overall width over skirting	3,755mm
Overall height	3,098mm
Belly clearance	508mm
Track on ground	4,128mm
Track width with battle tracks	826mm
Track width with narrow tracks	660mm
Track centres	2,794mm
Armour thicknesses:	
Turret front	180mm
Turret sides	80mm
Hull front	150mm
Superstructure sides	80mm
Tail plate	80mm

Armament:	
Main	8.8cm KwK 43 (L/71)
Auxiliary	Three 7.92mm MG34
	One smoke bomb-thrower in turret roof
Ammunition carried	72 × 8.8cm rounds (Porsche turret)
	84 × 8.8cm rounds (Henschel turret)
	63 × 8.8cm rounds (command tanks)
Power plant:	Maybach HL230
Type	V-12 water-cooled, petrol
Output	700 metric hp at 3,000rpm
Transmission	Maybach OLVAR w/8 fwd & 4 reverse speeds
Running gear:	
No. of road wheels	Nine double, overlapping, per side
Springing medium	Transverse torsion bars
Drive	Front sprocket
Performance:	
Max. speed (roads)	41.5km/hr
Range (roads)	170km
Fording depth	1.6m
Step	850mm
Trench crossing	2.5m

◀ The Tiger 2 with the Henschel production turret (Author's Collection)

▲ Rear view of the production Tiger 2 turret, showing the rear escape/loading hatch open. (Tank Museum)

▼ Side view of the Tiger 2 with the Porsche turret. (Author's Collection)

Five: The Tiger 2 (Royal Tiger) 79

▲ A Tiger 2 with Porsche turret, captured at the Henschel proving ground at Haustenbeck towards the end of the war. The gun has been destroyed by firng a round when the barrel was blocked. (Author's Collection).

▼ A captured Tiger 2 with Henschel turret at the British Department of Tank Design at Chertsey in early 1945. (Author's Collection)

▶ Rear view of a Tiger 2, showing the exhaust stacks; this vehicle is at the Bundeswehr Kampftruppenschule II at Munster(Lager). (Author's Collection)

With the Porsche turret, the Tiger 2 in action weighed 67 tonnes and with the Henschel production turret, 68.5 tonnes; thus, at its lightest, it was eleven tonnes heavier than the Tiger 1 and 22 tonnes above the weight class indicated by its VK 4503 project number. It nevertheless kept the same Maybach HL230 engine used to power its 11-tonne lighter predecessor and the 22 tonnes lighter Panther; its power/weight ratio of only 10.4 metric hp/tonne meant, therefore, that it was seriously underpowered, although its top speed on roads was only 1.5mph lower than that of Tiger 1. This is apparent when compared to the post-war German MBT Leopard 2, of comparable weight to the Tiger 1, whose 4-stroke multi-fuel turbo-charged engine has an output of 1,500 metric hp giving the tank a power/weight ratio of some 25 metric hp/tonne and a maximum road speed of 72km/hr. The Tiger 2 also suffered from a very high fuel consumption of some 7 litres per kilometre, with the result that, on its internal fuel tanks, it had a road range of only approximately 160 kilometres, compared with the 550km of the Leopard 2. It was the largest and heaviest turreted tank to appear in any army during the Second World War, although even larger and heavier tanks, such as the VK 7001 (Löwe, or Lion) by Krupp, the E-100 by Adler in association with Henschel and the 180-tonne Porsche Maus, of which mention has already been made, were in the pipeline, in various stages of design, prototype build or test.

By post-war NATO main battle tank standards, neither the Tiger 1 nor the Tiger 2 was unduly heavy or large; the Bundeswehr Leopard 2, and the British Chieftain, weigh about 55 tonnes and the Challenger about 62 tonnes, all, however, being very much faster, more effectively armoured, much more powerfully armed and more reliable than either of the Tigers. The unreliability of the Tigers related more to automotive aspects than to any other; the engines and gearboxes were overloaded and therefore prone to breakdown and catching fire, while the interleaved and overlapped road wheels of the Tiger 1 led to mud packing the suspension with consequent track-throwing. Lack of adequate recovery facilities, particularly in the early stages before the introduction into Tiger units of one Panther ARV (Pz Bergewagen Panther) to each company, meant that many broken down vehicles could not be recovered and had to be destroyed *in situ*.

Their record, considering the speed with which they had been designed and rushed into service, was, however, better than could have been expected; they were very effective tanks anyway, but had there been

Five: The Tiger 2 (Royal Tiger) 81

time fully to develop and get the 'bugs' out of them, they would have been more effective still, with less wastage due to broken-down tanks being beyond local repair. The Tiger 2 in particular, with its 8.8cm L/71 gun, was able to defeat any Allied tank at almost any range, while remaining frontally immune to any Allied tank or anti-tank gun; most Allied and German experts considered it to be the best all-round tank gun on either side to appear during the war. Various specimens of the Tiger 2 have survived, notably one restored to full working order in the French Tank Museum at Saumur, one in the Bovington Tank Museum (the only remaining specimen with the Porsche turret), one at the Kampfruppenschule II at Munster(Lager), one at the US Army Ordnance Corps Tank Museum at Aberdeen Proving Ground, Maryland, USA, and one at the Royal Military College of Science, Shrivenham.

As with the Tiger 1, command vehicle versions of the Tiger 2 were converted from normal gun tanks by the removal of stowage for 17 rounds of 8.8cm ammunition and the substitution of either the Fu7 or the Fu8 long-range radio.[16] The only other variant of the Tiger 2 to enter service was the 12.8cm self-propelled anti-tank gun on the Tiger B chassis, known as the Jagdtiger (Hunting Tiger) or Pz Jäg Tiger, Ausf B (Tank Hunter Tiger, Model B).

◀ The VK 7001 (Löwe or Tiger-Maus). (Author's Collection)

▼ The hull of the prototype E-100, captured at Haustenbeck at the end of the war. (Author's Collection)

CHAPTER SIX
THE HUNTING TIGER (JAGDTIGER)

AS WITH every other German tank to serve in the Second World War, the Royal Tiger was used as the basis for a self-propelled gun, in this case the 12.8cm PaK 44 or PaK 80 (L/55) anti-tank gun. With the gun mounted, with limited traverse to left and right, in a fixed, heavily armoured superstructure, this tank destroyer, the Jagdtiger, provided a good illustration of the German (and Russian) war-time philosophy with regard to anti-tank warfare; by substituting a fixed superstructure for the rotating turret of a conventional tank, it was possible to mount an anti-tank gun of larger calibre than the tank could take for little, if any, increase in vehicle weight and for a lower cost in man/hours than for a conventional turreted tank.

In this case, the leap in calibre and weight of shot was larger than the Western Allies had expected; the introduction of a 10.5cm gun of some 70 calibres in length to succeed the 8.8cm (L/71) PaK or KwK 43 seemed the obvious next step, and was, in fact, being investigated by the Germans as the future armament of the Tiger 2. The jump to 12.8cm, of which we had learned from PW and captured documents some time before the Jagdtiger was met in action, came therefore as something of a surprise. If such a gun were to be mounted on a Jagdpanther-shaped tank destroyer with a low silhouette, it would represent a potent threat; if, however, the higher silhouette of the Ferdinand/Elefant were adopted, the resulting ungainly size and large outline would make it at the same time more easily detectable, more difficult to camouflage and more vulnerable to attack in the flanks than a Jagdpanther design of vehicle.

▼ The wooden mockup of the Jagdtiger on its stand in the Henschel pattern shop at Kassel. (Bundesarchiv)

The question of which design the Jagdtiger would follow exercised the Allied army technical Intelligence agencies considerably during the last year of the war, and a high priority was attached to the interrogation of any prisoner who had had training in, or experience of, this vehicle. Conflicting answers were obtained, as is usual in such cases; in captured documents, any illustration of the Jagdtiger had been torn out before capture, even when illustrations of other tanks and SP guns were left in. Armour thicknesses of the new tank destroyer were known, but not the angle at which the plates were sloped; as a sloped glacis plate, as on the Jagdpanther, could make the equivalent thickness of the frontal armour more than twice that of the near-vertical front plate of an Elefant-type vehicle, the answer was crucial to Allied methods of attack of armour.

It was not until late 1944, just before the first Jagdtiger was met in action in north-west Europe, that the answer was obtained by MI 10 in the War Office from a captured notebook, containing excellent pencil drawings of most of the then current German tanks and SP guns but from which the Jagdtiger illustration had, as usual, been torn; however, some of the pencil from the torn out sheet had rubbed off on the back of the preceding page and it occured to me that, from this, Scotland Yard's forensic laboratory might be able, by the use of chemical means or of ultra-violet and infra-red light, to bring out a reasonable mirror image of the crucial drawing. This they were able to do, thus giving us our answer; that the front of the Jagdtiger was stepped after the fashion of the Elefant. This information was quickly circulated to all Allied operational units, in time for the correct method of attack to be employed when it was first encountered in December 1944, during the fighting in the Ardennes.

▶ A front 3/4 view of a Jagdtiger with the Porsche suspension. (Author's Collection)

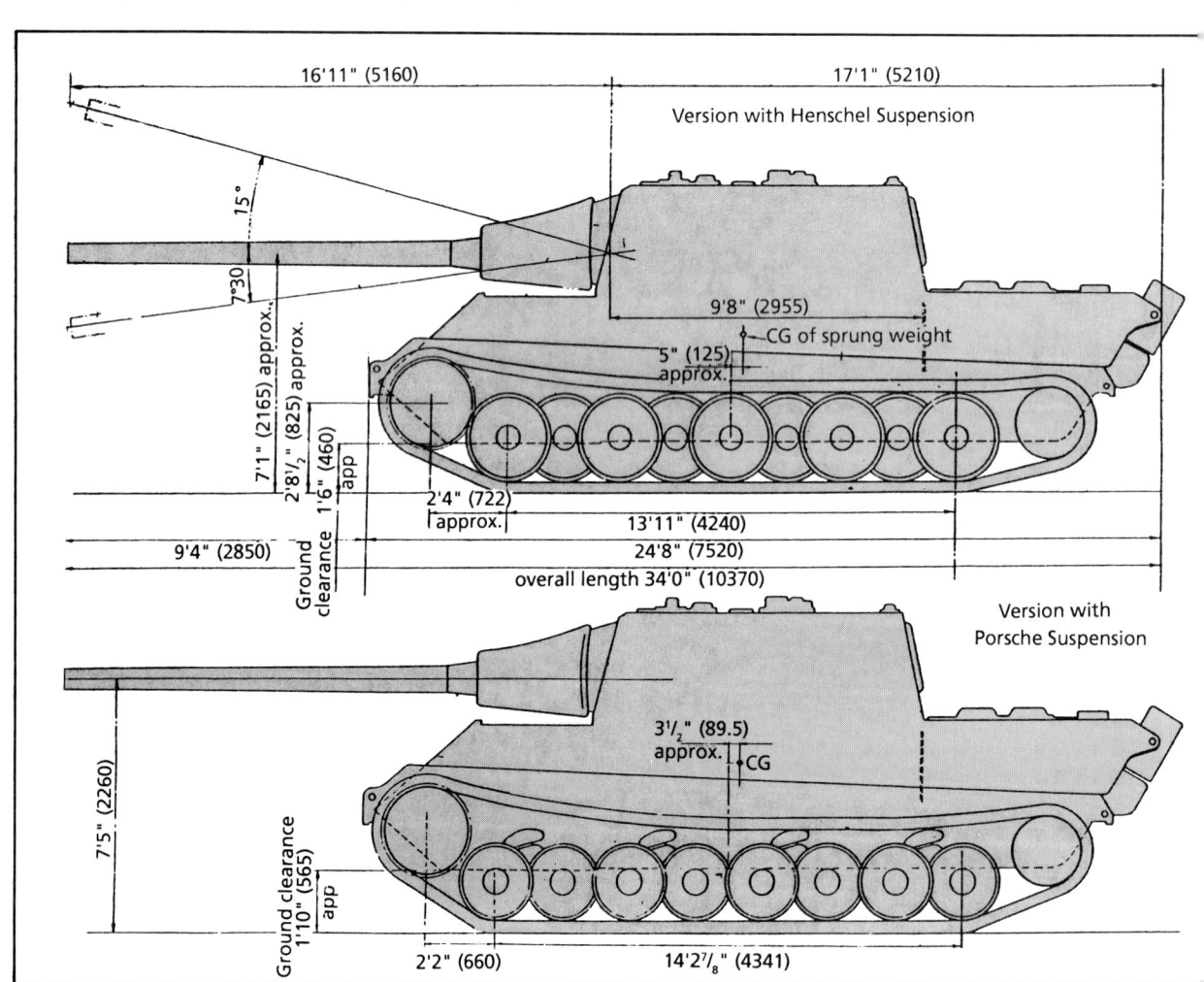

84   Six: The Hunting Tiger (Jagdtiger)

General arrangement drawing of the Jagdtiger, showing the differences between that fitted with the Henschel and that with the Porsche suspension. This drawing was circulated by MI 10 in August 1945, two months after the end of the war in Europe.

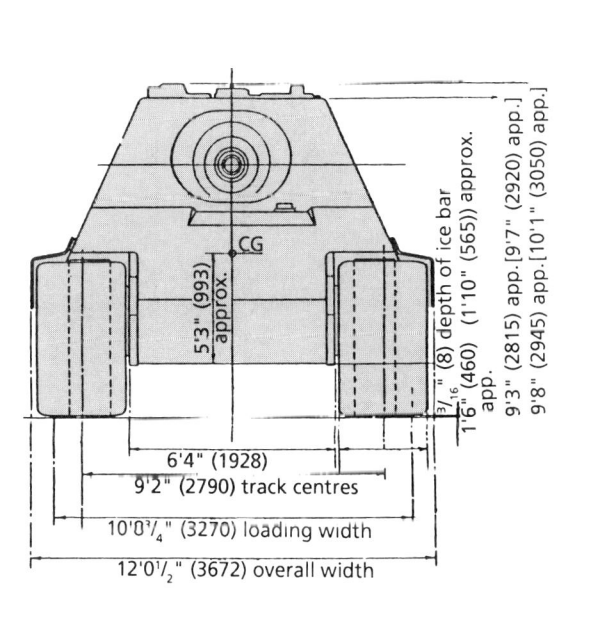

Allied, and particularly British military technical Intelligence was aware of the Jagdtiger's existence almost as soon as the wooden mock-up was shown to Hitler at the Arys proving ground in East Prussia on 20 October 1943. Based on the chassis of the Tiger 2 (Royal Tiger) lengthened by some 25cm (10in), the Pz Jäg Tiger, Ausf B (Sd Kfz 186) (Jagdtiger – Hunting Tiger) was a formidable vehicle, weighing some 75 tonnes and mounting either the 12.8cm PaK 44 (L/55) or the PaK 80, of similar calibre and calibre length, without a muzzle brake, in the 250mm thick front plate of a rigid armoured superstructure in the centre of the vehicle. The superstructure sides were formed in one piece as an upward extension of the Tiger 2 superstructure side plates, and were of the same thickness (80mm) and slope (25° to the vertical).

The ammunition for the 12.8cm gun was too long and heavy to have been loadable in one piece as 'fixed' ammunition; 'separate' ammunition, in which the projectile and the cartridge case were two distinct entities requiring to be loaded separately, was therefore employed. To speed up the loading process and ease the lot of the loader, two loaders were provided, bringing the crew of the vehicle to six men; the other members of the crew were, as normal in German AFVs, the commander and gunner in the fighting compartment and the driver and hull gunner/radio operator in the driver's compartment.

The remaining assemblies and components of the Jagdtiger were those of the Tiger 2 tank, although two vehicles, with chassis numbers 305001 and 305004,

Six: The Hunting Tiger (Jagdtiger)

were fitted with an alternative Porsche suspension of four bogie pairs of single overlapping road wheels, on each side, each bogie being sprung by a longitudinal torsion bar; the Henschel version had nine twin overlapping road wheels per side, each twin wheel being individually sprung on a transverse torsion bar as on the Tiger 2. The Porsche system was more economical in both man and machine hours, and was some 404,000 Reichsmarks cheaper to make and install; in its initial form, however, it was not robust enough, both the torsion bars and the bogie mounting brackets suffering frequent breakage, especially in cross-country travel. An order for the conversion of ten further vehicles to the Porsche suspension for troop trials was issued, but, due to the war situation, the scheduled troop trials could not be carried out.

After Hitler had approved the full-sized wooden mock-up of the Jagdtiger on 20 October 1943, an initial order for the building of 150 vehicles was given to Nibelungenwerke of St.Valentin, with an ultimate production rate of 50 per month envisaged. Chassis numbers were consecutive, starting at 305001. The first production vehicle was finished in time to be demonstrated to the Führer on his birthday, 20 April 1944, he having been shown the photographs of it a fortnight

▼ Side view of a Jagdtiger with the Henschel suspension, which consisted of nine overlapping road wheel stations per side, sprung on transverse torsion bars. (Rundesarchiv)

▶ A comparable view of a Jagdtiger fitted with the Porsche suspension, with eight overlapping road wheel stations per side, each sprung in pairs on short longitudinal torsion bars. (Bundesarchiv)

86 *Six: The Hunting Tiger (Jagdtiger)*

Six: The Hunting Tiger (Jagdtiger)

▲ A rear 3/4 view of a Jagdtiger with Henschel suspension. (Author's Collection)

▼ A front 3/4 view of the Jagdtiger with the standard (Henschel) suspension. (Author's Collection)

▶ Rear view of the Jagdtiger, showing the exhaust shields and rear track guards, as well as the loading/escape hatch in the superstructure rear plate. (Author's Collection)

88   Six: The Hunting Tiger (Jagdtiger)

earlier. A total of 60 vehicles had been completed by the end of January 1945, with the programme promising a further 13 in February, 40 in March, 37 in April and 25 each in the following months to August 1945; in fact, by the end of the war only a further 10 had been completed, bringing the total production of the Jagdtiger to 70 vehicles.[1] Due to a shortage of 12.8cm guns in March 1945, it would have been necessary to equip at least 25, and possibly as many as 50 Jagdtigers, as an interim measure, with the 8.8cm PaK 43/3 (L/71) of the Jagdpanther, had production continued; these vehicles would have been known as 'Pz Jäg Tiger für 8.8cm PaK 43/3 (Sf) (Sd Kfz 185)' (Tank Destroyer Tiger for 8.8cm Anti-Tank Gun 43/3).[2]

The Jagdtiger was the largest and heaviest tracked armoured vehicle to see service anywhere during the Second World War; it also mounted the largest calibre high-velocity anti tank gun of any such vehicle, firing the heaviest projectile at a muzzle velocity of 920 metres per second (3,030ft/sec). Slow and lumbering, with a high silhouette and an unreliable engine/transmission combination, with a slow rate of fire and only limited traverse, it was nevertheless a formidable, indeed almost invincible, anti-tank weapon. Its high silhouette and large size made it difficult to conceal but, once concealed, it was highly effective in defence and took a large toll of the lighter, under-armed British and US tanks which it met in action.

In his book *German Tanks of World War II* (p. 141), George Forty tells how, as an impressionable and newly commissioned subaltern, he visited the Ardennes battlefield three years after the end of the war in Europe and came across what seemed to him to be an entire regiment of knocked-out Sherman tanks; the author of this carnage had been 'a single Jagdtiger, whose immense bulk still occupied a perfect fire position in a farmyard at the top of a commanding hill feature. The Jagdtiger itself had been burnt out either by air attack or perhaps by its own crew when they ran out of ammunition.'[3] The Jagdtiger carried only 40 rounds of 12.8cm ammunition, not all of which would have been anti-tank rounds. The memory of this scene has remained with Lieutenant-Colonel Forty for nearly 40 years, as a perfect example of a tank destroyer doing its deadly work; but, when it was done and the ammunition expended, it was too large and relatively immobile a vehicle to move out of position and safely back for replenishment.

As far as is known, the Jagdtiger saw service in only two units, namely the s.Pz.Jäg.Abteilung 512 (Heavy Tank Hunter Battalion 512) and the s.Pz.Jäg.Kp.614; the latter was formed at Döllersheim, Austria, in late

Six: The Hunting Tiger (Jagdtiger)

1944 out of the disbanded Panzerjäger Abteilung 653 (Tank Hunter Battalion 653), formerly equipped with the Pz Jäg Tiger(P) (Elefant). The s.Pz.Jäg.Abt.512 was formed in the late autumn of 1944 at the PzErs.u.Ausb-Abt.500 (500 Armour Reinforcement and Training Battalion) in Paderborn, its personnel having been trained on the vehicle there from the arrival of their first Jagdtiger in June 1944; it was in action first in the area of the Remagen bridgehead on 3 March 1945 and later in the Ruhr, finally surrendering in Iserlohn on 16 April 1945.[4] Pz.Jäg.Abt.653 had fought on the Russian and Italian fronts when equipped with the Ferdinand/Elefant, but had returned to Austria to disband, to re-form as s.Pz.Jäg.Kp.614 and to re-equip with the Jagdtiger in 1944. The Jagdtiger seen by George Forty and which had caused so much destruction of Sherman tanks had probably belonged to this battalion, which deployed in the Ardennes in December 1944 and thereafter probably to Hungary.

Information on the Jagdtiger, as indeed on the Tiger 2 on which it was based, and on other AFVs, such as the Stu Mrs Tiger, introduced into the German service late in the war, is relatively sparse when compared to that available on the earlier Tiger 1. On the Allied side, this was due partly to the sheer quantity of captured new equipment available for examination and test, and partly to a lack of requirement for it to be examined, and information about it disseminated by Technical Intelligence, with the war so obviously near its end. On the German side, the urgency with which new equipment had to be put into service meant that the user handbooks for the later equipment were seldom properly printed and, as a result, were easily damaged or mislaid; when captured, at this late stage in the war, these handbooks were often retained as souvenirs by the finder, rather than being handed immediately to the nearest Intelligence officer or unit.

Similarly, photographs from Allied sources tend to show captured vehicles in very damaged condition, while those from German sources at this late stage in the war are understandably few and far between; they had little time for photography! Manufacturing drawings of, and files relating to, the later AFVs were gathered together by the truck-load from the factories where they had been built, as they fell into Allied hands; the Combined Intelligence Objectives Sub-Committee (CIOS) and British Intelligence Objectives Sub-Committee (BIOS) had been formed for this purpose and shipped the drawings and files back to UK and USA for examination, where they now languish (where they have not been destroyed) virtually untraceable in the inaccessible and ill-recorded archives of various British and US Government agencies.

Only two specimens of the Jagdtiger are known still to exist in the west; one is in the Bovington Tank Museum, and the other at Aberdeen Proving Ground, Maryland, USA, in the tank museum of the US Army Ordnance Corps.

12.8cm PaK 44 oder PaK 80 (L/55) auf Pz Jäg Tiger, Ausf B (Jagdtiger) (Sd Kfz 186)

Outline Specification

Weight in action	75 tonnes
Crew	6
Dimensions:	
Overall length incl. gun	10,654mm
Overall length excl. gun	7,514mm
Overall width over tracks	3,625mm
Overal width over skirting	3,755mm
Overall height	2,945mm
Belly clearance	508mm
Track on ground	4,240mm
Track width, battle tracks	826mm
Track width, narrow tracks	660mm
Track centres	2,794mm
Armour thicknesses:	
Superstructure front	250mm
Superstructure sides	80mm
Hull front	150mm
Tail plate	80mm
Armament:	
Main	12.8cm PaK 44 (L/55) or PaK 80 (L/55)
Auxiliary	One 7.92mm MG34 in ball mounting
	One smoke bomb-thrower in superstructure roof
Ammunition carried	40 × 12.8cm rounds
	1,500 × 7.92mm
Power plant:	Maybach HL230
Type	V-12 water-cooled, petrol
Output	700 metric hp at 3,000rpm
Transmission	Maybach OLVAR w/8 fwd & 4 reverse speeds
Running gear:	
No. of road wheels (Henschel)	Nine double, overlapping/side
(Porsche)	Eight single, overlapping/side
Springing medium	Torsion bar
	(Henschel – transverse, Porsche – longitudinal)
Drive	Front sprocket
Performance:	
Max. speed (roads)	40km/hr
Range (roads)	160km
Fording depth	1,750mm
Step	880mm
Trench crossing	2,500mm

Six: The Hunting Tiger (Jagdtiger)

CHAPTER SEVEN
TIGERS IN COMBAT

1. TIGER 1

ALTHOUGH originally intended as a replacement for the 20-tonne Pz Kpfw IV and to weigh only 50 per cent more, the tank which eventually became the Pz Kpfw Tiger, Ausf E, ended up weighing three times as much. It was obvious to the German Army that, at 56 tonnes, the Tiger 1 could never be produced in sufficient quantity, neither could its strategic and tactical mobility be adequate, to replace the Pz Kpfw IV on a one-for-one basis. As it would be difficult to find a suitable place for it in the standard panzer division/regiment organization, and, as a scarce resource, it could most economically be employed directly under the command of Army or Corps HQ, it was decided to create a new organization especially for it. This new organization was the (independent) schwere Panzer Abteilung (s.Pz.Abt. – heavy tank battalion).

The heavy tank battalions would be numbered in the 500 series, the Heavy Armour Reinforcement and Training Battalion at Paderborn in North Rhine/Westphalia and its outstation at Putlos on the Baltic being numbered 500 (s.Pz.Ers.– u.Ausb.Abt.500) and the heavy tank battalions from 501 up to, and including, 510. The number 511 was added when the former 502 Heavy Tank Battalion was re-numbered in 1945,[1] to avoid confusion with s.SS Pz.Abt.502. The number 512

▼ Pz Kpfw III Ausf L of 3 Platoon, No. 1 Company, 502 Heavy Tank Battalion at Fallingbostel in the autumn of 1942; the Tigers of this platoon will carry the turret numbers '131' and '132', but note that there are three Pz Kpfw III in this platoon instead of the more usual two. (Hartmann)

Tiger 1 91

ORGANIZATION OF HEAVY TANK BATTALIONS, 1942-3

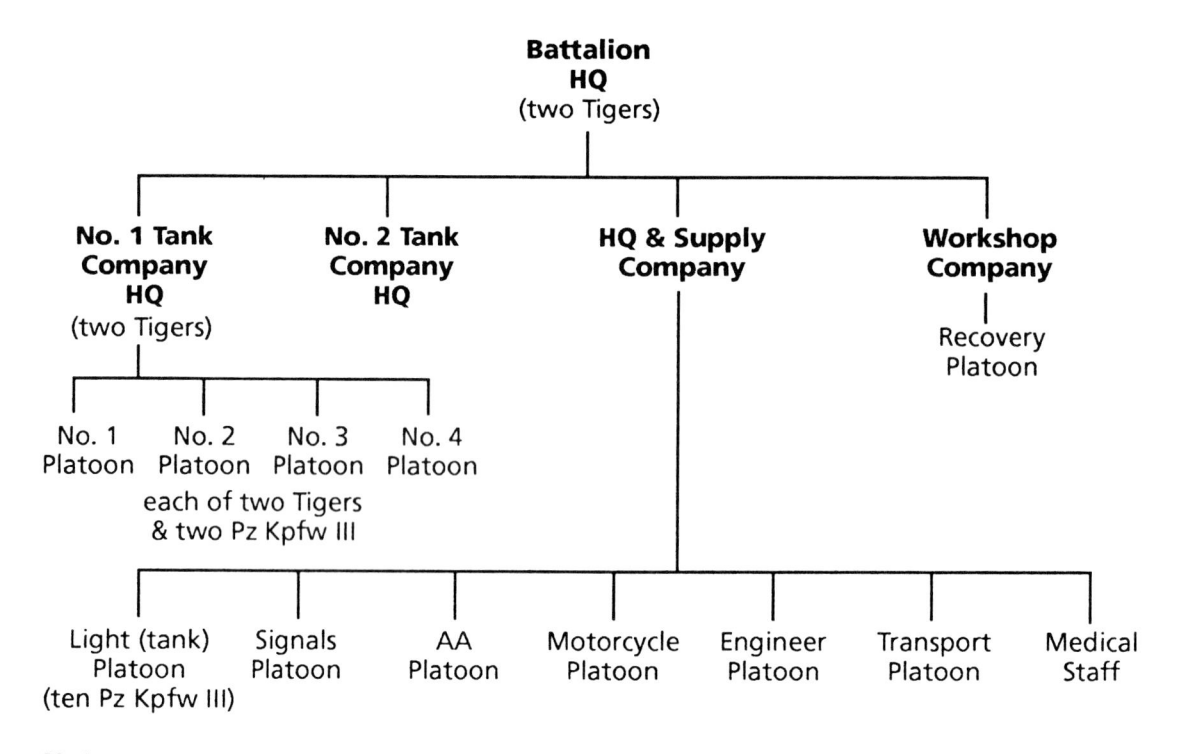

- **Battalion HQ** (two Tigers)
  - **No. 1 Tank Company HQ** (two Tigers)
    - No. 1 Platoon
    - No. 2 Platoon
    - No. 3 Platoon
    - No. 4 Platoon

    each of two Tigers & two Pz Kpfw III
  - **No. 2 Tank Company HQ**
  - **HQ & Supply Company**
    - Light (tank) Platoon (ten Pz Kpfw III)
    - Signals Platoon
    - AA Platoon
    - Motorcycle Platoon
    - Engineer Platoon
    - Transport Platoon
    - Medical Staff
  - **Workshop Company**
    - Recovery Platoon

Notes

1. The organisation of No. 2 Tank Company was identical with that of No. 1 Tank Company.

2. The War Establishment of Heavy Tank Battalions called for three tank companies but shortage of Tigers in late 1942 precluded formation of a third Tiger Company.

3. The Pz Kpfw IIIs in the Light Platoon were Ausf N. Those in the tank platoons could be Ausf J, K, L, M or N, according to availability.

4. Battalions were commanded by Majors and companies by Oberleutnants (Oblt).

was allocated to the heavy tank hunter battalion equipped with the Jagdtiger, whose personnel and training were also provided by 500 Heavy Armour Reinforcement and Training Battalion at Paderborn. The nomenclature position became less clear when the Waffen SS heavy tank companies in the SS Panzer Regiments were upgraded to battalions; they then became heavy SS tank battalions with numbers in the 100 series, that in the 1 SS Pz.Div.'Leibstandarte Adolf Hitler (LSSAH), for instance, becoming s.SS.Pz.Abt. 101. When, however, it was removed from the panzer regiment to become the corps Tiger battalion in I SS Pz.Korps in September 1944, it was renumbered as s.SS Pz. Abt.501 (Tiger), thus duplicating the number of the first Army heavy tank battalion and adding to the confusion, until the latter was re-numbered as s.Pz.Abt. 424 in December 1944 on also becoming a Korps Abteilung.

As originally planned, each battalion was to comprise three identical heavy tank companies, each consisting of an HQ platoon of two command Tigers and four tank platoons each of Two Tigers and two Pz Kpfw III Model H, L or M with 5cm guns. Battalion HQ consisted of two further command Tigers, while HQ company contained:

1. A Light Platoon equipped with ten Pz Kpfw III Model N, armed with the short 7.5cm KwK

92 *Seven: Tigers in Combat*

ORGANIZATION OF HEAVY TANK BATTALIONS, LATE 1943 TO LATE 1944

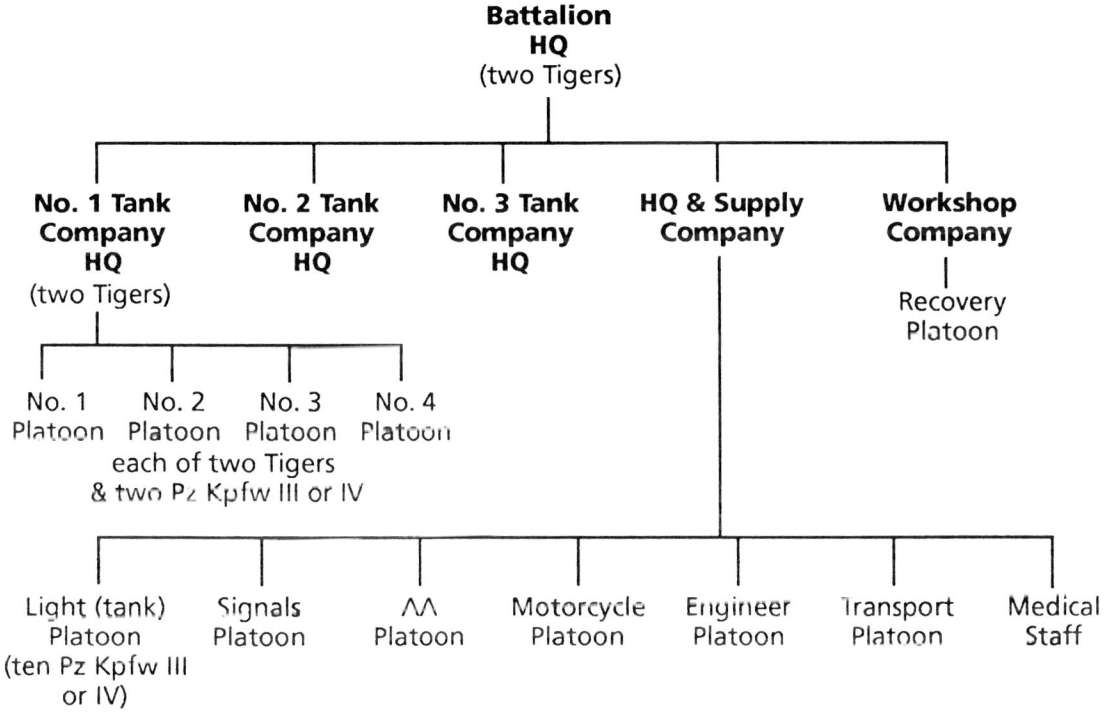

- **Battalion HQ** (two Tigers)
  - **No. 1 Tank Company HQ** (two Tigers)
    - No. 1 Platoon
    - No. 2 Platoon
    - No. 3 Platoon
    - No. 4 Platoon
    - each of two Tigers & two Pz Kpfw III or IV
  - **No. 2 Tank Company HQ**
  - **No. 3 Tank Company HQ**
  - **HQ & Supply Company**
    - Light (tank) Platoon (ten Pz Kpfw III or IV)
    - Signals Platoon
    - AA Platoon
    - Motorcycle Platoon
    - Engineer Platoon
    - Transport Platoon
    - Medical Staff
  - **Workshop Company**
    - Recovery Platoon

Notes

1. The organisation of Nos. 2 & 3 Tank Companies was identical with that of No. 1 Tank Company.

2. The Recovery Platoon originally had eight 18-tonne half-tracks (Sd Kfz 9); in 1944 they began to be replaced by two Panther ARVs [Pz Berge Wg Panther (Sd Kfz 179)].

(L/24) gun, for close support of the Tigers.
2. An engineer platoon.
3. A motorcycle reconnaissance platoon.
4. An anti-aircraft platoon.
5. A signals platoon.
6. A medical platoon.

The battalion also contained a workshop company, with a recovery platoon equipped with eight 18-tonne half-tracks s Zgkw 18 to, (Sd Kfz 9), and with a 10-tonne portable gantry crane on the establishment for turret and engine removal. The battalion organization is shown in the accompanying charts.

The idea of having mixed tank platoons each of two Tigers and two Pz Kpfw III was to enable the latter to provide the Tigers with close-in defensive support. If necessary, this could be thickened up with the Light Platoon's Pz Kpfw III Model Ns, whose 7.5cm guns carried a much greater high-explosive and anti-personnel punch than did the 5cm guns of the Pz Kpfw IIIs of the tank platoons. The Tiger 1, although surprisingly mobile for its size and weight, was seen primarily as a defensive weapon; its speed, and the low speed of its turret traverse, were limiting factors in the offensive role.

The 500 Heavy Armour Reinforcement and Training Battalion was formed at Paderborn in early

ORGANIZATION OF HEAVY TANK BATTALIONS FROM LATE 1944

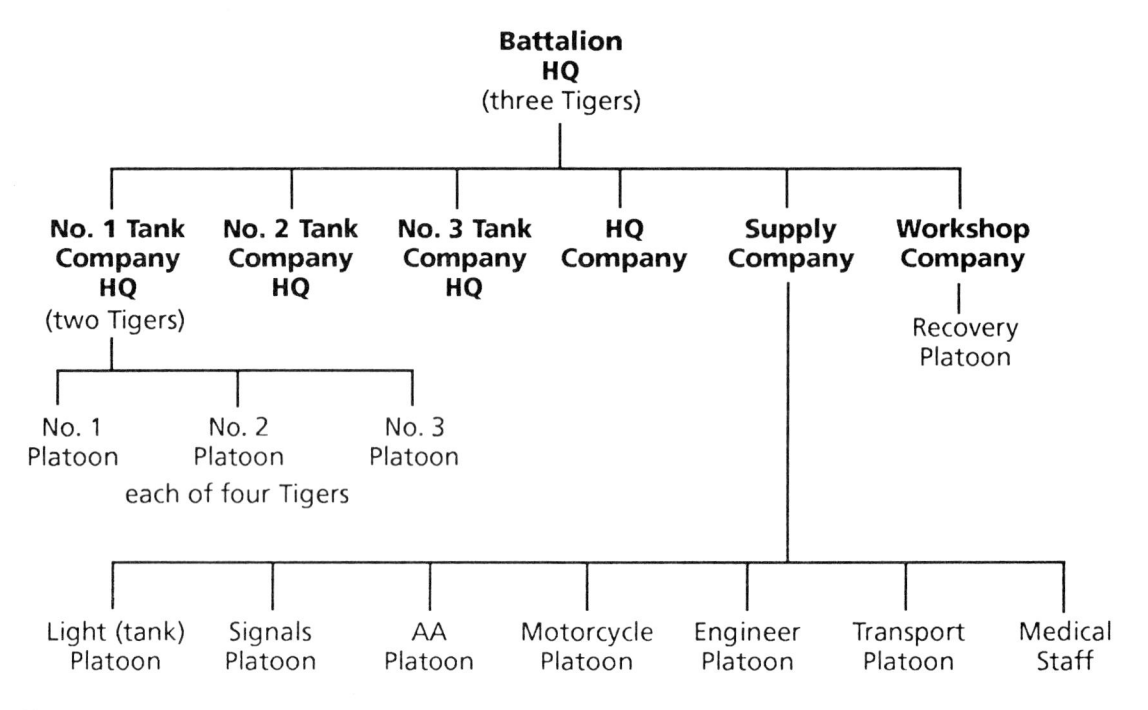

Battalion HQ (three Tigers)

- **No. 1 Tank Company HQ** (two Tigers)
  - No. 1 Platoon
  - No. 2 Platoon
  - No. 3 Platoon

  each of four Tigers

- **No. 2 Tank Company HQ**
- **No. 3 Tank Company HQ**
- **HQ Company**
  - Light (tank) Platoon
  - Signals Platoon
  - AA Platoon
  - Motorcycle Platoon
  - Engineer Platoon
  - Transport Platoon
  - Medical Staff
- **Supply Company**
- **Workshop Company**
  - Recovery Platoon

Notes

1. The organisation of Nos. 2 & 3 Tank Companies was identical with that of No. 1 Tank Company.
2. This re-organisation virtually doubled the Tiger strength of a Battalion from 22 to 45; three Companies each of fourteen and Bn HQ of three.
3. The Recovery Platoon's 18-tonne half-tracks were replaced by two Panther ARVs [Pz Berge Wg Panther (Sd Kfz 179)].
4. The Stabs Kompanie (HQ Company) was separated from the Supply Company.
5. The Light Platoon was now equipped with Pz Kpfw IV.

1942 and started accepting volunteers for the new heavy tank battalions from existing armoured units at the beginning of May that year. In the third week of May, cadres of the first four heavy tank battalions started to form: 501 in Erfurt, from the heavy tank companies (s.Pz.Kp.) 501 and 502 formed in February of that year, 502 in Bamberg and Putlos, 503 in Neuruppin and Putlos and 504 in Putlos. All four battalions came together in Fallingbostel in July and August 1942 to start their collective and vehicle training; all were at that time destined for the Russian front.

As fitted the senior battalion, s.Pz.Abt.501, under its commander Major Hans-Georg Lueder, had chosen a stalking tiger as its unit flash; 502, commanded by Major Richard Märker, had selected a mammoth, while 503, whose commander was Oberstleutnant (Lieutenant-Colonel) Post, appears not to have had a unit sign. The 504 Battalion, commanded by Major August Seidensticker, chose a flash based on the armour 'rhombus' tactical sign, the rhombus containing a heavy tank track pierced by a lance; this was not used on vehicles, however, the distinguishing marking on 504 Battalion's Tigers being a white 'rhombus' with a red stripe parallel to the leading edge and the company number (1 or 2) painted at the front end of each superstructure side plate.

► Pz Kpfw III Ausf N of the Light Platoon of 501 Heavy Tank Battalion, captured in Tunisia, at the School of Tank Technology in 1943; the 'stalking tiger' flash of s.Pz. Abt.501 can just be distinguished on the hull front vertical plate, above the red heavy tank rhombus symbol. (Author's Collection)

► The 'stalking tiger' flash of 501 Heavy Tank Battalion, with the heavy tank rhombus symbol beneath it. (Author's Collection)

▼ The distinctive rhombus unit flash of 504 Heavy Tank Battalion; the stripe parallel to the front edge was in red, while the number to the rear of it denotes the company to which the tank belongs. This flash is carried by the Tiger 1 in the Tank Museum at Bovington. (Author's Collection)

▼ The 'mammoth' unit flash of 502 Heavy Tank Battalion. (Author's Collection)

Tiger 1   95

The portable 10-tonne gantry crane of the Workshop Company in use for lifting the turret of a Tiger 1; from the white finish of the two Tigers in the background, this photograph was taken in the USSR. (Bundesarchiv)

The First Tiger Action

As the first pre-production Henschel Tiger 1s did not leave the Kassel factory until August 1942, in which month only eight were completed,[2] Hitler's aim, to have a Tiger unit of 25 tanks ready for action by 1 October 1942, proved impossible to achieve; in fact, Tigers were anticipated to be in such short supply throughout 1942 that the first four heavy tank battalions were formed with only two, instead of the planned three, Tiger companies in each. Hitler, however, could not resist the temptation to try the Tiger out in action on the Eastern Front, regardless of the shortage, and he therefore ordered No.1 Company of 502 Heavy Tank Battalion (1/502) to take its first four Tigers and one or two Pz Kpfw IIIs, together with half of the Workshop and HQ Companies and supporting soft vehicles, to the Leningrad front in support of Army Group North. Two Tigers arrived by train in Fallingbostel on each of the days 19, 20 and 30 August, together with some Pz Kpfw IIIs; the first four Tigers were taken over by 1/502 and the last two by s.Pz.Abt.501.[3]

1/502 left Fallingbostel on 23 August, three days after the arrival of their third and fourth Tigers, under command of the CO, Major Märker, arriving at Mga station on 29 August 1942.[4] Within a short time of unloading they were in action in the area of the station; not long afterwards, one of the Tigers had broken down with a broken gearbox, while, a few minutes later, a second one had an engine failure and a third, another failed gearbox. Thus the début of the 'invincible' tank, scheduled to drive to victory, had not got off to a very auspicious start.

Luckily, the Russians had not realized that the Tigers were unable to move and the Workshop Company was thus able to start their recovery that night, covered by the infantry but under heavy Russian mortar fire; three 18-tonne half-tracks had to be used for each Tiger, but their efforts were finally successful and all three vehicles were recovered with less trouble than had been feared. It was found that one of the causes of the gearbox and engine failure was overheating, resulting from jammed tracks caused by the soft mud packing tightly between the interleaved road wheels. The outer road wheels were accordingly removed, and this solution eased the problem.

▶ The first two prototype Tigers arrive at Fallingbostel by train in August 1942; the second vehicle can be seen sheeted up on the right of the picture. (Hartmann)

▼ Another view of the arrival of the first two Tigers at Fallingbostel; the lack of bolt holes for track guards on the superstructure sides of the prototype tanks is noticeable. (Hartmann)

◄ The unit tiger flash, the heavy tank battalion rhombus including the company number and the unit Field Post Number on the sign board for HQ No. 1 Company of 501 Heavy Tank Battalion, outside the entrance to Company HQ at Fallingbostel. (Hartmann)

All the defective parts were removed from the recovered vehicles and flown by Ju 52 transport aircraft back to Germany, where they were repaired by Henschel while replacement parts were flown back to the Battalion. Not until 15 September, however, could all four Tigers be reported as being once more ready for action. Six days later, on 21 September, the four Tigers with a few Pz Kpfw IIIs were put under command of 170th Infantry Division to act as the spearhead for the assault on the Soviet Second Shock Army beleaguered in Leningrad, despite Major Märker's pleas to higher command for the order to be rescinded in view of the total unsuitability for heavy tanks of the marshy ground over which they would have to fight. The order, however, had come from the Führer, who wished the Tiger to be tested in action, and was therefore immutable!

As dawn broke on 22 September, the German artillery opened fire and the bombers and Stukas of VIII Fliegerkorps pounded the Soviet divisions of the Second Shock Army trapped in the cauldron of Leningrad; the four Tigers of 1/502, accompanied by their supporting Pz Kpfw IIIs, moved forward across the start-line, and within minutes the first Pz Kpfw III was on fire and the first Tiger stalled and unable to engage a gear, due to an electrical fault which later set fire to the tank. All four Tigers were soon either knocked out by Soviet anti-tank guns or bogged in the soft going. Recovery of three, under heavy fire, would be possible; the fourth, however, the nearest to the enemy lines, was not recoverable and its destruction *in situ* was therefore recommended by Märker and his technical staff to prevent it falling into enemy hands. This course of action was not supported either by the OKH (Army High Command) or by Hitler, and Märker was told to re-examine the situation regarding its recovery; his re-examination, however, served only to confirm Märker's original opinion that recovery was impossible under the prevailing circumstances and with the available equipment. Accordingly, and reluctantly, the OKH at last gave orders for the demolition of the vehicle on 24 November. After removing all the optical instruments, radios, handbooks and machine-guns, and cutting off the barrel of the 8.8cm gun, the commander and men of the Workshop Company packed the vehicle full of explosives and blew it to pieces.

So ended the battle initiation of the Tiger 1; as with Winston Churchill's insistence on the use of the hitherto secret Churchill tank at Dieppe in August 1942, Hitler's order for the premature unveiling of the Tiger ended in dismal failure. Both leaders broke the basic rules for the employment of tanks, that they should be used in quantity rather than in penny packets, and that they should be used over ground suitable for their use. Needless to say, Hitler's search for a scapegoat needed to look no further than the CO of s.Pz.Abt.502, Major Märker; that unfortunate was summoned to the Führer's HQ on 21 November, where he was confronted by Goering with air photographs of the ground in which his Tigers had become bogged, and which he had stated to be unsuitable for the employment of heavy tanks, accompanied by the statement that they proved the 'going' to have been satisfactory. Poor Märker was removed from his command, his scheduled promotion to lieutenant colonel was rescinded and he was posted to command a company in Panzerregiment 31, where he was killed in action on 2 February 1943. Such is often the fate of those who prove their seniors wrong!

In Tunisia

Meanwhile, back in Fallingbostel, Tigers off the Kassel assembly line had been arriving in dribs and drabs to equip both the remainder of this battalion and the other battalions training there. As we saw earlier, it had been the original intention to send all four battalions to the Eastern Front; however, Hitler had, sometime previously, promised Rommel two battalions of Tigers to reinforce his Afrika Korps, and Rommel was by now querying the whereabouts of his promised reinforcements.

An Enigma cipher message from the OKH to Rommel dated 16 September 1942 advising the Panzerarmee of the Tiger dimensions was decrypted by the cryptanalysts of the British Government Code and Cypher School (GC & CS) at Bletchley Park; it was the first notification the British received associating the Tiger with North Africa, and it presented them with essential information confirming its size and weight. A second decrypt dated a month later from Rommel's Panzerarmee HQ to OKH queried the whereabouts of the promised forty Pz Kpfw III and forty Tigers; these numbers were the equivalent of two heavy tank battalions of two tank companies each, and warned the British what to expect. The decrypted reply from OKH stated that ten Tigers would be sent in November and a

▼ 501 Heavy Tank Battalion's No. 1 Company embarks its Tigers at Reggio/Calabria for the voyage to Bizerta in November 1943. This tank, with turret number 112, is the platoon sergeant's tank of I Platoon, No. 1 Company. (Hartmann)

Tiger 1   99

▲ The same Tiger 1, with wide tracks fitted, only just managed to clear the sides of the Siebel ferry; note the other Tigers and a Pz Kpfw III Ausf N of the Light Platoon, as well as some of the wheeled vehicles, waiting on the quayside for their turn to embark. (Hartmann)

◀ A close-up of the same tank. The chassis number is stencilled on the glacis plate and can be seen in the original photograph to be '250012'; this is the same vehicle that was shipped to the USA for examination at the end of the North Africa campaign and has been returned by the US authorities to Germany, where it now rests in the vehicle museum at Sinsheim. (Hartmann)

further ten in December 1942, thus warning the British when to expect them. Further intercepted and decrypted signals between OKH and Rommel's HQ, dated 23 and 24 November 1942, disclosed that the first Tigers of s.Pz.Abt.501 had by then been unloaded in Bizerta; the British now also knew the identification of one of the units involved, as well as the imminence of the threat.[5]

501 Heavy Tank Battalion, with the Field Post Number 25032, had received its first two Tiger 1s on 30 August 1942, at which time it was also designated to be the first of the two battalions promised to Rommel in North Africa.[6] It started its training for service in North Africa at the beginning of October, under the guidance of a Major Kummel, an Afrika Korps tank officer experienced in desert warfare. With the news of the Allied 'Torch' landings in Algeria and Morocco on 8 November, a new urgency attended the Battalion's preparations for its move; on 10 November, only two days after the landings, Hitler ordered it to proceed to

▲The same tank, nearly in position on the ferry. (Hartmann)

▼Tiger 112 in position at the forward end of the ferry. Note the exhaust covers, each with three horizontal slits on each side, typical of the early production model Tiger 1. (Hartmann)

Tunisia with all speed. No.1 Tank Company (1/501) was the better prepared, as it had in any case been expecting to move to Africa as the unit with the ten Tigers promised to Rommel for November; its vehicles had already been painted in German desert yellow, its turret numbers painted inconspicuously in white outlines only, its Tigers fitted with the Feifel air pre-cleaners on the tail plate and all unit flashes and tactical signs removed.

The second Tiger company, 2/501, not scheduled to reach Rommel until December, was meanwhile diverted to Vichy France to assist in the German occupation, with the result that it did not reach Tunisia until the beginning of January 1943; most of its vehicles on arrival there were still painted in the olive green colour used in western Europe, with turret numbers in red with white outlines and the unit Tiger flash and red Panzer rhombus on the left of the front vertical plate and on the right of the tail plate; the company commanders of the Battalion seem to have had considerable autonomy concerning the painting and marking of their tanks.

The Battalion commander, Major Lueder, accompanied by his ordnance officer, Oberleutnant W. Hartmann, flew to Tunis in a Ju-52, arriving there on 22 November 1942. The Battalion moved by rail in six transport trains from Fallingbostel to Italy, the tracked vehicles to Reggio/Calabria, whence they were shipped on Siebel ferries to Bizerta starting on 20 November, and the wheeled vehicles to Palermo. The personnel of the Battalion were mostly flown to Africa in Me-323 'Gigant' and Ju-52 transport aircraft. The speed with which the Battalion move was carried out showed a creditably fast reaction to the Allied landings, which had taken place only two weeks previously, particularly in view of the shortage of Tigers for training and the numerous vehicle modifications called for, both as a result of its development trials and of its forthcoming use in the hot and dusty environment of North Africa. On their arrival, Lueder and his men were accommodated in the Maréchal Foch barracks in Tunis.

While the first Tigers of 1 Company were still en route, Lueder received orders to support the 5th Parachute Regiment, together with two companies of Pz.Abt.190 of 10th Panzer Division, as part of Kampfgruppe Koch (Battle Group Koch) in the area of Medjez-el-Bab. He briefed his battalion on their task on 24 November and, as soon as they were ready, the first three Tigers of No.1 Company (those mentioned in the decrypt of 24 November) moved off. They took part in their first action, at Medjez-el-Bab station, at 11.00 on 25 November, only seven days after leaving Fallingbostel. The No.2 Tiger Company (2/501), occupied in Vichy France, did not start to arrive in Tunisia until the

102 *Seven: Tigers in Combat*

◀ Soft-skinned vehicles of 501 Heavy Tank Battalion being unloaded at Tunis in November 1942. (Hartmann)

▶ A Battalion 1-tonne half-track Sd Kfz 10/4 of the AA Platoon, a self-propelled mount for the 2cm Flak 38 anti-aircraft gun, being unloaded on the Tunis quayside. (Hartmann)

▼ A Tiger 1 of 501 Heavy Tank Battalion on the move in the Pont du Fahs area of Tunisia during Operation 'Eilbote I', January 1943. (Hartmann))

Tiger 1 103

beginning of January 1943. All the Tigers of s.Pz.Abt. 501 used in Tunisia were of the early type (see chart in Chapter 3), with narrow front track guards, turrets with two pistol ports and slotted exhaust pipe covers.

For some weeks after the arrival of the first Tigers in Tunisia, the only opposing tanks were the reconnaissance Stuarts/Honeys and the 6pdr-armed Crusaders and Valentines of the British 6th Armoured Division, and the M-3s and M-4s of the US 1st Armored Division, in the Allied invading force. All were overmatched at ranges out to 2,000m by the Tiger's 8.8cm KwK 36 gun, while at ranges greater than 600m even the Tiger's flanks were immune to the armour-piercing shot of the Allied tanks' 6pdr and 75mm guns.[7] Under these circumstances, therefore, it is not surprising that the only Tiger casualties during their first actions were due to mechanical breakdown rather than to enemy action. In fact, it was not until 20 January 1943 that the first two Tigers, of 2 Company, 501 Heavy Tank Battalion, were knocked out by Allied fire, namely the 6pdr anti-tank guns of No.2 Troop of 'A' Battery of 72nd Anti-Tank Regiment, RA, on the road from Robaa to Pont du Fahs. The Germans were able to recover the second tank, but the first gave the Allies the first details of the type and thickness of its armour, as well as other details of its equipment. The official British history of the Second World War quotes a date of 31 January for this event, but contemporary unit and Intelligence documents are quite clear on the 20 January date.[8]

The British first reported contact with the Tiger in the attack on Djedeida, on 28/29 November; in an Enigma decrypt of 30 November, the Germans claimed the destruction of 30 out of 50 tanks in this attack.[9] The Tigers of 1 Company, s.Pz.Abt.501, were next involved in the battle for Tebourba from 1 to 4 December 1942; after the capture of Tebourba by Axis forces on 4 December, 134 burnt-out Allied tanks were counted on the battlefield. After this battle, in which personnel, but no Tiger losses were sustained by the Battalion, 1/501 Heavy Tank Battalion returned to Tunis.

On 18 December, the Battalion moved from the Maréchal Foch barracks in Tunis to a new camp in La Manouba, a suburb to the south-west of Tunis where, with the worsening of the weather and the consequent reduction in operations, a period of consolidation, training and acclimatization set in. By 25 December, the Battalion strength in Tunisia had increased to twelve Tigers and sixteen Pz Kpfw III, plus a workshop platoon, while, by the beginning of January 1943, the No.2 Company (2/501) had started to arrive from its former station in Vichy France. By mid January 1943, both Tiger companies were at full vehicle strength in Tunisia for the first time.

104 *Seven: Tigers in Combat*

▲ A Valentine III or V of the British 6th Armoured Division, also knocked out in the November 1942 battle for Tebourba. (Hartmann)

◄ British 6pdr Crusader cruiser tanks, knocked out by 501 Heavy Tank Battalion near Tebourba in November 1942. (Hartmann)

► A US M-3 tank of the US 1st Armored Division lying burnt out in the olive grove in which it was knocked out by 501 Heavy Tank Battalion in November 1942. (Hartmann)

▲ The first Tiger to be captured in Tunisia; it was knocked out on 20 January 1943 by 6pdr anti-tank guns of 2 Troop, 'A' Battery of 72nd Anti-Tank Regiment, RA. The Valentine next to it was blown up on a mine. (Author's Collection)

▼ In this captured photograph, the turret of the Tiger shown embarking at Reggio in earlier photographs, with turret number 112, is being lifted by the portable 10-tonne gantry crane of the Workshop Company of 501 Heavy Tank Battalion. (Author's Collection)

The period of training and consolidation had enabled the Battalion to practise the tactical employment of Tigers in conjunction with Pz Kpfw III and IV. In the attack, the role of the Tiger was that of supporting the lighter tanks by fire; the latter led, followed by the heavier Tigers, and, when contact with the enemy armour was made, the screen of lighter tanks deployed outwards to the flanks, leaving the Tigers to engage frontally. In defence, the Tiger would usually be sited in a covered and defiladed position, from where it was a particular danger to Allied tanks. Despite the comparatively slow traversing rate of its turret, the Tiger proved a very effective defensive weapon, able to cover a wide area with anti-tank fire. Its wide tracks enabled it to reach good hull-down positions over difficult ground, from which no amount of artillery fire was able to force it to withdraw. Pz Kpfw III and IV tanks rarely took up good defensive positions on their own, but were used to watch the flanks of positions occupied by Tigers. The lighter tanks were often used in small groups to counter-attack from concealed positions on the flank.[10]

In January 1943, von Arnim, who had just taken over command in Tunisia, was directed by Kesselring, Commander-in-Chief, South, to seize all five passes through the Tunisian eastern Dorsal, with a view to giving the Axis forces control of all entrances into the Tunisian plain, as well as a footing on the plateau beyond. With Operation 'Eilbote I' (Special Messenger I), which he proceeded to put into effect on 18 January, he planned to roll up the Allied positions in the eastern Dorsal from north to south, the purpose of this offensive being to safeguard the communications between his army in the north and that of Rommel in the south, as well as to make the good airfield areas in the coastal plain safe from Allied interference. In this operation, 501 Heavy Tank Battalion formed part of a battle group under the command of General Weber, GOC 334th Division, and was deployed in the area of Pont du Fahs and Zaghouan; their advance was halted by Allied minefields covered by the 6pdr anti-tank guns of 72nd Anti-Tank Regiment RA, and it was in this action that the first two Tigers, mentioned above, were knocked out by them. 2/501 continued to occupy positions in the area south-west of Pont du Fahs, while 1/501 reached Zaghouan after several night marches.

1/501 was next employed, under command of 10th Panzer Division, in Operation 'Frühlingswind' (Spring Breeze), an operation designed to destroy the US forces in the area of Sidi bou Zid, west of Faid. Reconnaissance in the Faid area had been hindered for several days by a heavy sandstorm, and the attack did not, as a result, go in until the early hours of 14 February; on that first day, 68 US tanks were knocked out, of which

▼ Tanks and crews of 3 Platoon, No. 1 Company of 501 Heavy Tank Battalion in harbour near Pont du Fahs, Tunisia, prior to Operation 'Eilbote I'. (Hartmann)

▲ Camouflaging-up in harbour; the two Tigers of 3 Platoon, just before the start of Operation 'Eilbote I' in January 1943; both Tigers are of the early production model. (Hartmann)

▼ 501 Heavy Tank Battalion on the march south towards Kairouan at the beginning of 'Eilbote I' on 18 January 1943. Note the sandbags and extra track links with which the hull frontal armour of the Light Platoon Pz Kpfw III Ausf Ns were reinforced. (Hartmann)

▲▼ Moving into harbour on the flooded Tunisian plain, during Operation 'Eilbote I'. (Hartmann)

▲ The Battalion preparing to move out of harbour on 'Eilbote I'. (Hartmann)

▼ Surveying the damage after 'Eilbote I'; this Tiger has been hit several times on the frontal hull armour, with little effect on the vehicle. (Hartmann)

fifteen had been accounted for by 1/501. One undamaged Sherman was recovered in this action by a Tiger driver of 1/501, taken to Tunis by the Battalion recovery staff and from there sent back to Germany for detailed examination. A seriously wounded US officer commanding one of the knocked out Shermans complained bitterly to his captors that the 8.8cm gun of the Tiger was 'not fair'! On the afternoon of 16 February, the Company received orders to destroy a concentration of US armour at a cross-roads fifteen kilometres northwest of Sidi bou Zid; in a surprise attack from the north, large numbers of US tanks were again knocked out and many wheeled vehicles captured. In this action, the company commander, Oberleutnant Schmidt-Bonarius, was fatally wounded and Oberleutnant Hartmann took over command. By the end of Operation 'Frühlingswind', 1/501 had helped to destroy 165 US tanks and to capture some 2,000 US troops.

For the next operation, 'Béja', the two tank companies of 501 Heavy Tank Battalion were reinforced by fifteen PzKpfw IV 'Specials', with the long-barrelled 7.5cm guns, and II Battalion of 7th Panzer Regiment (PR 7) as the core of Kampfgruppe (battle group) Lang. The aim of the operation, which started on the morning of 26 February 1943, was to capture Béja, and it was part of the larger Operation 'Ochsenkopf' (Ox Head), the objective of which was to capture Medjez-el-Bab.

'Ochsenkopf' was a failure, although initially it gained a lot of ground; Kampfgruppe Lang's drive on Béja was a disaster, running into a well-laid British anti-tank gun trap at Hunt's Gap, a defile ten miles northeast of Béja. On withdrawal it had lost 22 tanks, with a further 49 damaged but recovered; of the nineteen Tigers of 1/ and 2/501 that went into action, only four survived. Eight Tigers were irrecoverably lost here on mines alone; the remainder fell to anti-tank guns, artillery fire, the boggy ground and ground-attack aircraft (Allied air superiority was at last beginning to make itself felt). Two troop leaders and thirteen other tank crewmen were killed, while the Battalion commander, Major Lueder, the commanders of both Tiger tank companies, the signals officer, the commander of the light platoon and the Adjutant were wounded and evacuated to Italy. It is thus not surprising that, in the

▼ Tiger 141 of 501 Heavy Tank Battalion camouflaged in harbour during the march to Sidi bou Zid on Operation 'Frühlingswind'. (Hartmann)

Tiger 1   111

▲ A Sherman of US 1st Armored Division, knocked out in the action on 14 February 1943. (Hartmann)

▼ Another Sherman of US 1st Armored Division, captured intact by 501 Heavy Tank Battalion, and the first to be captured in this condition, was shipped to Germany for detailed examination and testing. (Hartmann)

▲ The new meets the old on Operation 'Frühlingswind'. (Hartmann)

▼ The heavy going, caused by the exceptionally heavy rains of February 1943, gave considerable problems to the Tiger 1, due to mud packing tightly between the interleaved road wheels. (Hartmann)

◀ Remains of Tigers knocked out in Operation 'Béja'; the turret numbers 823 and 833 indicate that these tanks belonged to the eighth company of a Panzer regiment, in this case No. 2 Company of 501 Heavy Tank Battalion, which had come under command of 7th Panzer Regiment as its third battalion. (IWM)

▶ Tiger 132 of No. 1 Company of 501 Heavy Tank Battalion, renumbered as 732 after the Battalion had come under command of 7th Panzer Regiment, thus making the Company the seventh company of the Regiment. (Author's Collection)

▼ Another shot, taken during Operation 'Béja' on 26 February 1943, showing the very muddy conditions encountered. (Hartmann)

114   Seven: Tigers in Combat

history of s.Pz.Abt.501, Béja is known as the 'Tiger Grave' and Lang as 'Tank Killer'.

With the situation in North Africa now very much more serious than it had been when Hitler had promised Rommel his 40 Tigers, the provision of the second instalment of twenty assumed a higher priority; **s.Pz.Abt.504,** by this time formed and beginning to receive its quota of Tigers in Fallingbostel, was therefore earmarked as the second Tiger battalion for Rommel. The CO, Major August Seidensticker, was appointed on 8 February 1943 and the Battalion was warned for service in North Africa five days later.[11] The tanks were finished in desert yellow, turret numbers were in small solid red numerals and the unit company signs were painted on the forward end of each superstructure side plate and on the tail plate. All 504 Battalion's tanks were of the middle production model (see chart in Chapter 3), and thus can be distinguished easily in photographs from those of s.Pz.Abt.501.

504 Battalion's departure for Tunisia, originally scheduled to start on 13 February, was delayed first until 16 and then to 26 February as the training and equipment of the Battalion were, not surprisingly, incomplete. The first transport train left Fallingbostel during the night of 27 February, and Major Seidensticker himself reached Tunis on 17 March, by which time 501 Heavy Tank Battalion had been reduced by Allied action to only four Tigers. The remnant of 501 Battalion was therefore taken under command by Major Seidensticker in a combined 504/501 Tiger Company; only one Tiger company of 504 Battalion had, in the event, reached Tunisia, as the No.2 Company (2/504) had been diverted to Sicily in view of the deteriorating situation in Tunisia.[12]

The combined unit of the remnants of s.Pz.Abt.501 and 1/504 under the command of the CO of 504 Battalion, Major Seidensticker, was formed and given the task of moving 400 kilometres on its tracks to the area of the Maknassy Pass, as part of Kampfgruppe Lang, with a view to preventing the Allied advance eastwards through the pass to the coast. The combined unit, with approximately twelve Tigers, arrived in the Maknassy Pass area on 19 March. The successful completion of this march was a tribute not only to the unit fitters; it was a quite remarkable achievement when it is considered that the first tanks of 504 Battalion had not left Fallingbostel until early on 28 February and that the Battalion prior to that date had had very little training on the Tiger. The combined unit also had to run the gauntlet of several heavy air attacks *en route* and an attack by eighteen Flying Fortresses on arrival at the Maknassy Pass.

▲ A Tiger 1 in the markings of s.Pz.Abt.504; the turret numbers were much smaller than those of 501 Battalion and were in red with no white outlines. (Author's Collection)

Early on 20 March, after heavy artillery concentrations and massive air attacks, elements of the US 9th Infantry Division, 1st Armored Division and Combat Command 'C' (Brigade Group 'C') attacked, while Combat Command 'A' feinted towards the Maknassy – Gafsa road. The long range of the Tigers' guns enabled the attack towards Maknassy to be repulsed; an official Wehrmacht report on 24 March stated that 44 Allied tanks had been destroyed in the attack. What it did not state was that this damage had been inflicted by only twelve Tigers!

Ten days later, the combined Tiger battalion moved to the Hermann Goering Division sector, stretching from Bizerta to Medjez-el-Bab. The build-up for 'Vulcan', the final Allied attack to clear Tunisia of Axis troops, was now nearing completion; against von Arnim's fifteen depleted divisions with only 110 fit tanks, including only thirteen Tigers, the Allies could field nineteen fully manned and equipped divisions, well supported logistically, with overwhelming artillery and air superiority and with more than 1,000 tanks.

Preliminary Allied re-grouping started on 17 April, and on 20 April the Hermann Goering Division mounted a spoiling attack, code-named 'Fliederblüte', to the south from the direction of Medjez-el-Bab; the counter-attacking force consisted of four Tigers and four Pz Kpfw III of s.Pz.Abt.501/504, five attached Pz Kpfw IV 'Specials' and 12 Company of 5th Parachute Regiment (Jägerregiment Hermann Goering).[13] The attack was launched on the night of 20/21 April against the British 1st Infantry and 4th Mixed Divisions in the centre, and achieved both surprise and some initial success, among other things driving through and shooting up the HQ of the British 21 Army Tank Brigade near Testour.[14] After much confused fighting, the German force withdrew and the rearguard took up defensive positions in the area north-east of 'Handley Cross' on the Djebel el Mehirigar and Djebel Djaffa. A British attack by 1/6th Battalion of the East Surrey Regiment, part of 10 Infantry Brigade, and 'A' Squadron of 48th Royal Tank Regiment in the afternoon of 21 April failed to dislodge them and cost the loss of two Churchill tanks, one of them the author's, and two more damaged; the British troops were withdrawn at dusk and the German rearguard withdrew later that night.[15]

Examination of the battlefield the next morning revealed a burnt-out Pz Kpfw III near the two burnt-out Churchills and another Pz Kpfw III with a track off further to the rear. Farther still, behind the shoulder of

▲ Tiger 131 of 504 Heavy Tank Battalion after being knocked out by Churchills of 'A' Squadron of 48th Royal Tank Regiment on 21 April 1943; a Churchill and Dingo scout car of 48 RTR are in the background. (IWM)

Djebel Djaffa, was a virtually undamaged Tiger, its turret jammed by a lucky 6pdr shot from one of the Churchills of 'A' Squadron 48th RTR, another Tiger penetrated by anti-tank fire which had killed the commander, Oberleutnant Schröter, a Pz Kpfw III and a Pz Kpfw IV, both also with only minor damage.[16] Thus the first virtually undamaged Tiger 1, of 3 Platoon, 1/504, and bearing the turret number 131, at last fell into British hands; it is now in the Tank Museum at Bovington Camp in Dorset, England.

The end of both 501 and 504 Heavy Tank Battalions came on the Cap Bon peninsula on 8 May 1943 with their surrender to the British. Their tanks and crews, despite their small numbers (no more than 32 Tigers were landed in Tunisia between November 1942 and the end of the campaign, and never more than twenty were serviceable at any one time) created a legend of the Tiger's invincibility which lasted throughout the war and up to the present day, while the number of tank casualties inflicted upon US and British units was out of all proportion to the number of Tigers employed. It reflected great credit on the officers and men of the two battalions that they managed, despite chronic shortage of vehicles and training time, to attain such a high standard of professionalism.

In Sicily

The No.2 Company of **504 Heavy Tank Battalion**, under the command first of Oberleutnant Hummel and later of Oberleutnant Herbert Heim, was meanwhile awaiting events in Sicily. In the absence of the originally planned third Tiger company, 2/504 was all that remained of that Battalion after the surrender in Tunisia; at that time, it had only nine Tigers to its name and few Pz Kpfw IIIs, most of the latter having been sent to North Africa as reinforcements. Instead of Pz Kpfw III, therefore, it took over some Pz Kpfw IVs from 15th Panzer Battalion of 15th Panzer Grenadier Division and eight more Tigers arrived later, bringing the company Tiger strength up to seventeen.[17]

The Allied landings on Sicily started during the night of 10 July 1943; resistance was fierce, but the outcome was inevitable, and the Tigers of 2/504 were defeated in detail as the Allies advanced. With the Allied capture of Messina on 17 August 1943, German resistance in Sicily ended; by this time, all except one of the Tigers of 2/504 had been destroyed and this remaining one was evacuated to the Italian mainland on the last ferry to cross the Straits of Messina, together with its crew, commanded by Leutnant Goldschmidt.

Thus ended the story of s.Pz.Abt.501 and 504 in North Africa and Sicily. Both battalions were, however, later re-formed, each with the correct number of three Tiger companies, 501 at Paderborn in September 1943 and 504 in the winter of 1943/4 on the troop training area of Wezep bei Zwolle in Holland.[18]

On the Eastern Front

Of the four heavy tank battalions to be formed at Fallingbostel in the latter half of 1942, 501 and 504 had been dispatched to North Africa as reinforcements for Rommel's Afrika Korps, but 502 and 503 were destined for the Eastern Front, as were the majority of the heavy tank companies and battalions. The record of 502's doings and movements being more complete than that of any other Battalion in this theatre, its story will be recounted here in more detail than that of any of the other heavy tank battalions on the Eastern Front, and may be taken as being typical of the experiences of them all; the histories of the other heavy tank battalions and companies will be told in broad outline only, particularly as the records relating to some of them were lost in the closing stages of the war.

As has been seen, No.1 Tiger Company of **s.Pz.Abt.502** had already been dispatched prematurely, at Hitler's whim, to the Leningrad front, with only four Tigers, and with the disastrous results that might have been foreseen; the remainder of the Battalion was to follow in stages, as equipment became available. Six months after the Battalion's formation, however, 2/502 was still not complete at Fallingbostel while 1/502 still languished, with few tanks, before Leningrad; 2/502 received its first Tiger at Fallingbostel on 25 September, but the remainder did not arrive until December 1942. Their drivers, the workshop staff and specialist personnel were therefore trained by s.Pz.Abt.503, located beside them at Fallingbostel.[19]

On 23 December 1942, a telex message was received by the Battalion ordering 2/502 to move to the Eastern Front, where it would come under command of Army Group Don (FM von Manstein). HQ Company had meanwhile already moved to the Gory area at the beginning of December. 2/502 detrained at Proletarskaya on 7 January 1943 and, after a 10-hour march of some 110 kilometres arrived in the Ssungar-Kuberle sector of the front, where, under command of 17th Panzer Division, it took part in some minor actions. It then came under command of the newly arrived s.Pz.Abt.503, with whom it moved in stages to Rostov, which it reached on 22 January.

▼ A Tiger of No. 2 Company, 504 Heavy Tank Battalion, knocked out in Sicily. (IWM)

118 *Seven: Tigers in Combat*

The No.1 Company of 502 Heavy Tank Battalion, meanwhile, had been in action in the Lake Ladoga area, under the command of various divisions. One Tiger which had been heavily bogged was finally recovered using two Pz Kpfw III as anchors and four 18-tonne half-tracks to do the pulling, in an operation spread over three nights. As a result of this difficult operation and many similar ones in the boggy conditons prevailing, it was recommended that the 18-tonne recovery half-tracks be fitted with spades, as designed by the Workshop Officer of s.Pz.Abt.502; after the successful trial of prototypes at Paderborn, they were put into production and issued to the heavy tank battalion recovery platoon half-tracks. The proposed development of a recovery vehicle on the Tiger chassis had, it will be remembered, been stopped by Hitler, and it was not until the highly successful Panther armoured recovery vehicle was issued to the heavy tank battalions that they had adequate means of recovering their bogged or broken-down Tigers. The Panther ARV had a winch with a 40-tonne capacity, whereas that of the 18-tonne half-track was only 2.8 tonnes.

By mid June 1943, 1/502 had been joined in the Leningrad area by the newly formed 3/502, as well as by the HQ and Workshop Companies. 2/502 had earlier been sent to France to help in the occupation, presumably instead of 2/501 which had been sent to Tunisia, and did not arrive in Russia until 22/23 July; it was in action immediately after off-loading in Mga. By 21 July 1943, the remaining action-ready components of s.Pz.Abt.502 were standing-to before Leningrad, ready for the third battle of Lake Ladoga, which started on the 22nd. The Battalion was withdrawn from the battle on 5 September to rest and reform, and it was not until two months later, on 4 November 1943, that it was again in action, this time in the defence of Nevel.

From January 1944, the Battalion was withdrawn piecemeal back to the Leningrad area, where it was involved in the Narva bridgehead battle from February to April 1944. In this battle, the Battalion knocked out its 500th enemy tank on 23 February, in honour of which the Battalion Commander, now Major Jahde, issued a special order of the day In May, however, Major Jahde left the Battalion to attend the Officers' School at Eisenach and a new CO, Major (Dipl.Ing.) Hans-Joachim Schwaner, took command. In June 1944 the Battalion participated in the defence of Ostrov, and then moved to Dunaburg between 3 and 7 July; it was significant that each succeeding action in which the Battalion was involved had been heavier than the

▼An early production Tiger 1 on a rail flat, with portable unloading ramp in position, this ramp was for use in places where there was no station platform at which to unload. (Author's Collection)

preceding one, and they were becoming increasingly difficult as the Soviet tank and self-propelled anti-tank guns became ever more numerous and larger in calibre. Increasingly the actions were defensive in nature, followed by withdrawal, which made recovery of both tank and personnel casualties more difficult as well as having a lowering effect on morale. During this period, the Russians first employed the newly introduced IS-2 heavy tank, mounting a 122mm long-barrelled gun, the 122mm heavy anti-tank gun and the T-34(85), a version of the T-34 medium tank mounting an 85mm gun in a larger, redesigned turret.

After suffering heavy losses of both Tigers and crews, s.Pz.Abt.502 was withdrawn into Army reserve to Jucava, 40 kilometres south of Riga, on 5 August 1944. On the same day, Hauptmann Leonhardt, the commander of 3/502, temporarily assumed command of the Battalion, as Major Schwaner had broken an ankle; his successor, Hauptmann von Foerster, took over on 25 August. It was not long, however, before the Battalion, with all its fit Tigers, was again committed, this time in support of 81st Infantry Division, to help to stem a Soviet breakthrough towards Riga near Suostas. After a hard-fought but ultimately unsuccessful defensive action lasting several days, the Battalion was ordered to move during the night of 26 August to come under command of X Army Corps; the Russians had reached the East Prussian border, their breakthrough towards Riga had succeeded, and the summer battle in the area of Ostrov, Roskiskis, Schönberg and Dunaburg had ended.

By now, s.Pz.Abt.502 was short of Tigers, having received no replacements for those that it had lost in the preceding battles; it was accordingly ordered to deliver all spare soft-skinned vehicles to a collection point at Tukkum, whence they would be distributed to other

Seven: Tigers in Combat

◀ A Tiger unit on the move by train; note the portable gantry crane, on the flat wagon between the two Tigers. Note also the tank crew's bivouac attached to the gun barrel on the nearest rail flat. The nearest Tiger is a late-production model with steel-tyred road wheels and the latest commander's cupola. (Bundesarchiv)

▲ Side view of the Pz Berge Wg Panther ARV, showing the spade at the rear and the box-type crew compartment. (Author's Collection)

▼ A captured Panther recovery vehicle undergoing test on Chobham Common by the School of Tank Technology in 1945; it is recovering a Churchill up a steep slope. (Author's Collection)

Tiger 1   121

▲ A Tiger 1 of the middle production model with a broken track on the Eastern Front; note the white snow camouflage, extending even to the exhaust covers. (Author's Collection)

▼ The heavy tank battalion's workshop company using its portable 10-tonne gantry crane to remove the turret of a Tiger 1. (Author's Collection)

122   Seven: Tigers in Combat

units in Kurland. Crewmen, soft-skinned vehicle drivers and echelon personnel thus released were formed into an infantry alarm-unit under command of HQ Company. The Battalion was then committed, under command of Eighteen Army, in the Riga bridgehead, in a series of actions in which, by 4 October, the Tigers had knocked out some 83 enemy tanks, mostly T-34(85); on 26 September, they knocked out their 1,000th enemy tank since their campaign on the Eastern Front had started in the autumn of 1942, making a total of 500 knocked out since February 1944 alone.

The last German troops evacuated Riga on 13 October; in mid October, s.Pz.Abt.502 moved to an area 30 kilometres to the east of Libau, less eight Tigers of 3/502, which were temporarily placed under the command of s.Pz.Abt.510. On 24 October, the German I Army Corps, with 4th, 12th and 14th Panzer Divisions, counter-attacked towards Memel, East Prussia; this counter-attack was led by s.Pz.Abt.510, with its eight additional Tigers of 3/502, in an attack eastwards towards Preekuln, in which five of the eight Tigers of 3/502 were knocked out and the Soviet troops lost 60 anti-tank guns. On 12 November, 3/502 handed over their last six Tigers to 510 Heavy Tank Battalion and left Kurland for Paderborn, where they became the first company of s.Pz.Abt.502 to be equipped with the new Tiger 2; the remainder of the Battalion, meanwhile, was in the Memel bridgehead, later to be cut off in besieged Memel itself.

On 10 January 1945, the two remaining Tiger companies of the Battalion were ordered by General Gollnick, commanding XXVIII Army Corps, to take part in Operation 'Silberstreifen' ('Silver Stripes') with the aim of breaking out to Kurland with a view to keeping open a line of retreat to East Prussia. After a short artillery and rocket-launcher bombardment, under the cover of which the engineers cleared routes through the minefields, the two Tiger companies moved forward at 12.45. On the morning of 13 January at 07.00 the Third White Russian Front opened its offensive against East Prussia with three hours of artillery drum fire, from 350 batteries and rocket-launchers, and, on the 15th, strong Soviet forces broke through the German positions south of Schlossberg; s.Pz.Abt.507 took much of the brunt of the attack, and inflicted heavy losses on the attacking units. The Soviet

▼ Summer on the Eastern Front. Repairing the idler wheel and track of a Tiger 1. (Author's Collection)

Tiger 1 123

aim was to by-pass Kurland and make straight for East Prussia; by the end of January, Russian troops had reached the Vistula Lagoon, severing most of East Prussia from the rest of Germany.

In view of the Soviet success, Colonel-General Guderian asked Hitler to release from the Memel bridgehead those units belonging to Third Panzerarmee for action in East Prussia. As the first unit involved, s.Pz.Abt.502, now re-numbered as **s.Pz.Abt.511** by an Army General Staff order dated 5 January 1945 to prevent confusion with the newly formed s.SS.Pz.Abt.502, was ordered to make all speed to East Prussia; this it did by sea, on the rail ferry boats *Deutschland* and *Preussen-Sassnitz* and a marine pontoon ferry. It reached the Pillau roadstead, after a quiet night voyage, in the early morning darkness of 24 January 1945 and moved off north-eastwards into the Samland. By 7 February, after conducting a lengthy fighting withdrawal and an unsuccessful attempt to relieve the beleaguered fortress of Königsberg, 511 Heavy Tank Battalion found itself in the area of Neuhausen. There it was able to enjoy a well-earned rest period; all, that is, except the Workshop Company, which had ten Tigers to repair and make battle-worthy.

On 19 February, the counter-attack towards Königsberg from the west started, with the aim of clearing the road from Königsberg through to Pillau via Fischhausen; s.Pz.Abt. 505 was in the Königsberg perimeter, together with 1st and 561st Infantry and 5th Panzer Divisions. After many sharp actions in which many individual acts of great bravery were performed, the Russian attack was temporarily halted, and again the Battalion was able to enjoy a well-earned rest; this was the last of the war and lasted six weeks, in which time 1/511 handed over its remaining Tigers to 2/511 and itself re-equipped with the Jagdpanzer 38 (Hetzer). The men of the Company could not understand how they could be expected to counter the heavy Soviet tanks with so light a vehicle, armed only with the 7.5cm PaK 39(L/48) anti-tank gun; it was no tank, only a lightly armoured self-propelled anti-tank gun, suitable for the infantry!

On 29 March 1945, the Soviet Front Commander announced the fall of Gdansk and Gdynia. The big attack on Königsberg began on 6 April; the German commander surrendered the city on the 9th. The Soviet

▼ A captured Pz Jäg 38(t) Hetzer, the type with which No. 1 Company of s.Pz.Abt. 511 was re-equipped, much to their disgust. Armed only with the 75mm (L/48) gun, and relatively thinly armoured, they felt it was no match for the heavy Russian tanks and SP anti-tank guns then being encountered. (Author's Collection)

commander called for the surrender of all German troops in Samland in leaflets dropped from the air, pointing out that the Allies were 300 kilometres east of the Rhine and had occupied Bremen, Hanover, Brunswick, Leipzig and Munich. Königsberg had fallen and the Russians had occupied Vienna and were at the gates of Berlin. The end was near; the last battle in Samland began for s.Pz.Abt.511 on 13 April 1945 near Thierenberg station, in a fighting withdrawal that lasted until the 16th and ended in the Neuhauser Forest. Here the Workshop Company was hidden, and worked feverishly to repair the remaining damaged Tigers. Nearly all the Hetzers of 1/511 had been destroyed and their crews either wounded or taken prisoner; the rest of the Battalion sought to escape through the bottleneck of Fischhausen to Pillau, hoping from there to be evacuated by sea, in a Dunkirk-style operation, back to Germany. The majority found themselves on the Frischen Nehrung by the 18.5 kilometre stone, together with the Battalion's last Tiger, turret number 217, which the Workshop Company had managed to make battle-worthy; this was used to guard their rear, and it in fact knocked out eight Russian tanks on 26 April and a further six or seven the following day. The Tiger blew up from an unknown cause that evening; the last two armoured troop carriers of the Battalion had to be destroyed the same evening.

In the evening of 8 May 1945, 250–300 men of the Battalion waited on the beach at Nickelswalde for the possibility of evacuation; none materialized, and on the following morning, therefore, they piled their small-arms, formed up into ranks and awaited the arrival of the Russian troops at 11.00

That was the end of the story of the s.Pz.Abt. 502/511,[20] a typical heavy tank battalion, equipped with Tiger 1s, on the Russian Front. Other battalions engaged there and also equipped with the Tiger 1 were:

■ **s.Pz.Abt 501.** Re-formed at Paderborn in September 1943 from 150 members of the earlier 501, destroyed in Tunisia. Again destroyed July 1944 in Vitebsk area. Mid July 1944, again re-formed, in Ohrdruf/Thuringia with Tiger 2. In December 1944 re-numbered as s.Pz.Abt.424, to prevent confusion with newly formed s.SS Pz.Abt.501.[21]

■ **s.Pz.Abt.503.** Formed in spring 1942 at the same time as s.Pz.Abt.502, and already encountered in this Chapter. Originally scheduled to be equipped with the Tiger(P). Took part in Operation 'Citadel' (July 1943). April 1944 to Lemberg, thence to Ohrdruf/Thuringia to re-equip. Thereafter employed on Western Front and in Hungary. In December 1944, renamed s.Pz.Abt. 'Feldherrnhalle' to prevent confusion with newly formed s.SS Pz.Abt.503.[22]

■ **s.Pz.Abt.505.** Formed end-January 1943 at Fallingbostel, with personnel from Armoured Reinforcement Battalions 5 and 10; at full strength by 18 February. Originally earmarked for North Africa; exchanged personnel and equipment with s.Pz.Abt.504 and placed under command Heeresgruppe Mitte on 1 May 1943. Took part in Operation 'Citadel' (July 1943). July 1944 to Ohrdruf/Thuringia to re-equip with Tiger 2. Thereafter employed on Eastern Front from mid September 1944.[23]

■ **s.Pz.Abt.506.** Formed July 1943 out of third battalion of Panzerregiment 33 (III./PR33) at St Polten. Sent in September 1943 to Heeresgruppe Sud. Withdrawn in July 1944 to Ohrdruf/Thuringia to re-equip; thereafter employed on Western Front.[24]

■ **s.Pz.Abt.507.** Formed with three Tiger companies in September 1943 at Vienna/Mödling out of the first battalion of Panzerregiment 3 (I./PR 3). Tactical sign – blacksmith forging sword on anvil, in shield with RH corner cut out. From March 1944 with Heeresgruppe Mitte. Re-formed March 1945 with Tiger 2.[25]

■ **s.Pz.Abt.509.** Formed September 1943 out of PR204 in Schwetzingen. Trained at Pz.Ers.u.Ausb. Abt.500 Paderborn and equipped with 45 Tiger 1 and 90 Pz Kpfw IV at Mailly le Camp, France. To Eastern Front end-October 1943. Returned in early September 1944 to Sennelager to re-equip with Tiger 2.[26]

■ **s.Pz.Abt.510.** Formed at Paderborn in June 1944 and equipped with Tiger 1 as not enough Tiger 2 available. Personnel from Workshop Company of s.Pz.Abt.504, Tank Company of Company Commanders' School, Versailles, and Pz.Ers.-u.Ausb.Abt.500, Paderborn. Trained at Ohrdruf. Moved to northern sector of Eastern Front early August 1944. Surrendered to Russian troops on 8 May 1945.[27]

■ **Pz.Gren.Div.'Grossdeutschland'. 13 Company of the PR 'Gross-deutschland'** was equipped with fourteen Tiger 1s and was in action on the Eastern Front in February 1943. In spring 1943, the third battalion of this Panzerregiment (**III/PR'GD'**), with 9, 10 and 11 Companies, was equipped with Tigers at Cottbus – 9 Company was the former 13 Company, 10 Company formed from what should have been 3 Company s.Pz.Abt.501 and 11 Company from 3/504. Moved to Eastern Front in August 1943. December 1944 became s.Pz.Abt.'Grossdeutschland' and re-equipped.[28]

■**Waffen-SS.** Each of the Waffen-SS panzer and panzer grenadier divisions contained a heavy tank company, equipped with Tiger tanks, in its panzer regiment. In 1st SS Panzerregiment 'Leibstandarte SS Adolf Hitler'(LSSAH) it was 13 (heavy) Company, while in 2nd SS Panzer Grenadier Division 'Das Reich' and 3rd SS Panzer Grenadier Division 'Totenkopf' it was 8 (heavy) Company. All saw action on the Eastern Front. These heavy tank companies were up-graded into heavy tank battalions in October 1943, that in 3rd SS PzG Division becoming **s.SS Pz.Abt 103,** that in 2nd SS Panzer Grenadier Division 'Das Reich' becoming **s.SS Pz.Abt.102** and that in 1st Panzer Division 'LSSAH' becoming **s.SS Pz.Abt. 101.** The formation of s.SS Pz.Abt.104 as the Corps Heavy Tank Battalion of IV SS Panzer Korps is questionable. In September 1944, SS heavy tank battalions were removed from the divisions to become corps Tiger battalions and were again re-numbered, 101 to 501, 102 to 502 and 103 to 503 SS Heavy Tank Battalions. Organization of SS Tiger companies and heavy tank battalions was similar to that of equivalent Army units, as was turret numbering. The 501 SS Heavy Tank Battalion was first in action as Corps troops in June 1944 in Normandy although many of its members had already seen much action on the Eastern Front with 13/SS-PR1 'LSSAH' and s.SS Pz.Abt.101. 102 SS Heavy Tank Battalion also saw heavy action in France from June to August 1944 before being sent to Paderborn for re-equipping and re-forming as s.SS Pz.Abt.502.[29]

In Italy

Only two heavy tank battalions, both equipped with the Tiger 1, served in Italy; they were the re-formed **s.Pz.Abt.504,** the original Battalion having been destroyed in Tunisia and Sicily, and **s.Pz.Abt.508.** The Italian Campaign started on 3 September 1943, when troops of the British Eighth Army crossed the Straits of Messina and established themselves on the toe of the Italian mainland at Reggio/Calabria; the Axis forces withdrew before the Eighth Army, who were thus able to make very rapid progress through the mountainous country of Apulia. On 9 September 1943, the US Fifth Army assaulted the beaches of Salerno, breaking out of the beachhead on 29 September and capturing the city of Naples. Taranto, Brindisi and Bari were soon in Allied hands, and by 8 November the Eighth Army had reached the River Sangro. The end of 1943 found the Fifth and Eighth Armies stretched across Italy from Ortona to the River Garigliano. The winter rains had come with a vengeance; most of the roads were not built to carry heavy army traffic and collapsed in the wet weather, while the fields would no longer support the weight of a vehicle. And the country in which the fighting was now taking place was broken and mountainous.

On 22 January 1944, therefore, an attempt was made to turn the flank of the Axis defensive positions, and the US VI Corps landed at Anzio, some 30 miles south of Rome; Axis forces, however, succeeded in containing the Allied landing within the beachhead until their final breakout at the end of May. Meanwhile, the Axis forces, far from relinquishing their hold along the Garigliano, constructed two formidable lines of defence. The most forward was known as the Gustav Line, and stretched from Cassino along the Garigliano to Gaeta; behind this position lay the second, the Adolf Hitler Line, in the Liri valley, the most practicable route to Rome. The Allied assault on the Gustav Line started on 11 May 1944 and met with great success; Cassino was captured, the Gustav Line was broken and the Adolf Hitler Line was also smashed. On 4 June 1944, the Allies entered Rome.

The **504 Heavy Tank Battalion** was re-formed at the troop training area of Wezep bei Zwolle in Holland in the winter of 1943/4, largely from members of the former Battalion who had been wounded in the earlier campaigns, who had been away from the Battalion on courses or leave at the time of its destruction or who had escaped from Tunisia and Sicily at the time of the surrender. They were collected together by Leutnant Karl Goldschmidt, who had escaped from Sicily with his Tiger and crew and who was put in command of 3 Company. The Battalion commander was Hauptmann Friedrich Kühn; his Adjutant was Leutnant Harkort, 1 Company was commanded by Leutnant Steuber and 2 Company by Oberleutnant Heim, all three having served in the original 504 Battalion with Goldschmidt. The majority of the remaining personnel of the Battalion came from Pz.Abt.18, which had been destroyed on the Eastern Front in November 1943. Training in the Tiger took place at 500 Armoured Reinforcement and Training Battalion at Paderborn.

At the beginning of May 1944 the Battalion was sent to the Parthenay area, where it took part in several training exercises with 17th SS Panzer Grenadier Division 'Goetz von Berlichingen'. On 2 June 1944 orders came for it to entrain at Ulm for the Italian front; when the Allied landings in France came on 6 June, everybody expected these orders to be changed and the Battalion committed against the invasion, but no change came and the Battalion moved as ordered in the second week of June. They unloaded in the heavily bombed-damaged stations of Pontremoli, Sarzana and Massa before setting out on a road march of more than 150 kilometres to the front; they could only move by night, thanks to Allied air superiority. By this time, the battle for Monte Cassino had ended and the breakout of the US Fifth Army from the Anzio beachhead had ended in the capture of Rome.

The Battalion re-assembled in a pine wood near San Vicenzo, north of Piombino, after a march fraught with technical problems with the Tigers; their first action was by 1 Company in co-operation with 362nd Infantry Division on 20/21 June 1944, when they mounted a counter-attack south of Montepescali (north of Grosseto). Also on 21 June, 2 Company was in action against US troops; a massed US tank attack on 22 June on Parolla, SE of Massa Marittima, saw Officer Cadet Röhrig of 1 Company defeating 23 Shermans, eleven of which were knocked out by the Tiger's 8.8cm gun and the other twelve abandoned by the headlong flight of their crews on seeing the damage inflicted on their comrades' tanks. As a result of his action, Röhrig was awarded the Ritterkreuz in July 1944.

The recovery platoon, now commanded by Leutnant Goldschmidt, achieved miracles of recovery in the difficult country in which the Tiger companies were fighting; not only were the recovery situations difficult in themselves, but recovery had to be undertaken under heavy bombardment from fighter-bombers and artillery and the recovered vehicles towed 90 kilometres daily back to the Workshop Company location. Had it not been for the efforts of the recovery platoon, some twenty Tigers, nearly half the Battalion Tiger strength, would have been lost. Despite the outstanding performance against the lighter Allied tanks, however, the officers and crewmen of the Battalion would have preferred a lighter, more flexible tank than the Tiger in the country through which they were having to fight; and this message was passed by Reichsminister Speer to Hitler in October 1944 as if it were the preference of all German tank crews, which was definitely not the case. At the same time, the US tankers were expressing dissatisfaction with their Shermans, a captured US document saying that they were 'shot like ducks on a pond', so it would seem that neither Tiger nor Sherman was giving satisfaction in Italy!

After the withdrawal in the valley of the Cecina, s.Pz.Abt.504 was placed under command of 24th Panzer Grenadier Division, while 3 Company came under command of 17th SS Panzer Grenadier Division and the commanding officer, now Major Kühn, with some of his HQ, reported to the commander of XXXXVI Army Corps. 3 Company, together with the Sturmgeschütz Battalion of 17th SS Panzer Grenadier Division, secured the Pisa area, 2 Company waited in the area south of Verona for re-equipment with new Tigers and 1 Company was on anti-partisan security duties on the road from Castelnuovo di Garfagnano, which wound through the wild country of the Serchio valley. On 12 August 1944, the whole Battalion was re-united under Marshal Graziani's Ligurian Army in the area of Tortona and on 10 September moved into reserve for rest and recuperation in the area of Forlimpopoli, before again going into action, less 1 Company, against the Allied drive on Rimini. No.1 Company had meanwhile been sent to Vienna, where, in the Army Group tank repair workshops, they were learning to use the Tiger 2 which they were destined never to receive.

The Battalion, less 1 Company, was in action around Rimini, which fell to the Allies on 21 September, and the south-eastern sector of the River Po from September 1944 and through the winter of 1944/5. In November 1944, 3 Company moved to Vienna, to the tank repair workshop of Army Group South-West, having handed its Tigers over to 1 Company; the latter had returned to the battalion fold, and was soon in action again, this time against the British and the Canadians in the battle for the River Senio. The withdrawal to the line of the Senio took place on 20 December and the front remained there until April 1945. This gave the Battalion the chance of a quiet Christmas in the area of Lugo–Cotignole. Towards the end of January 1945, 3/504 rejoined the Battalion from Vienna, without tanks; as the s.Pz.Abt.508, which had been in Italy only a few months, was short of personnel, 3/504 was able to take over the remaining Tiger 1s of 508 Heavy Tank Battalion and thus again reach its establishment strength in tanks.

On 20 February, the Battalion again moved into front reserve and had a quiet time until 8 March 1945. When the Allied offensive opened at noon on 9 April, 3 Company was in the area of Lugo, 1 Company between Lugo and the Santerno and 2 Company in front of Massa Lombarda. The Tigers' positions were obviously known, and attracted heavy Allied artillery fire down on them; the British 21 Tank Brigade summary of their operations in Italy in April 1945 stated that 'there were estimated to be 25 to 30 Tigers in the LUGO – MASSA LOMBARDA area'. The Battalion retreated gradually back towards the Po, losing many Tigers both to enemy fire and to accident; on 28 April the Battalion's last Tiger was blown up by its crew on the road to Bassano, when one of its tracks fell into an underground water-course and the one remaining recovery half-track was unable to winch it out.

The Battalion was in the Agordo valley, together with Corps HQ and a small battle group of 29th Panzer Grenadier Division, when the written capitulation order, dated 2 May 1945, was received from the commander of LXXVI Panzer Armee Korps; on 3 May the remains of the Battalion moved back to the outskirts of Belluno, then, two weeks later, by way of Bologna and the Via Emilia to the large prisoner-of-war compound north of Rimini and into captivity.[30]

The other heavy tank battalion to see service on the Italian front was the **s.Pz.Abt.508**, whose tactical sign was a charging bull in a shield. Unfortunately, little is now known of the personnel of the Battalion or of its movements and the actions in which it fought in the Italian campaign. The Battalion was formed in August 1943 from the remains of Panzerregiment 8, it was training at Paderborn at the beginning of 1944 and its only recorded action was in the Nettuno area in June 1944. It handed its remaining Tiger 1 tanks over to 3/504 in January 1945.[31]

In France and Germany
By the time of the Allied invasion of Normandy on 6 June 1944, the Tiger 1 was beginning to be replaced by the Tiger 2 in the heavy tank battalions. As production of the Tiger 2 was insufficient to replace all Tiger 1s, however, some battalions were equipped with a mixture of both types while others were fully equipped with one or the other.

503 Heavy Tank Battalion, between 11th and 17th June, received its first Tiger 2s, but, as there were not enough for the whole Battalion, only No.1 Company was equipped with them; it was the first operational tank company in Germany to be so equipped. The remaining two Tiger companies received new Tiger 1s. Little is now known of the part played by this Battalion in the battle for north-west Europe, due to the destruction and loss of war diaries at this stage of the war. It is known that the Battalion moved from Ohrdruf to Normandy in eight trains at the end of June 1944; it took them five days to reach Paris, because of Allied interdiction of the rail lines, and they unloaded in Dreux on 2 July. On 11 July, the Battalion came under command of PR 21 of 21st Panzer Division and was in action near Colombelles; it returned to Paderborn in September 1944 for re-equipment with Tiger 2s, of which it received 45, and its subsequent movements are described later. In December 1944, it was renamed **s.Pz.Abt. 'Feldherrnhalle'** to avoid confusion with the re-numbered s.SS Pz.Abt.503.[32]

The only other Tiger units engaged in north-west Europe were **s.Pz.Abt.506**, equipped with Tiger 2s and also described later, and the Waffen SS Heavy Tank Battalions 101 and 102. The **s.SS Pz.Abt.102** had only just been re-equipped with 45 brand-new Tiger 1s at the Wezep bei Zwolle training area when the Allied invasion of Normandy began.

On 30 June, this Battalion took part in the counter-attack on Caen and was under command of the 12 SS Panzer Division 'Hitler Jugend' to 20 August 1944. During this time it was heavily involved in the battle for Hill 112, on the reverse slope of which several of its Tigers were so well dug-in that they were able to meet Allied attack from any direction; 7th Royal Tank Regiment lost eight tanks and 'A' Squadron of 9th RTR lost twelve out of fourteen on 10 July to the Tigers of s.SS Pz.Abt.102 dug-in on Hill 112. In August, however, the Battalion lost most of its own tanks in the withdrawal through the Falaise Gap and, in mid September 1944, it was sent to Paderborn to re-form as **s.SS Pz.Abt.502** and to re-equip with Tiger 2.[33]

Meanwhile, **101 SS Heavy Tank Battalion,** the heavy tank battalion of I SS Panzer Korps, was located in Belgium with 1st SS 'Leibstandarte' Panzer Division; on 12 June 1944 it reached the battle area, with 2 Company, commanded by Sturmbannführer Michael Wittmann, located in a small wood to the north-west of Villers Bocage and 1 Company on its right. Wittmann, who had served with the Battalion and with its predecessor, 13 Company of SS Panzer Regiment 1, since their formation, was the German tank commander with the most 'kills' to his credit during the Second World War, and, in view of his performance in Normandy in 1944, deserves particular mention here.[34]

Wittmann had joined the Army in the ranks in October 1934, at the age of 20; he joined the SS two years later and, in November 1937, was promoted to the rank of Sturmmann. He was an armoured car commander in the invasion of Poland in September 1939 and in the invasion of France in May 1940. Sent to Greece in October 1940 with LSSAH, then an assault gun unit equipped with StuG IIIs, he moved with his unit to the Eastern Front in time for Operation 'Barbarossa', the German invasion of the Soviet Union, in June 1941. In July of that year he was awarded the Iron Cross 2nd Class, in August he was wounded in the face by shell fragments during the drive to Rostov and in September he was awarded the Iron Cross 1st Class. Still in command of a StuG III, he was again wounded in October 1941 and was recommended for officer training, from which he was commissioned on 12 December 1942.

After training on the Tiger tank from January to March 1943, he rejoined 13 (Heavy) Company of SS

128   Seven: Tigers in Combat

▲A late-production model Tiger 1 moving through a French town in 1944. (Bundesarchiv)

▼Wittman's company of s.SS Pz.Abt 501 moving in column along a French road in 1944. (Author's Collection)

Panzer Regiment 1 'LSSAH' on the Eastern Front in time for the battle of Kursk in July 1943; in this battle he gave an indication of his ability by knocking out 30 Soviet T-34 tanks and 28 anti-tank guns in the area of Bjelgorod. Two days later he destroyed seven more T-34 and nineteen more anti-tank guns; further successes followed in November of that year, and by 6 December his tally had reached 60 tanks destroyed.

By 13 January 1944 his total number of tank kills was 88, as a result of which he was awarded the Knight's Cross; the next day he destroyed a further nineteen tanks and three SP guns, for which he received the Iron Cross with Oak Leaves and was promoted to Obersturmbannführer. In February 1944, a further nine T-34s and thirteen SP guns fell to his gun while operating in the area of Boyarka, bringing his total of enemy AFVs destroyed to 119. In the same month he assumed command of 2 Company of s.SS Pz.Abt.101 and took his Company to Belgium with 1st SS Panzer Division 'LSSAH'.

On 13 June 1944, in the battle for Villers Bocage, Wittmann's single tank knocked out 25 various armoured vehicles belonging to the British 4th County of London Yeomanry, of 22 Armoured Brigade,[35] in less than five minutes; as a result, on 22 June he was awarded the Swords to the Knight's Cross and shortly afterwards promoted to Hauptsturmbannführer (captain). At this time, his tally was 138 enemy tanks and at least 132 anti-tank guns destroyed. While not in any way attempting to minimize the exploits of an undoubtedly talented tank commander, however, one must remember that the sights were laid and the gun fired by his gunner, Balthasar (Bobby) Woll; a quite extraordinary understanding and empathy developed between the two men, and it was in combination that they achieved this exceptional number of enemy tank and anti-tank gun 'kills'.

Wittmann and his crew were killed two months later, on 8 August, during Operation 'Totalize', the Canadian, Polish and British attack on Falaise, when his Tiger was attacked from three sides by five Sherman 'Firefly' tanks armed with 17pdr guns; just before this, he had accounted for three more enemy tanks, this time from the Polish Armoured Division.[36] By a strange quirk of fate, Woll had temporarily left the Battalion on sick leave the week before his commander and fellow crewmen met their deaths, and survived the war. One cannot help wondering if his absence at the crucial time could have been a contributory cause of the tank being knocked out; a slower than expected reaction to Wittmann's fire orders by the replacement gunner could have enabled the Shermans to survive where normally Woll would have ensured that they did not.

A recent book on the Waffen SS tank units by Hauptmann a.D. Will Fey (*Panzer im Bild* – see Bibliography) states that Wittmann's tank was hit by either a rocket fired from a Typhoon aircraft or by a large-calibre artillery shell and was blown apart. We shall probably never know which version is correct.

By the time of the Ardennes offensive in December 1944, 101 SS Heavy Tank Battalion had been re-numbered (in September 1944) as **s.SS Pz.Abt.501** and re-equipped with the Tiger 2; this phase of its career is described later, in the section dealing with the Tiger 2 in action.

2. STU MRS TIGER

This variant of the Pz Kpfw Tiger, Ausf E was produced only late in the war, and in very small numbers, by Alkett of Berlin/Spandau; Tiger 1s sent back to Germany for repair or re-work had their turrets removed and a heavily armoured fixed superstructure, mounting the 38cm naval rocket-launcher RW 61, built on to the Tiger 1 hull and automotive components.

A mild steel prototype was demonstrated to Hitler in October 1943 and, after trials in Germany, was sent for user trials to Warsaw in the late summer of 1944.[37] Nothing is known of its actions there and, needless to say, the close-mouthed and suspicious Soviet authorities, following their constant practice during and after the war, said nothing of having encountered it to their Western Allies; it accordingly came as something of a surprise to the British when they captured a document in December 1944 in which a new unit, the armoured assault mortar Tiger company (Pz.Stu.Mrs.Kp.Tiger), was mentioned.[38]

Two of these companies, **Pz.Stu.Mrs.Kp.1000 and 1001,** were formed to operate the Stu Mrs Tiger; by the end of September 1944, seven vehicles had been built by Alkett, of which 1000 Company received four and 1001 Company, three.[39] Nothing is known of the organization and other equipment of these two companies, but it would have been logical for each to have had two or three Stu Mrs platoons, each with two Sturmmörsers and possibly one or two Pz Kpfw III or IV for local protection. It is known that the original intention had been to provide each vehicle with an ammunition-carrying tracked vehicle, based on a tank chassis, to supplement the fourteen rockets which could be carried in each Sturmmörser, but none was ever captured, at any rate by the Western Allies. Alkett had managed to build a total of sixteen Stu Mrs Tigers by the end of the war.[40]

▲ A Sturmmörser Tiger in Germany in 1945. (Author's Collection)

In December 1944, **Pz.Stu.Mrs.Kp.Tiger 1000** was in the Trier area; it went into action on the Alsace border, but with only one Sturmmörser, as three had broken down and were beyond local repair. Its sister company, **1001**, was in the Eifel in November/December 1944, and saw action in the Düren-Euskirchen-Bonn area in the middle of January 1945.[41] According to post-war German sources, the RW 61 was a dangerous weapon with an enormous morale effect, especially at night; on one occasion one round from the 38cm launcher demolished a West Wall bunker occupied by Allied troops, and on another a troop of Sherman tanks in a village was knocked out by one round.

Because of the enormous damage it caused to buildings, equipment and morale, the Americans made great efforts to locate the individual vehicles by air reconnaissance, espionage and other means; when found, they would bring down heavy concentrations of artillery fire on them, with the result that the Stu Mrs were unable to stay long in any one location. For this reason, in March 1945 Pz.Stu.Mrs.Kp.1001 moved, with three Stu Mrs Tigers, eastwards from Bonn across the Rhine on a tank ferry and into the Ruhr Gebiet; shortly afterwards the last rocket was fired and the remaining vehicles destroyed.[42]

Only one Stu Mrs Tiger seems to have survived the war, at least in the west; this was shipped to UK in 1945 for preliminary examination and then to the USA for detailed examination and trials. For several years it rested in the Tank Museum of the US Army Ordnance Corps at Aberdeen Proving Ground, Maryland, but it has now been returned to the Federal Republic of Germany and lies in the Technical Defence Studies Collection (Wehrtechnische Studiensammlung) of the Bundesamt für Wehrtechnik und Beschaffung (BWB) at Mayener Strasse 85–87, Koblenz.

3. PZ JAG TIGER (P) – ELEFANT

It had been the original intention that the Porsche VK 4501(P) would be put into production, and the heavy tank battalions equipped with it; in fact, s.Pz.Abt.503 had arrived at Fallingbostel expecting to receive the Porsche Tiger rather than the Henschel version.

However, when it was decided to convert the 90 Porsche Tigers, already ordered and in production, from tanks to self-propelled mountings for the 8.8cm PaK 43 (L/71), their unsuitability as equipment for a heavy tank battalion was obvious; it was accordingly decided by the OKH (Supereme Army HQ) that they would be used to equip a tank hunter regiment of two battalions. This regiment was the **Panzerjäger Regiment (Pz.Jäg.Regt.)656,** and it comprised two battalions, **schwere Panzerjägerabteilungen (s.Pz.Jag.Abt) 653** and **654,** each equipped with 45 Pz Jäg Tiger (P) (Elefant, formerly Ferdinand).[43] The s.Pz.Jäg.Abt.653 was formed in March 1943 in Bruck/Leitha out of the Sturmgeschütz Abt 197; 654 became the second battalion of Pz.Jäg.Regt.656 in June 1943, but became independent again in September of that year when it re-equipped with Jagdpanther.

The conversion of the Porsche Tiger from tank to self-propelled tank destroyer was ordered in September 1942, and was carried out by Nibelungenwerke in Austria in conjunction with Alkett in Berlin/Spandau, who designed the fixed superstructure for the gun and mounting. The air-cooled engines specified by Dr. Porsche were replaced by twin water-cooled Maybach HL120s and mounted in the middle of the vehicle rather than at the rear, and the frontal armour was thickened up to 200mm by means of appliqué plates bolted to the basic armour. Due to the urgency of the programme, vehicles were delivered to the Army in ones and twos, as they were completed.

All 90 were completed by the end of May 1943 and Pz.Jag.Regt.656 was then sent, fully equipped, to the Eastern Front Central Army Group (Heeresgruppe Mitte) in time to take part in the Kursk offensive, with Oberstleutnant (Lieutenant-Colonel) von Jungenfeldt in command. Of the two battalions of the Regiment, 653 was commanded by a Major Steinwachs and 654 by Major Noak.

In action, the Elefant was used as a mobile pillbox, although its mobility was severely restricted by difficulties with the limited-travel torsion bar suspension, of Porsche design, and with the electric final drive motors; the high performance of the long 8.8cm gun enabled it to take on any enemy tank or anti-tank gun from a range at which it was itself impervious to the enemy weapon. Nevertheless, the lack of any close-in defensive weapon meant that it was always necessary for it to be accompanied by protective infantry in combat.

In the battle for Kursk, Pz.Jäg.Regt.656 was on the German northern flank, under XXXXI Corps, in support of 86th Infantry Division; 653 Battalion reached Alexandrovka in support of 292nd Infantry Division, while 654 Battalion supported 78th Assault Division. By 27 July 1943, so a Wehrmacht report dated 6 August stated, the Regiment had accounted for 502 Soviet tanks, 20 anti-tank guns and 100 artillery pieces.

▼A Panzerjäger Tiger (P) (Elefant) knocked out in Italy in 1944. (Bundesarchiv)

A further Wehrmacht report dated 26 November 1943 told of a further 54 Soviet tanks knocked out by the Regiment in the Nikopol bridgehead. In Operation 'Citadel'. Pz.Jäg.Abt.653 alone accounted for 320 Soviet tanks for the loss of 24 killed and missing, and thirteen Elefants.

After this action, the remaining Elefants were sent to Italy, where their numbers were gradually whittled down by Allied action, vehicle breakdown and by the destruction of those vehicles disabled beyond recovery. No.1 Company of the Battalion was destroyed in Italy in September 1944; No.2 Company was renamed in 1945 as the 614 Heavy Tank Destroyer Company (**s.Pz.Jäg. Kp.614**) and, after refresher training at Döllersheim, near Vienna, it was equipped with Jagdtiger 12.8cm tank destroyers[44] with which it served in the Ardennes and Saarpfalz.

4. TIGER 2

The loss of unit war diaries and other unit records as the German forces were driven back in retreat and destroyed in the last year of the war, particularly in the burning of the Army archives at Potsdam in April 1945, makes difficult the piecing together of the story of the Tiger 2 in combat; it was, of course, during this period that those heavy tank and heavy tank destroyer battalions re-equipped with the Tiger 2 received the new tank. The loss of records is particularly true of those battalions in action against the Russian Army, as the Soviet authorities did not return most prisoners of war until some ten years after the war, by which time memories had become dim. Neither have the Soviet authorities since the war allowed access by foreign historians to captured German military documents, if indeed they were ever retained. These are the reasons why this section is less detailed than that, for example, dealing with the Tiger 1 in combat.

Not all the heavy tank battalions had their Tiger 1s replaced by Tiger 2. Of those which were fully or partially re-equipped with Tiger 2, 501, 505, 507, 509, s.Pz.Abt.'Grossdeutschland' and s. SS Pz.Abt.502 are known to have served only on the Eastern Front, 503 and s. SS Pz.Abt.501 on both the Western Front and in Hungary, and 506 only on the Western Front.

On the Eastern Front

s.Pz.Abt.501 re-equipped with the Tiger 2 in July 1944 and was in action in southern Poland as Corps 'fire brigade' shortly afterwards, together with 507 and 509 Heavy Tank Battalions and 3rd Panzer Division. The

▼ Tiger 2s with Porsche turrets, camouflaged in France in 1944. (Bundesarchiv)

Battalion unloaded at Kielce, 40–50 kilometres from the front, in early August 1944; the road march to the front caused many vehicle breakdowns, mainly of final drives, and only eight Tigers arrived at the front during the evening of 11 August. The following day the Battalion was in action, in support of 16th Panzer Divison.

The Workshop Company was meanwhile reinforcing the final drives of the broken-down tanks, as well as removing the projectile racks from the turrets; a hit on the turret of one of the Battalion Tigers had caused the turret ammunition stowage to explode, with disastrous results both to the crew and to the tank, and removal of the projectiles to a safer stowage place seemed a wise precaution. The final-drive faults led to a rumour of deliberate sabotage at the factory, but it is more probable that the heavier weight of the Royal Tiger overstressed a final drive taken virtually unchanged from the 12-tonne lighter Tiger 1.

In December 1944, the Battalion became the Corps Heavy Tank Battalion in XXIV Panzer Korps, and was re-numbered **s.Pz.Abt.424,** to prevent confusion with the newly renumbered s. SS Pz.Abt.501. The Battalion moved east on ever shorter notice, but no orders came to send it into action; eventually the Battalion was overwhelmed in the big Russian attack launched in January 1945. Without most of their tanks, the Battalion personnel made their way through to Sorau, whence they were routed to the Pz.Ers.u. Ausb.Abt.500 at Paderborn, where a substantial number were posted into s.Pz.Jag.Abt.512, equipped with the Jagdtiger. Thus ended, for the third and final time, the 501 Heavy Tank Battalion, by now known as 424 Heavy Tank Battalion.[45]

The **s.Pz.Abt.505** was re-formed at Paderborn in September 1944 and re-equipped with Tiger 2. On taking over the tanks, many technical deficiencies were noted during training and sorted out with the Henschel representatives; in particular many vehicles caught fire, three brand-new ones being burnt out. By 5 September the Battalion was ready to move; alerted for the Eastern Front, it loaded on 8 September and arrived at Nasielsk on 11 September. On arrival, with three command tanks and 35 gun tanks fit, it was committed to the Narev bridgehead, but was put into Army reserve with effect from 13 September. For Operation 'Sonnenblume' ('Sunflower'), an operation to eliminate the Narev bridgehead which began on 4 October, the Battalion was placed under command of 3rd Panzer Division. The Battalion was involved in the retreat from Königsberg to Pillau/Fischhausen, where it took part in the last stand with s.Pz.Abt.502/511.[46]

The **507 Heavy Tank Battalion** was reformed at Paderborn and partially re-equipped with Tiger 2 in March 1945. Due to shortage of Tiger 2, it received only fifteen, the remainder of the battalion receiving Tiger 1. It was involved in the retreat to the Harz against US troops, in actions at Bad Driburg, Borgholz and Gieselwerder, where the River Weser was crossed. At Osterode, all its fit tanks were handed over to an SS unit; the Battalion then made its way through the Harz to Magdeburg, where it was supposed to pick up new tanks. As no tanks were there, the still intact Battalion moved to the Milowicz training area, south of the road from Prague to Königsgratz, where it eventually re-equipped with 3.7cm SP anti-aircraft guns on Pz Kpfw IV chassis. The Battalion surrendered to Russian troops on 7 May 1945.[47]

s.Pz.Abt.509 was formed at Paderborn in the middle of September 1944 and equipped with Tiger 2. By mid January 1945 it had received 45 Tiger 2 and was sent, via Dresden and Prague to Hungary. It reached Vesprem on 15 January, unloaded from the trains and moved into the Hungarian Artillery School at Hajmasker. Under command of IV SS Panzer Corps, the Battalion was involved in the counter-attack to relieve Budapest on 17 January, with 1st Panzer Division, 3rd SS Panzer Division 'Totenkopf' and 5th SS Panzer Division 'Wiking'. It was subsequently involved in heavy fighting, and, in a report dated 15 February, the Wehrmacht announced that the Battalion had knocked out 203 Soviet tanks and assault guns, 145 guns and five aircraft for the loss of ten of their own tanks; by the end of that month, Battalion Tiger strength was down to 15–20 tanks. On 13 March the Battalion met the Soviet ISU-122 in action for the first time; 24 were knocked out by sixteen Tigers.

By 9 April 1945, however, after several heavy actions, the Battalion had only nine Tigers fit for action. On the 13th, the Battalion was ordered to entrain at St. Polten for Gratkorn im Muntal and thence to Laa on the Thaya where, on the line between Laa and Hollabrünn, one of the trains carrying two Royal Tigers, the reconnaissance platoon and part of HQ company was in collision with an oncoming train; sixteen men of the Battalion were killed in this accident. On 7 May, the order to withdraw to the demarcation line on the River Moldau, near Kaplitz, was given; the withdrawal began the next day, but with great interference from Russian tanks and infantry. These were engaged by the last five Royal Tigers in what turned out to be the Battalion's last engagement of the war, one enemy tank being knocked out and a surrounded SS unit relieved. The last five Tigers were then blown up

134 *Seven: Tigers in Combat*

by their crews, personnel loaded on trucks and the convoy moved back at 23.00 on 8 May. At 18.00 on 9 May, the Battalion surrendered to US forces, was redirected south to Linz in Austria and there put in a prisoner-of-war camp.[48]

Until 13 December 1944, the s.Pz.Abt. 'Grossdeutschland' had been serving on the Eastern Front as the third battalion of Panzer Regiment 'Grossdeutschland'; on this date it was renamed and re-equipped with new tanks, although it is not known whether these were new Tiger 1s or Tiger 2s. After re-equipment, it fought in the Narev bridgehead, in the area of Ortelsburg, East Prussia, at Allenstein and Zinten. In the heavy defensive battles in the Heiligenbeil cauldron from 17 to 22 April 1945, the Battalion lost its last tanks, after which the personnel were taken prisoner either by the Russians or, the majority, by the British in Schleswig-Holstein.[49]

The Heavy SS Tank Battalion 502 was re-formed and re-equipped with Tiger 2 at Paderborn/Sennelager in the late autumn and winter of 1944/5. It took the first tanks over on 27 December 1944 and had received a total of 37 by 6 March 1945. It received orders to move to the Frankfurt/Oder bridgehead at the end of February and moved by train on 17/18 March to Bergenbrück, via Eberswalde, Berlin and Fürstenwalde, thence by road to Briesen to come under command of Ninth Army. By 3 April it was in the area of Diedersdorf and Litzen, in readiness for the forthcoming battle for Berlin; the Russian attack on Berlin began on 16 April 1945, and the Battalion's last action was on 1 May near Hasenfelde and Steinhofel. After losing its last tanks the Battalion joined with personnel from other SS units of Ninth Army; many crossed the Elbe into US hands.[50]

In Normandy and the Ardennes

s.Pz.Abt.503 was only partially re-equipped with Tiger 2 when it re-formed in June 1944; one company only (1/503) received Tiger 2, the other two Tiger companies receiving new Tiger 1s. After re-equipping, the battalion was sent by rail to France de-training in Dreux, 80 kilometres west of Paris, on 2 July. After four nights of road marches (movement had to be by night, due to Allied interdiction by air of all road and rail movement by day), the Battalion was in the area of Rupierre, twelve kilometres east of Caen. Here it remained, ready for action, throughout the British bombardment of Caen on the evening of 7 July and the British attack on the 8th; it was not until the early morning of 11 July, after several changes of orders, that the Battalion was finally committed, in support of Pz.Regt.21 of 21st Panzer Division, to a counter-attack on Colombelles. When Colombelles was re-taken it was

▼ France 1944. A Tiger 2 has been blown up by its crew. (Tank Museum)

found to be empty, but British armour was spotted 3 kilometres away and attacked; a squadron of fourteen Shermans was knocked out, two command tanks being captured intact, documents captured in the tanks indicating that they belonged to the 148th Regiment, RAC.

Early in the morning of the 18th, three Allied air fleets with 2,100 bombers carpet-bombed the area for four hours, hitting 3/503 locations and knocking out several Tigers. The Battalion now withdrew 10 kilometres to a new defence line around Cagny; in a Wehrmacht report dated 19 July 1944, the Battalion was credited with the destruction of 40 enemy tanks. Shortly after this, 3 Company of the Battalion was ordered to the Mailly le Camp training area, where it was re-equipped with Tiger 2 tanks and on 8 August entrained for Paris; it was in action with its new tanks north of the Seine. After the last of these was knocked out, the tank-less crews were shipped back to Sennelager, to be re-equipped with the rest of the Battalion.

By 22 September 1944, the Battalion had received its full establishment of 45 Royal Tigers and spent the period up to 11 October in platoon, company and battalion training in the Sennelager training area. On 12 October the Battalion entrained for Hungary, and detrained at Budapest on the 14th; it was then based in Taksony, 30 kilometres south of Budapest. On 21 December, the Battalion was re-named s.Pz.Abt. 'Feldherrnhalle', to avoid confusion with the newly renumbered SS Heavy Tank Battalion 503, although the news did not reach the Battalion until 4 January 1945, by which date only thirteen of its Tigers were fit. In January 1945, as we have seen, sixth SS Panzer Army had arrived from the Ardennes to retake Budapest; by 12 January, 5th SS Panzer Division had got to within 21 kilometres of Budapest, but could get no closer. By 2 May 1945, the Battalion had withdrawn to Socherl, where it stayed until 6 May and where twelve Tiger 2s were made fit for action by the Workshop Company; by this time, US troops were at the gates of Prague. The Battalion moved west, its rear guarded by its twelve remaining tanks until, after destroying the remaining tanks and other vehicles on 10 May, the personnel were split up into parties of 10–12 men to make their way across the Czech frontier and back to Germany. More than twelve officers and 400 men made it into US captivity, only to be handed over to the Russian Army by the US authorities fourteen days later.[51]

The s.Pz.Abt.506 had been reorganized and re-equipped with the Tiger 2 at Ohrdruf in August 1944; in this reorganization, the supply and repair elements of the Tiger companies were combined into a new Supply Company, incorporating the anti-aircraft platoon. Commanded by Major Lange, the Battalion received its full establishment of 45 Tiger 2s between 20 August and 12 September 1944. During the conversion training on the new tank, many vehicle fires occurred; these were attributed to looseness of the many fuel line junctions, not fully tightened at the factory during build. The Battalion entrained for the Western Front from 22 to 24 September, moving via Cologne and Wesel to Holland. After unloading, the Tiger companies were placed directly under the command of First Parachute Army and located in the area of Oosterbeek and west of Arnhem, where they went into action against Allied air-landed troops; here they had their first experience of bazooka-armed infantry and suffered their first losses during Operation 'Market Garden'.

At the beginning of October, the Battalion again entrained, this time for Apeldoorn, Zutphen and Bocholt, in five trains on the 10th, four on the 11th and one during the night of 13 October; during the journey, the AA platoon shot down, from the train, a fighter-bomber attacking it; the aim of the move was to help to relieve surrounded Aachen, under command of Seventh Army. Involved in heavy fighting between Eschweiler and Geilenkirchen, the Battalion lost ten killed on 21 October.

With the German line resting on the River Roer, the Battalion moved into the Grevenbroich area to rest in December 1944, where it was joined by a fourth Tiger company, s.Pz.Kp. Hummel, commanded by Oberleutnant Hummel, a former company commander of s.Pz.Abt.504, who had been wounded in the battle for Sicily. This company had been formed in Münster in July 1944 as an 'alarm unit', and had been 'stood-to' in Sennelager, equipped with Tiger 1, in mid September 1944. It had entrained for Bocholt, de-trained there and marched some 80 kilometres on its tracks to the Aachen area, where it came under command of 10th SS Panzer Division 'Frundsberg'.

In mid December 1944, the Battalion entrained for the Eifel, and was in action near Malmédy and Bastogne in the centre of the Ardennes front; it retreated further and further until US troops reached the West Wall. By 2 April 1945, the Battalion, less tanks and with no hope of obtaining replacements, was under the command of a company of s.Pz.Jäg.Abt.512 equipped with Jagdtiger, acting as infantry in the defence of Iserlohn.[52]

Little is known about s. SS.Abt.501 during this period. At some time between late 1944 and the Battle of the Bulge, probably in October 1944, it is believed to have been re-equipped with Tiger 2 tanks, but it is not known where and the date is not confirmed. In the

▲ Another Tiger 2, with Henschel turret, knocked out in France in 1944. (Tank Museum)

Ardennes, the Battalion formed part of Panzer Regiment 1, which at that time had only one battalion; it was later in Hungary.[53]

5. HUNTING TIGER (JAGDTIGER)

The Pz Jäg Tiger Ausf B (Jagdtiger) was almost the last of the heavy AFVs to come into service in the Wehrmacht during the Second World War, and did not start to come off the production line until April 1944; the planned production rate of 50 vehicles per month was never attained, the total number produced by Nibelungenwerke being approximately 70 by the end of the war, of which 48 had been built in 1944 and a further twelve in January 1945.[54]

The organization designed to receive and operate the Jagdtiger was the heavy tank hunter battalion (s.Pz.Jäg.Abt.), an organization which comprised two tank hunter companies in the event, although, like the heavy tank battalions, originally intended to consist of three. As with the equipment of the early Tiger 1 battalions, shortage of vehicles dictated the reduced establishment. How the rest of the battalion was organized, and with what vehicles and in what quantities it was equipped, is not now known.

Two heavy tank hunter units were formed in the autumn of 1944: the first was the **s.Pz.Jäg.Kp.614**, formed at Döllersheim in Austria in September 1944 out of the former s.Pz.Jäg.Abt.653, which had been disbanded in Italy and had previously been equipped with Pz Jäg Tiger (P) (Elefant).[55] The 614 Company was equipped with the Jagdtiger, and it is believed that it served first in the Ardennes, in December 1944, and thereafter in Hungary until the end of the war.

The second unit was the **s.Pz.Jäg.Abt.512**, which was formed in the late autumn of 1944 at the s.Pz.Ers.u.Ausb.Abt.500 at Paderborn. Due to shortage of vehicles, the Battalion consisted of only two tank destroyer companies, but in this case neither was given its full complement of Jagdtigers; only twenty were available altogether for this Battalion, and initially only four for one company and three for the other. The Battalion was commanded by Hauptmann (later Major) Scherf, who had previously commanded 503 Heavy Tank Battalion, while No.1 Company was commanded by Hauptmann Albert Ernst, an experienced tank destroyer commander, and No. 2 Company by Oberleutnant Otto Carius, a former tank platoon commander of 502 Heavy Tank Battalion.

Of the Battalion's two companies, No.1 was the first into action, against the Remagen bridgehead on 10

Hunting Tiger (Jagdtiger) 137

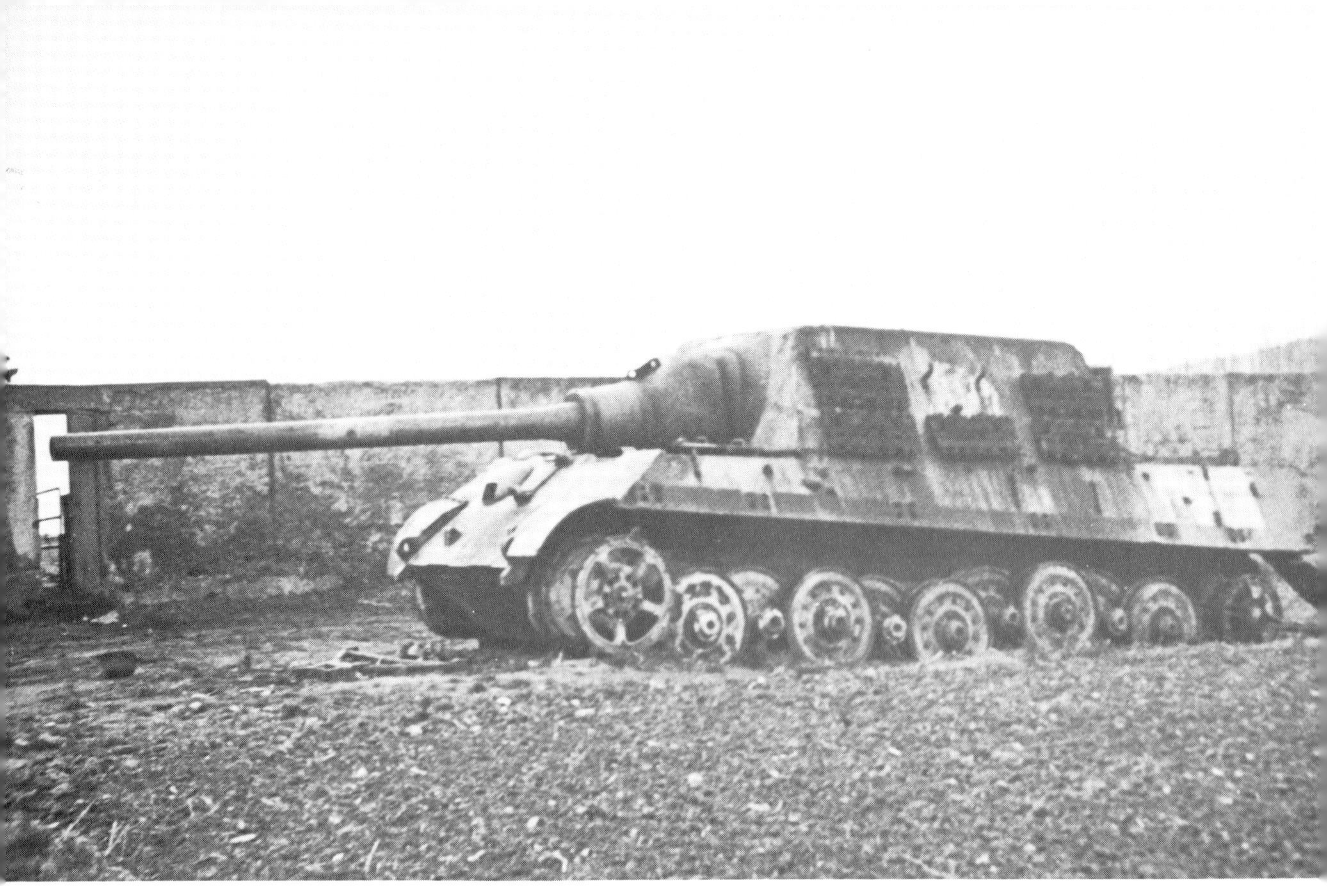

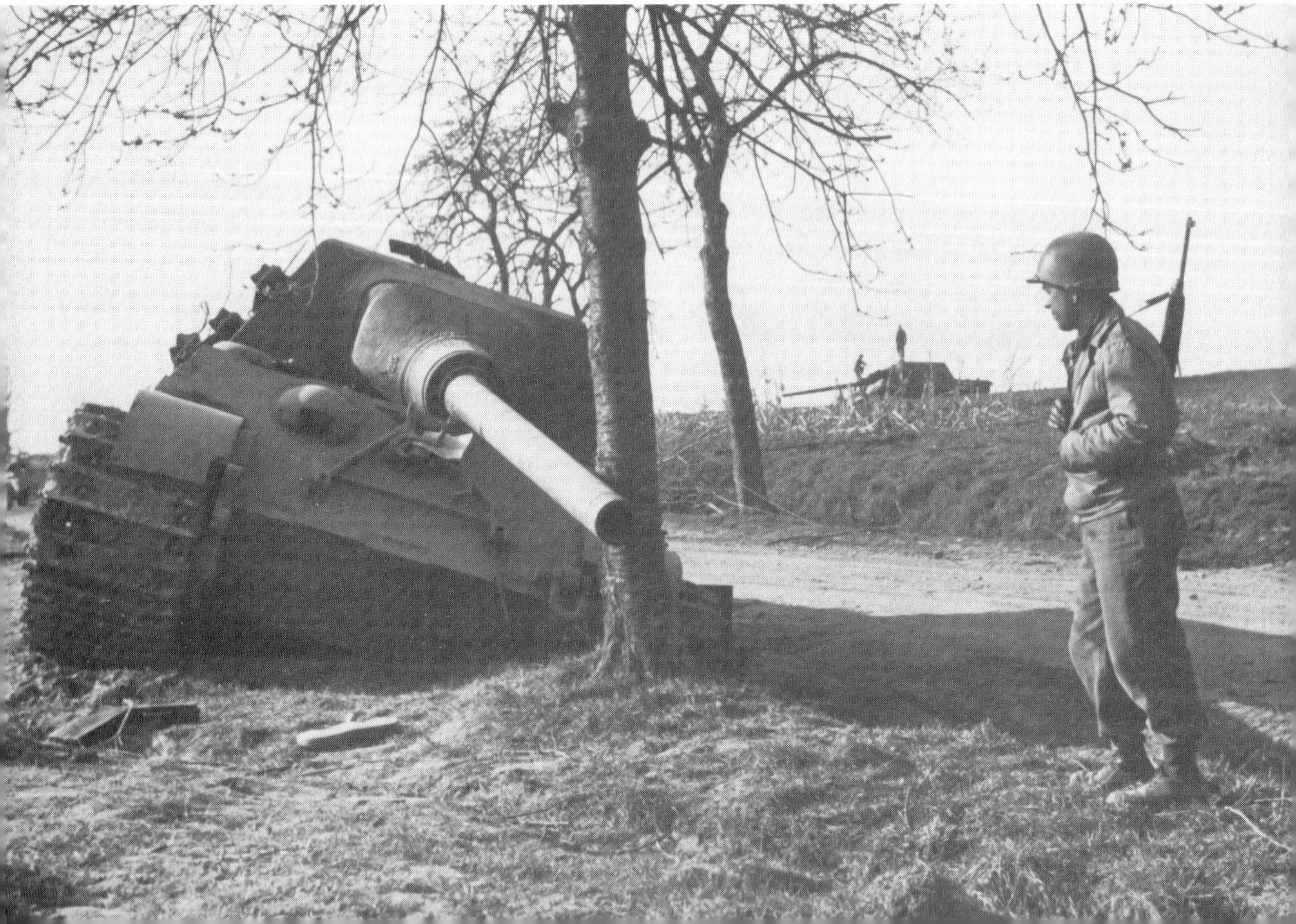

◀ A Jagdtiger of s.Pz.Jäg. Abt.512 knocked out near Hagen (Ruhr) in April 1945. (Author's Collection)

March 1945; at this time, No. 2 Company was still in the Sennelager training area and had to be transported by rail to the front with great urgency. By the time action was broken off, No.1 Company had only six fit Jagdtigers and withdrew to the Siegen area; here it was put in support of Generaloberst Harpe's Army, in a battle group with the 'Freikorps Sauerland' as covering infantry and with a platoon of assault guns, another of quadruple AA guns and a few Pz Kpfw IV under command. The battle group passed through Meinerzhagen and Lüdenscheid to Altena, where Hauptmann Ernst received orders to entrain for Iserlohn, it detrained at Menden and moved by road through Hagen to the relief of Unna, which had fallen to the Americans on 9 April. In the Unna area it briefly joined up with its No. 2 Company, commanded by Oberleutnant Carius.

Carius had been faced with a problem as, although his company personnel were at Paderborn, the company Jagdtigers had to be collected from Döllersheim, near Vienna; this had entailed numerous trips between the two places, collecting his Jagdtigers in ones and twos and trying to train his Company in their use in between trips. Despite all, by 8 March 1945 the Jagdtigers were loaded on to railflats, destined for Siegburg, near Bonn; however, the panic induced by the US bridgehead over the Rhine at Remagen, together with the Allied bombing of rail targets in general and Sennelager station in particular meant that the trains could only move by night, lying up in tunnels and cuttings by day, and that destinations and routes had constantly to be changed. There was now no chance of the Company going into action at Remagen, so, on arrival at Siegburg, Carius immediately received orders to re-load his vehicles for Duisburg, where he would come directly under the command of LIII Panzer Korps. On arrival, he had to report the total loss of two Jagdtigers from fighter-bomber attack during the journey; they had been so badly damaged that they had to be blown up by their crews.

His few Jagdtigers were now scattered thinly along the Corps front, until Carius received orders direct from Field Marshal Model to take all his Jagdtigers to

◀ Two more Jagdtigers, this time from the re-equipped s.Pz.Jäg.Kp.614, knocked out in the Ardennes in December 1944. (Tank Museum)

Unna and to defend the town. With his four remaining fit Jagdtigers, Carius made his way to Unna, losing one Jagdtiger en route when it fell into a bomb hole; there, he came under command of an *ad hoc* town commandant's staff; the US forces, however, largely by-passed Unna on their way to Dortmund, and the Company saw little action there. The next night, Carius and the remains of his Company slipped out of Unna and made their way to Ergste; Unna fell on 9 April 1945, and six days later the Company destroyed its weapons and surrendered at Ergste.

Meanwhile, with the fall of Unna, the No.1 Company had moved north with its battle group and across the River Ruhr at Langschede; on 11 April 1945 its armoured cars had reached the heights around the Bismarckturm, and from there had reported strong US vehicle columns moving to the south. Ernst accordingly ordered his battle group, consisting of four Jagdtigers, four assault guns, three Pz Kpfw IV and four quadruple 3.7cm AA guns, to take up positions along the ridge, and, as the enemy came within firing range, ordered them to open fire; the eleven AFVs did so almost simultaneously, knocking out the two leading Shermans and setting fire to, or blowing up, several trucks. The Jagdtigers, having a slow rate of fire, engaged targets at the longer ranges, out to about 4 kilometres. The US column's drive to the south, to the heart of the Ruhr cauldron, came to a halt with 50 vehicles, including eleven Shermans, destroyed; in the ensuing fighter-bomber attacks, the 3.7cm AA guns were destroyed one by one. One Jagdtiger was knocked out by a fighter-bomber rocket which hit the commander's hatch, killing all six of the crew, and another was damaged; Ernst ordered his troops to disengage slowly, and the next morning received orders from LIII Panzer Korps to hold the airfield at Deilinghofen for 24 hours.

Ernst took up positions in Hemer, and in the afternoon of 12 April during an American attack, two more Shermans were knocked out; on the 13th, all was quiet, although Menden, only a few kilometres to the north, fell that day. Because of the many hospitals in Hemer, Ernst tried to find a senior officer to negotiate the town's surrender with the US forces; unable to find one, he negotiated the surrender himself, to Major Boyd H. McCune of the US 394th Infantry Regiment.

During the night of 15 April, Ernst learned of the destruction of Carius's No.2 Company; by this time, the Americans were investing Iserlohn from all sides, and, as Ernst had also heard of the surrender of Generalleutnant Fritz Bayerlein and the Corps HQ, he surrendered the town of Iserlohn, and his Company, to the Americans on 16 April 1945.[56]

Hunting Tiger (Jagdtiger) 139

POSTSCRIPT

TODAY, when examined with the hindsight of nearly 50 years, and at a time when most main battle tanks are of comparable size and weight and mount even bigger guns, it is difficult to understand the grip which the Tigers took on their opponents' imaginations; certainly their influence on tank design thinking was very much greater than would have been expected from the comparatively small numbers of these tanks built and deployed. For instance, in Operation 'Citadel', the German operation to retake Kursk in July 1943 and which involved the largest tank battle in history, only 146 Pz Kpfw Tiger Ausf E were employed. In Tunisia in 1942/3, no more than 32 Tiger 1s were landed in North Africa, of which never more than twenty were serviceable at any one time; in Sicily, only seventeen Tigers were deployed. The same was true of every theatre, and the total Tiger production from 1942 to the end of the war was only 1,995 vehicles, of which 1,350 were Tiger 1, 90 were Tiger(P), 485 were Tiger 2 and 70 were Jagdtiger.

Of the hulks of knocked out Tigers scattered throughout the USSR, Hungary, North Africa, Sicily, Italy and north-west Europe, most have been broken up and disposed of as scrap; in Tunisia for example, fifteen definite and two possible Tiger hulks, as well as two 'runners', were located and recorded on 9 June 1943 in a survey carried out by officers of the British 104 Tank Workshops REME, but only the two marked as 'runners' survive.

One of these, a middle-production vehicle with the chassis number '250122' and the turret number '131' in small red figures, was the vehicle abandoned in the action against 'A' Squadron of 48th RTR on 21 April 1943. It had belonged to s.Pz.Abt.504 and had been the platoon commander's tank of 3 Platoon of No.1 Company. After the German surrender in North Africa, it was refurbished by 104 Tank Workshop REME from captured spares, thoroughly examined by them (and the resulting technical Intelligence report rushed back to MI 10 in London), emblazoned front and rear with the First Army shield and the 21 Army Tank Brigade diabolo, and temporarily put on display in Tunis.

From then on, Tiger '131' led the life of a VIP; most British troops who got to Tunis saw her, and she was

◀ The first Tiger to be captured intact, turret number 131, of 504 Heavy Tank Battalion, being inspected by Winston Churchill in Tunis in June 1943. (Author's Collection)

▶ The same tank after its return to the UK, during its automotive trials at FVPE, Chertsey, in early 1944. (Author's Collection)

examined there with great interest by Winston Churchill on 2 June and by HM King George VI on 18 June 1943. On the 26th of that month, it was driven to the port of La Goulette for shipment on LCT 568, arriving in Bizerta on 3 August; it was then trans-shipped to the SS *Empire Candida* for the journey to Bône, where it was discharged on 11 August. It finally left North Africa for UK, accompanied by Major A. D. Lidderdale, AMIMechE, REME, the officer commanding 104 Tank Workshop, and a tank crew from the same unit, in the SS *Ocean Strength* on 20 September. On reaching UK it was sent for detailed testing and examination to the School of Tank Technology (STT) at Chertsey in Surrey, a branch of the Military College of Science responsible, in conjunction with the Department of Tank Design and the Fighting Vehicle Proving Establishment, both located next door at Chertsey, for the examination of, and the issuing of reports on, all foreign AFVs of interest received in the UK.

STT issued a preliminary report, written by Major Lidderdale, in November 1943, and in the same month Tiger '131' was exhibited on Horse Guards' Parade in London. The very detailed final report was issued by STT in stages in loose-leaf form between March and November 1944, but, due to the influx of vehicles of later design and greater technical interest after the Allied landings in north-west Europe, was never completed, and interest in the vehicle waned.

After the war, when STT moved from Chertsey to Bovington Camp, its collection of Allied and enemy tanks moved with it and formed the nucleus of the present Tank Museum there. Tiger 131 is still there, now unfortunately without many of its internal components and without its unique and distinctive British markings; unfortunately these were painted out when the tank was repainted some years ago, and at the same time the turret numbers were incorrectly painted in red with white outlines and in numerals of too large a size. At the time of writing, the Tank Museum has plans to rebuild the vehicle as a 'runner', using a Maybach HL230 engine in place of the original HL210, and also to restore its First Army and 21 Army Tank Brigade flashes. It is still an impressive tank, even if it is now somewhat dwarfed by its later compatriots standing nearby.

The other Tiger remaining from the North Africa campaign is an early model, formerly belonging to 1 Platoon of No. 1 Company of s.Pz.Abt.501, with the chassis number '250012' and the turret number '712'

Postscript 141

(formerly '112', but changed when the remnant of this Battalion came under command of Panzer Regiment 7 as its third tank battalion, 1 and 2 Companies then becoming 7 and 8 Companies, respectively). Earmarked to go to the USA in the survey of Tiger remains carried out in June 1943 by 104 Tank Workshop REME, Tiger '712' ended up in Aberdeen Proving Ground, Maryland, for examination by US Army Ordnance personnel; after the war, she was transferred to the outdoor tank museum there, where she lay for many years. She has recently been returned to the land of her birth, and now rests in the Autotechnik Museum at Sinsheim, near Heidelberg.

Only two other Tiger 1s are known to exist outside the Soviet Union; one, a late-production model is in the French Tank Museum at Saumur; the other, also in France, lies at the roadside at Vimoutiers in Normandy.

Despite the small numbers encountered, the Tiger 1s deployed in North Africa had an effect both on Allied troop morale there at the time and on British tank design thereafter. The Tiger's effect on the morale of the Allied troops encountering it and, by rumour, on those who had not yet done so, was out of all proportion to the number of Tigers employed. The effect on British tank design is still to be seen in the emphasis placed by the British users on the importance of firepower in relation to the other tank characteristics, mobility and protection. Before and during the Second World War, firepower had had to come a very poor third when British tank design priorities were laid down, due to the lack of suitable weapons and ammunition. The advent of the Tiger changed this, and, from the introduction of the Centurion to the present day, firepower has been given, and retains, the top priority which it deserves.

The ability of the Tiger 1 to operate submerged under twelve feet of water impressed the tank designers of all nationalities and, although only the first 495 Tigers had this facility, several post-war main battle tanks have incorporated the snorkel air-breathing method of submerged operation.

Of the Sturmmörser Tiger, only one specimen is known to have survived the war. Again, this was originally in the US Army Ordnance Corps tank

▼ The same tank in November 1943 on Horse Guards' Parade in London to present it to Winston Churchill as a gift from Lieutenant-General Sir Kenneth Anderson, Commander First Army. Major Lidderdale, the OC of 104 Tank Workshop REME, who was responsible for bringing the vehicle to UK, stands in front of it, flanked by the skeleton British crew which accompanied him. (Lidderdale)

▲ The same tank in its present resting-place at the Bovington Tank Museum, sadly deficient of its identifying spare track link bar and step, as well as of its First Army and 21 Army Tank Brigade flashes, and with incorrectly white-outlined turret numbers. (Author's Collection)

▼ The other runner Tiger captured in Tunisia (turret number 712 of No. 1 Company, 501 Heavy Tank Battalion) after its arrival at Aberdeen Proving Ground, Maryland, in 1943. This tank is now back in its native country, at the Sinsheim vehicle museum. (US Army Ordnance)

Postscript 143

▲ The same tank, after completion of its examination by the US Army, in the Aberdeen Proving Ground museum collection. (APG)

collection at Aberdeen Proving Ground, where it arrived after having undergone preliminary examination in England at STT; now it too has been returned to its native country, where it is located in the collection of the Wehrtechnische Studiensammlung (Technical Defence Studies Collection) of the Bundesamt für Wehrtechnik und Beschaffung (BWB) at Koblenz.

The Pz Kpfw Tiger Ausf B (Tiger 2 or Royal Tiger) is better represented in the west than its predecessor, the Tiger 1. The French Tank Museum at Saumur has a specimen in full mechanical working order. The Kampftruppenschule II of the Bundeswehr at Munsterlager in Lower Saxony has another specimen, mounted outdoors on a plinth; this vehicle, also formerly in the collection of the US Army Ordnance Corps at Aberdeen Proving Ground, Maryland, was presented to the Kampftruppenschule by the US Army. Another stands by the roadside in the Belgian village of La Gleize, where it was knocked out, and there is a further specimen in the Soviet Union in their tank museum; the Russian collection is for Services use only, as is that at the British Royal Military College of Science. All of these vehicles have the Henschel production turret, with the flat front.

The United Kingdom has two specimens: one, the only survivor with the Porsche turret, has the chassis number '280002', was found at Haustenbeck in 1945 and is now in the Tank Museum at Bovington Camp, while the other, with a Henschel production turret, is in the private collection of the Royal Military College of Science at Shrivenham, where it is used in the training, in tank design, of Army officers.

Of the Jagdtiger, only two are known to be in existence; that in the Bovington Tank Museum is the only survivor of the two vehicles known to have been fitted with the Porsche-designed bogie suspension with longitudinal torsion bars, and is thus now unique. The other Jagdtiger, with Henschel suspension, is in the US Army Ordnance Corps collection at Aberdeen Proving Ground, Maryland.

The Panzerjäger Tiger (P) served only in the USSR and in Italy; in addition, only 90 were built, so it is understandable that very few survived the war. One, however, is, held by the US Ordnance Corps in their collection at Aberdeen Proving Ground, Maryland, and it is possible that there is another in the Soviet tank museum; no others are known in the tank museums of the west.

These then are all that remain of the once all-conquering Tiger tanks of the Second World War. They became legends in their time among Allied troops, after the first shock of meeting them in action,

▲ The Tiger 2 with Henschel turret which is now in the vehicle collection of the Royal Military College of Science at Shrivenham. (Author's Collection)

▼ The same vehicle, with a late camouflage pattern added. (Author's Collection)

Postscript 145

and there is no doubt that they were ahead of their time in many respects. Had more time been available for their development and the elimination of the 'bugs', had more material and production capacity been available for the building of adequate numbers and had the German tank industry been able to concentrate its resources on these tanks and the Panthers, instead of frittering them away on so many dead-end projects, the Tiger might have been a war-winner. As it was, it was a story of too few too late; well-crewed and well-maintained as they were by the heavy tank and tank destroyer battalions, they were beaten by the overwhelming numbers of inferior but more mobile tanks pouring out of the factories of the USSR and the USA.

Several of the features of the Henschel Tigers have been copied by post-war tank designers of both east and

▶ The other Tiger 2 in British hands is the only remaining one with the Porsche turret, and is in the Bovington Tank Museum collection. (Author's Collection)

▼ Rear 3/4 view of the Bovington Tiger 2, with the rear turret loading/escape hatch cover removed. (Author's Collection)

Opposite page, bottom: The Kampftruppenschule II of the Bundeswehr at Münster (Lager) was presented with this example of the Tiger 2 with Henschel turret by the US Army in 1961. (Author's Collection)

146   Postscript

Postscript

Postscript

◀ A rear 3/4 view of the Bundeswehr Tiger 2 in its present location in the tank collection at Kampftruppen schule II. (Author's Collection)

west. The single lateral torsion bar suspension has been used in almost all post-war main battle tanks to date, the only exception being those of Great Britain; Britain was the first to refuse to pay the height penalty imposed on a tank by the necessity for a false floor to accommodate the torsion bars, and instead mounted its suspension outside the hull between the top and bottom runs of the track. Only now that the limitations of the metal spring, in giving the greater vertical road wheel movement required by higher cross-country speeds, have been realized are other types of springing, such as the gas spring, coming to the fore, and the torsion bar, although still one of the best compromises for the springing of armoured fighting vehicles, is gradually being replaced; nevertheless, the Tiger and other German tanks of the Second World War led the world in the employment of torsion bars for many years.

Other features of the Tiger running gear, such as the interleaved road wheels and the interchangeable narrow/wide tracks, were felt to be disadvantages by other nations and were not copied; the interleaved road wheels were obviously too prone to jamming from mud packing between the wheels, while the cost and the logistic problem of supplying two sets of tracks for every tank were felt to be too great.

Another feature of the Tiger that has been copied post-war, however, is its stationary-eyepiece gunner's sighting telescope; slavish reproductions of it have been a feature of most Russian post-war main battle tanks, the Russians having preferred this type to periscopic sights for use with weapon stabilization, as the gunner does not need to move his head, when sighting on the move, to accommodate the movement resulting from elevation and depression of the gun.

The provision on the first 495 Tigers 1s of means to enable the tank to travel underwater made a great impression on the more important tank-producing countries, and most of the post-war main battle tanks produced in the Soviet Union incorporated this facility; so did the West German Leopard 1, despite the fact that the Wehrmacht had abandoned it on the Tiger after the first 495 vehicles and never employed it on any subsequent tanks produced during the war.

What else remains to recall the legendary Tigers,

◀ The French Army's Tiger 2, in their Tank Museum at Saumur; this vehicle is in working order, and carries the Henschel production turret. (Author's Collection)

apart from the few remaining specimens in various tank collections around the world and those of its design innovations which were thought worthy of copying by various post-war tank designers? The graves of many of their crewmen are scattered through the foreign lands in which they died, reminding all who see them that, legendary though the Tigers may have been, they were far from immortal; those who survived had their memories, which several of them have recorded for posterity in various publications to enable a wider public to share them.

The companies that designed and built the Tigers still exist; so do their factories. The original buildings were largely destroyed in the Allied air raids towards the war's end, but new ones have sprung up since the war from the ruins. Henschel is still at Kassel, although now a part of the Thyssen empire rather than the independent company that it used to be. It is still in the fighting vehicle business, although not in the pre-eminent position that it once occupied; this has been yielded to Krauss Maffei who, in conjunction with Porsche KG, also still very much involved in AFV design, has been responsible for the design of all, and the production of most, of the Federal Republic of Germany's post-war main battle tanks and their variants. The diving tank at the Henschel proving ground at Haustenbeck, near Sennelager was still in use after the war, and served as the model for the tank built at Chertsey for the British tank design and proving establishment. Steyr Daimler Puch, whose Nibelungenwerke factory at St. Valentin was responsible for the building of the Porsche Tiger, the Pz Jäg Tiger(P) and the Jagdtiger, is also still active in AFV design and construction, although of rather lighter type than the Tigers.

The barracks at Fallingbostel and Paderborn and the training areas near them are still used by armoured troops, this time British, as the author can testify; he has been stationed in both since the war, as a member of one Royal Tank Regiment or another, and has spent several months in total, in various stages of discomfort and sleeplessness, on the adjacent training areas of Soltau, Hohne and Sennelager; Ohrdruf too has been in constant use, but by troops of the Russian Forces in Germany, since 1945.

These then are all that remain of the once so powerful Tigers; a legend in their time, they are still a legend with a new generation of tank enthusiasts, most of whom can know them only by the photographs, the plethora of plastic model kits, the few remaining museum specimens and the multiplicity of books such as this, written by the people who had personal wartime experience of the tank itself.

Postscript 149

◀ A view of the rear plate and exhaust stacks of the French Tiger 2. (Author's Collection)

▼ One of the only two Jagdtigers known still to be in existence, at the Bovington Tank Museum; the other is in the USA. This vehicle is one of only two fitted with the experimental Porsche suspension. (Author's Collection)

SOURCE NOTES

Abbreviations Used:

IR	Illustrated Record of German Army Equipment 1939–1945, Volume III – Armoured Fighting Vehicles (MI 10, The War Office, 1947).
Spielberg	Der Panzerkampfwagen Tiger und seine Abarten by Walter J. Spielberger (Motorbuch Verlag, Stuttgart, 1977).
HWA	Notes made by author from Heereswaffenamt (Wa-Prüf 6) files in 1945-6.
Kniepkamp	MS notes of conversations between author and Herr Kniepkamp in 1945.
Schilling	'History of German Tank Development' by Robert Schilling, US Army Ordnance (CIOS report dated 25 June 1945).
Heydekampf	MS notes of conversations between author and Dr. Stieler von Heydekampf, 1945.
Oswald	Kraftfahrzeuge und Panzer der Reichswehr, Wehrmacht und Bundeswehr by Werner Oswald (Motorbuch Verlag, Stuttgart, 1971).
Kleine/Kühn	Tiger – Die Geschichte einer Legendären Waffe by Egon Kleine/Volkmar Kühn (Motorbuch Verlag, Stuttgart, 1976).
25 Tk.Bde.	25 Army Tank Brigade Technical Intelligence Summary No. 1 dated 25 February 1943.
48 RTR	48th Battalion Royal Tank Regiment War Diary for April 1943 and Appendix II thereto.
Porsche	MS notes of conversations in 1945 with Dr.Ing.h.c. Ferdinand Porsche and other Porsche KG personnel.
Fletcher	Tiger! – The Tiger Tank: A British View by David Fletcher (HMSO, London, 1986).
Forty	German Tanks of World War Two by Lieutenant-Colonel George Forty (Blandford Press, London, 1987).
US Ord.	US Army ETO Ord. Tech. Intell. Report No. 184.
WOTIS	War Office Tech. Int. Summary (MI10, The War Office, various dates).
Hinsley	British Intelligence in the Second World War, vol 2, by F. H. Hinsley, et al (HMSO, 1981).
Liddell Hart	The Tanks. vol 2, by B. H. Liddell Hart (Cassell, 1959).
Jackson	The North African Campaign, 1940-43 by General Sir William Jackson (Batsford, 1975).
Tessin	Verbände und Truppen der Deutschen Wehrmacht und Waffen SS, 1939–45 by Georg Tessin (Biblio Verlag, Osnabruck, 1975).

INTRODUCTION
1. 25 Tk.Bde
2. 48 RTR
3. Reproduced in Fletcher *Tiger! – The Tiger Tank: A British View*
4. IR
5. HWA
6. Ibid

CHAPTER ONE
1. Oswald
2. Kniepkamp
3. HWA
4. Ibid
5. Ibid
6. Ibid
7. Ibid
8. Oswald
9. Schilling
10. Ibid
11. HWA
12. Heydekampf
13. Ibid
14. Schilling
15. HWA

CHAPTER TWO
1. Schilling
2. HWA
3. Spielberger
4. Ibid
5. HWA
6. Spielberger
7. Ibid
8. Ibid
9. Ibid
10. Kleine/Kühn
11. Spielberger
12. Kleine/Kühn
13. Spielberger
14. IR
15. Spielberger
16. Ibid
17. Ibid
18. Porsche
19. Forty (p.144)
20. IR
21. Porsche/Kniepkamp

CHAPTER THREE
1. Kniepkamp
2. Spielberger
3. Ibid
4. Kniepkamp
5. Aders
6. Spielberger
7. Ibid
8. IR
9. Spielberger
10. IR
11. Ibid
12. Spielberger
13. Ibid
14. Ibid
15. Forty
16. Kniepkamp
17. Aders
18. Kniepkamp
19. IR
20. Spielberger
21. Kniepkamp
22. Ibid
23. Spielberger
24. Aders
25. Spielberger
26. Schiller
27. Spielberger
28. Ibid
29. Fletcher

CHAPTER FOUR
1. WOTIS 135 (19 July 1944)
2. HWA
3. WOTIS 157 (20 Dec 1944)
4. WOTIS 183 (9 Aug 1945)

5 Kniepkamp
6 WOTIS 170 (28 Mar 1945), para 7
7 WOTIS 171 (4 April 1945)
8 US Ord
9 WOTIS 169 (21 Mar 1945), Appx D
10 Kniepkamp

CHAPTER FIVE
1 HWA
2 Ibid
3 Spielberger
4 IR
5 Ibid
6 Spielberger
7 Ibid
8 HWA
9 Spielberger
10 Ibid
11 IR
12 Spielberger
13 IR
14 Ibid
15 Ibid

16 Forty

CHAPTER SIX
1 HWA
2 Spielberger
3 Forty
4 Kleine/Kühn

CHAPTER SEVEN
1 Tessin
2 HWA
3 Kleine/Kühn
4 Ibid
5 Hinsley
6 Notes & recollections of Wilhelm Hartmann and BG a.D. H-G Lueder, members of s.Pz.Abt.501
7 Fletcher
8 HQRA 6th Armoured Division letter RA/O/2/5 of 15 Feb 1943
9 Hinsley
10 'Notes from Theatres of War No. 16 – North Africa, November

1942–May 1943' (The War Office, 1943)
11 Kleine/Kühn
12 Ibid
13 Ibid
14 'Notes from Theatres of War No. 16'
15 Ibid
16 48 RTR
17 Kleine/Kühn
18 Ibid
19 Ibid
20 Ibid
21 Tessin
22 Ibid
23 Ibid
24 Ibid
25 Ibid
26 Ibid
27 Ibid & Kleine/Kühn
28 Tessin
29 Kleine/Kühn
30 Ibid
31 Ibid
32 Ibid
33 Ibid

34 Monograph on Michael Wittmann by Gary L. Simpson
35 Liddell Hart (p. 344)
36 Kleine/Kühn
37 Spielberger
38 WOTIS 156 of 13 Dec 1944
39 Kleine/Kühn
40 Spielberger
41 Kleine/Kühn
42 Ibid
43 Ibid
44 Ibid
45 Ibid
46 Ibid
47 Ibid
48 Ibid
49 Ibid
50 Ibid
51 Ibid
52 Ibid
53 Ibid
54 Spielberger
55 Tessin
56 Kleine/Kühn

GLOSSARY

AA	Flugabwehr	anti-aircraft
Abt	Abteilung	Battalion
AgK	Amtsgruppe Kraftfahrwesen	Directorate of Motor Vehicles
AHA	Allgemeine Heeresamt	General Army Branch (of War Ministry)
AOK	Armee Oberkommando	Army HQ Staff
ARV	Panzerbergewagen	Armoured Recovery Vehicle
Ausb	Ausbildung	Training
Ausf	Ausführung	Model, Mark
Bde	Brigade/Regiment	Brigade
Bef Wg	Befehlswagen	Command Vehicle
Bn	Abteilung	Battalion
BW	Bataillonsführerwagen	Battalion Commander's Vehicle
CC	Kampfgruppe	Combat Command (US) Brigade Group (UK)
Char (de combat)	Panzerkampfwagen	Tank
Coy	Kompanie	Company
DTD		Department of Tank Design
DW	Durchbruchwagen	Breakthrough Vehicle
E	Einheits-	Standard
Ers	Ersatz	Replacement, Spare
FlaK	Flugabwehrkanone	Anti-aircraft gun
FPNr	Feldpostnummer	Field Post Office No.
Fu	Funk	Radio
Führer		Commander
Gep	Gepanzerte	Armoured
GOC	Divisions-Kommandeur	General Officer Commanding
HEAT } Hl/gr }	Hohlladungsgranate	Hollow charge shell (HE anti-tank)
Hptm	Hauptmann	Captain
HQ	Hauptquartier	Headquarters
HWA	Heereswaffenamt	Army Weapons Directorate
In	Inspektion	Inspectorate
Jäg	Jäger	Hunter (Destroyer)
Jagdpanzer	Panzerjäger	Tank Destroyer
K	Kanone	Gun
Kp	Kompanie	Company
KwK	Kampfwagenkanone	Tank Gun
LaS	Landwirtschaftliche Schlepper	Agricultural Tractor
LKA	Leichte Kampfwagen A	Light Tank Model A
Lt	Leutnant	2nd Lieutenant
MG	Maschinengewehr	Machine-gun
Mrs	Mörser	Howitzer
NbFz	Neubaufahrzeug	New design of vehicle
Nb.K	Nebelkerze	Smoke candle
Oblt	Oberleutnant	Lieutenant
OKH	Oberkommando des Heeres	War Ministry
OTL	Oberstleutnant	Lieutenant-Colonel
OKW	Oberkommando der Wehrmacht	Defence Ministry
PaK	Panzerabwehrkanone	Anti-tank gun
PR	Panzerregiment	Armoured regiment (equivalent to British brigade)
Pz	Panzer	Tank or armoured
Pz Bef Wg	Panzerbefehlswagen	Command tank
Pz Berge Wg	Panzerbergewagen	Armoured recovery vehicle
Pz Jäg	Panzerjäger	Tank hunter or destroyer
Pz Kpfw	Panzerkampfwagen	Tank
Pz Sfl	Panzerselbstfahrlafette	Armoured SP mounting
RW	Raketenwerfer	Rocket-launcher
s	Schwer(e)	Heavy
Sd Kfz	Sonderkraftfahrzeug	Special vehicle (used in Ordnance Vocabulary)

Glossary 153

Sf }	Selbst-	Self-propelled	Treibsatz		Rocket motor
SP	fahrende		Uffz	Unteroffizier	Corporal, NCO
Sprgr	Sprenggranate	High-explosive shell	V	Versuchs-	Experimental vehicle
Sqn	Kompanie	Squadron		fahrzeug	
STT		School of Tank Technology	VK	Vollketten- fahrzeug	Tracked vehicle
Stu	Sturm	Assault	WaPrüf	Waffenprüf-	Weapons Testing Branch
Stu G	Sturmgeschütz	Assault gun		ungsamt	
SW	Sturmwagen	Assault vehicle	Zg	Zug	Troop, platoon
SW	Schwerewagen	Heavy vehicle	ZW	Zugführerwagen	Troop commander's vehicle
Tk	Panzerkampf- wagen	Tank			

BIBLIOGRAPHY

1. PUBLISHED SOURCES

CARELL, Paul. *Die Wüsten Fuchse*. Henry Nannen Verlag, Hamburg, 1958.

CHAMBERLAIN, Peter, DOYLE, Hilary L. and ELLIS, Chris. *Encyclopedia of German Tanks of World War Two*. Arms & Armour Press, London, 1978.

FEY, Will. *Panzerkampf im Bild*. Munin Verlag, Osnabrück, 1987.

FLETCHER, David. *Tiger – The Tiger Tank: A British View*. HMSO, London 1986.

FORTY, Lieutenant-Colonel George. *German Tanks of World War Two*. Blandford Press, London, 1988.

HART, R. H. Liddell. *The Tanks*. vol. II. Cassell, London, 1959.

HINSLEY, Professor F. H. et al. *British Intelligence in the Second World War*, vol. 2. HMSO, London, 1981.

JACKSON, General Sir William. *The North African Campaign, 1940–43*. Batsford, London, 1975.

KLEIN, Egon and KÜHN, Volkmar. *Tiger – Die Geschichte einer legendären Waffe, 1942–45*. Motorbuch Verlag, Stuttgart, 1976.

OSWALD, Werner. *Kraftfahrzeuge und Panzer der Reichswehr, Wehrmacht und Bundeswehr*. Motorbuch Verlag, Stuttgart, 1971.

PLAYFAIR, Major General I. S. O. et al. *History of the Second World War*. HMSO, London, 1966.

SPIELBERGER, Walter. *Panzerkampfwagen Tiger und seine Abarten*. Motorbuch Verlag, Stuttgart, 1977.

TESSIN, Georg. *Verbände und Truppen der Deutschen Wehrmacht und Waffen-SS, 1939–45*. Biblio Verlag, Osnabrück, 1975.

HARTMANN, Wilhelm. 'Schwere Panzer-Abteilung (Tiger) 501.' In *Die Oase*, magazine of the Verband Deutsches Afrika-Korps e.V., Rommel-Sozialwerk e.V., April 1972.

WAR OFFICE. *Vocabulary of German Military Terms and Abbreviations*. HMSO, London, 1943.

2. UNPUBLISHED SOURCES

a. Official Papers

THE WAR OFFICE. *Illustrated Record of German Army Equipment 1939–1945, Vol. III, Armoured Fighting Vehicles*. MI 10, London, 1947.

— *German Pz Kw VI (H)*. MI 10, London, September 1943.

— *Notes From Theatres of War, No. 16 – North Africa, November 1942–May 1943*. London, 1943.

— *Technical Intelligence Summaries (WOTIS)*. MI 10, London, various dates.

MILITARY COLLEGE OF SCIENCE SCHOOL OF TANK TECHNOLOGY. *Preliminary Report No. 19 – Pz Kw VI (Tiger)*. Chertsey, November 1943.

— *Report on Pz Kw VI (Tiger) Model H*. Chertsey, Parts I, II & IX, January and September 1944, Part IV March, April and September 1944. Remaining Parts not completed.

— *Glossary of German Tank Terms*. Chertsey, December 1942.

— *Revised Glossary of German Tank Terms*. Chertsey, March 1943.

48TH BATTALION, ROYAL TANK REGIMENT. *War Diary – April 1943 and Appendices II, III and IV thereto*.

HQ 25 TANK BRIGADE. *Technical Intelligence Summary No. 1*. 25 February 1943.

COMBINED INTELLIGENCE OBJECTIVES SUB-COMMITTEE. Report by Mr. Robert Schilling, US Ord. *History of German Tank Development*. G-2 Division, SHAEF (Rear), APO 413. 25 June 1945.

Pz AOK 5 AFRIKA. *War Diaries* – IWM reference numbers 1041, 1307 and 1387.

GENERALINSPEKTEUR DER PANZERTRUPPEN OKH ('D' Vorschriften):

D 656/23 Pz Kpfw Tiger, Ausf E (Sd Kfz 181) – May 1944 (Driver's Handbook).

D 656/27 Tigerfibel (Tiger Primer) – August 1943.

D 656/42 Pz Kpfw Tiger Ausf B (SD Kfz 182) – Sept 1944 (Turret Handbook).

D 656/43 Pz Kpfw Tiger, Ausf B (Sd Kfz 182) – Sept 1944 (Driver's Handbook).

FILES OF THE GENERALINSPEKTEUR DER PANZERTRUPPEN (Guderian) in the Bundesarchiv – Militararchiv (Inventory Number RH 10), Freiburg i. Br., Germany.

b. Private Papers

PERSONAL NOTES FROM:

Brigadegeneral (Rtd) H-G Lueder, former commander of s.Pz.Abt.501.

Herr Wilhelm Hartmann, former Ordnance Officer and Company commander of s.Pz.Abt.501 and s.Pz. Abt.506.

Dr. (med) R. Hautmann, former member of s.Pz.Abt. 504.

MANUSCRIPT REPORT, by Capt Wightman, REME and Lieutenant Sewell to OC 104 Tank Workshop REME, on all known captured and knocked-out Tigers in Tunisia – dated 9 June 1943.

AUTHOR'S MS NOTES OF CONVERSATIONS IN 1945 WITH:

Dr.Ing. Stieler von Heydekampf (Managing Director, Henschel und Sohn, and President, from December 1943, of the Panzer Kommission).

Dr.-Ing.habil. Erwin Aders (Head of Tank Development, Henschel und Sohn)

Dipl.-Ing. Ernst Kniepkamp (Head of WaPrüf 6, HWA)

Dr.-Ing, h. c.. Ferdinand Porsche

INDEX

I. NUMERICAL INDEX OF FORMATIONS AND UNITS

(Note: page nos. in italic indicate illustrations)

1 (German) Army Korps, 123
1 Panzer Division, 134
1 (German) Parachute Army, 136
1 SS Panzer Division 'LSSAH', 128–9
1 SS Panzer Korps, 128
1st (US) Armoured Division, *105, 112, 114,* 116
1st (British) Army, 140–1, *142–3*
1 (British) Infantry Division, 116
2 (Soviet) Shock Army, 98
3 Panzer Army, 124
3 Panzer Division, 133–4
3 Panzer Regiment, 125
3 SS Panzer Division, 134
3 (British) Mixed Division, 116
4th County of London Yeomanry, 129
4 SS Panzer Korps, 134
5 Panzer Division, 124
5 (German) Parachute Regiment, 116
5 SS Panzer Division, 134, 136
5th (US) Army, 127
6 (British) Armoured Division, 104, *105*
6 SS Panzer Army, 136
7th (US) Army, 136
7 Panzer Regiment, *61,* 111
7th Royal Tank Regiment, 128
9 (German) Army, 135
9 (US) Infantry Division, 116
9th Royal Tank Regiment, 128
10 (British) Infantry Brigade, 116
10 Panzer Division, 102, 107
10 SS Panzer Division, 136
12 SS Panzer Division, 128
14 Panzer Division, 123
15 Panzer Battalion, 117
15 Panzer Grenadier Division, 117
16 Panzer Division, 134
16 SS Panzer Grenadier Division, 126
17 Panzer Division, 118
17 SS Panzer Grenadier Division, 127
18 (German) Army, 123
21 (British) Army Tank Brigade, 7, *10,* 127, 141, *143*
21 Panzer Division, 128, 135
21 Panzer Regiment, 128
22 (British) Armoured Brigade, 129
24 Panzer Grenadier Division, 127
25 (British) Army Tank Brigade, 7
29 Panzer Grenadier Division, 128
33 Panzer Regiment, 125
48th Royal Tank Regiment, *9,* 116, *117*
53 Panzer Korps, 139
72 Anti-tank Regiment RA, *106,* 136, 138
76 Panzer Armee Korps, 128
78 (German) Assault Division, 132
79 (British) Armoured Division, 63
81 (German) Infantry Division, 120
86 (German) Infantry Division, 132
101 SS Heavy Tank Battalion, 128, 130
102 SS Heavy Tank Battalion, 126
103 SS Heavy Tank Battalion, 126
104 SS Heavy Tank Battalion, 126
104 Army Tank Workshop REME, 7, *142*
148 Regiment RAC, 136
197 Sturmgeschütz Battalion, 132
204 Panzer Regiment, 125
334 (German) Division, 107
362 (German) Infantry Division, 127
394 (US) Infantry Regiment, 139
424 (German) Heavy Tank Battalion, 134
500 Armoured Reinforcement and Training Battalion, 126
501 (German) Heavy Tank Battalion, 53, 55, *61,* 95, *98–101,* 100, *102–16,* 125, 134, *143*
501 SS Heavy Tank Battalion, 92, 126, *129*
502 (German) Heavy Tank Battalion, *91,* 95, 98–9, 118–20, 123–4, 137
502 SS Heavy Tank Battalion, 91, 124, 126
503 (German) Heavy Tank Battalion, 125, 128, 137
503 SS Heavy Tank Battalion, 125, 126
504 (German) Heavy Tank Battalion, 7, 55, *116–18,* 117, 125–8, *140, 142–3*
507 (German) Heavy Tank Battalion, 55, 134
508 (German) Heavy Tank Battalion, 127–8
509 (German) Heavy Tank Battalion, 125, 133
510 (German) Heavy Tank Battalion, 123, 125
511 (German) Heavy Tank Battalion, 124–5
512 (German) Heavy Tank Destroyer Battalion, *139*
614 (German) Heavy Tank Destroyer Company, 133, 137, *139*
653 (German) Tank Hunter Battalion, 132–3, 137
654 (German) Tank Hunter Battalion, 132
656 (German) Tank Hunter Regiment, 132
1000 (German) Armoured Assault Mortar Company, 130–1
1001 (German) Armoured Assault Mortar Company, 130–1

II. GENERAL INDEX

(Note: Page nos. in italic indicate illustrations)

AA MG 34, 56
AA MG mounting, 46
AA MG mounting ring, 56
Aachen, 136
Aberdeen Proving Ground, 142, *143–4*
Aders, Dr.-Ing.habil. Erwin, 11, 31, 43–4
Adler, 81
Adolf Hitler Line, 126
Afrika Korps, 45, 99–100, 118
AgK, 13
Agordo valley, 128
AHA, 13
air raids, 24, 77
Alexandrovka, 132
Algeria, 100
Alkett, 15, 22, 32, 36, 65, 68, 130, 132
Allgemeine Heeresamt, 13
Altena, 139
ammunition carriers, armoured, 63
ammunition, AP, 22; AP40, 22; APC, 22; APCBC, 22; AP/CR, 22; fixed, 21, 85; separate, 85
Amtsgruppe Kraftfahrwesen, 13, 23
anti-tank gun, self-propelled, 11
Anzio, 126–7
Apeldoorn, 136
appliqué armour, 17, 21
Ardennes, 84, 89–90, 130, 133, 135–7
armament, tank, 21
armour, appliqué, 17, 21; arrangement, 21; cast, 21; -piercing, 22
armoured ammunition carrier, 63; assault mortar Tiger company, 130; command vehicles, 41, 63, 65, 82; OP, 63, 65; recovery vehicle, 34, *34,* 49, 63, 63–4, 65, 81, 119, *121*
Armoured Reinforcement Battalion, 125
Army Group Don, 118
Army Group North, 96
Army Group South-West, 127
Army High Command, 98
Arnhem, 136
Arnim, General von, 107, 116
artillery, self-propelled, 18
ARV, 34, *34,* 49, 63, 63–4, 65, 81, 119, *121*
Arys training area, 65
assault bridge, armoured infantry, 63
Ausführung, 10, 11

Bad Driburg, 134
Baillie Stewart, Captain Norman, 11
Bamberg, 94
Bari, 126
Bassano, 127
Bastogne, 136
Bataillonsführerwagen, 11, 15
battalion, corps Tiger, 92; Heavy Armour Reinforcement and Training, 91–3; Heavy Tank, 65, 91, 94, 96, 99; heavy tank hunter, 92; heavy SS tank, 92
Bayerlein, LtGen Fritz, 139
Béja, 111–30
Belgium, 128–9
Belleville washer, 21
Belluno, 128
Bergenbrück, 135
Berka, 31
Berlin, 135
BIOS, 90
Bizerta, 100, 102, 116, 141
Bletchley Park, 99
BMM, 22
Böblingen, 24, 36
Bocholt, 136
Bofors, 13
Boge und Sohn, 37
Bologna, 128
bomb thrower, 2in, 76
Bône, 141
Bonn, 131, 139
Bordsprechanlage B, 65
Borgholz, 134
Bovington Camp, 6, 8, 46, 117, 141, *143,* 144
Boyarka, 129
brake, muzzle, 21, *57*
bridge-layers, armoured, 63
Briesen, 135
Brindisi, 126
British Intelligence Objectives Sub-Committee, 90
Bruck/Leitha, 132
BT medium tank, 9, 37
Budapest, 134, 136
Bulge, Battle of the, 136
Bundesamt für Wehrtechnik und Beschaffung (BWB), 131
Bundesamtes für Wehrtechnik und Beschaffung, Wehrtechnische Studiensammlung des, 68
Bundeswehr, 26
BW medium tank, 11, 15, *25,* 38
BWB, 68

Caen, 128, 135
Cagny, 136
Cap Bon peninsula, 117
capped shot, 21
Carius, Oblt Otto, 137, 139
Cassino, 126–7
Central Army Group, 132
Centurion main battle tank, 19, 142
Challenger main battle tank, 81
Char B heavy tank, 9, 18
Chertsey, 7–8, 141
Chieftain main battle tank, 81
Churchill infantry tank, 7, 19, 116, *117*
Churchill, Winston, 7, 20, 99, 141
CIOS, 90
collaboration, German/Soviet, 37
Cologne, 136
Colombelles, 128, 135
Combat Command A, 116
Combat Command C, 116
Combined Intelligence Objectives Sub-Committee, 116
command vehicle, 82
commander's cupola, 46
commander's tanks, Pz.Kpfw.III, 65
companies, heavy tank, 65, 94, 126
companies, Waffen SS heavy tank, 92
Company Commanders' School, Versailles, 125
Company, Workshop, 124–5
Corps Heavy Tank Battalion, 134
Cotignole, 127
Cottbus, 125
Crusader cruiser tank, 104, *105*

D-Vorschriften, 11
Daimler Benz, 11–15, 22, 26, 36–9
deep wading equipment, 45, 149
Deilinghofen, 139
Demag, 22
Department of Tank Design, 8, 25, 141
Deutsche Eisenwerk, 22

Index 157

Diedersdorf, 135
Dieppe, 99
diesel engine, air-cooled, 35–6
dischargers, 'S'-Mine, 56
diving tank, 46
Djedeida, 104
Döllersheim, 89, 133, 137, 139
Dortmund, 139
Dortmund Hoerder Hüttenverein, 46
Dresden, 134
Dreux, 128, 135
DTD, 8, 25, 141
Duisburg, 139
Dunaburg, 119–20
Durchbruchwagen 1, 37–8
Düren, 131
DW 1, 37–8
DW 2, 38–9

E-5, 24
E-100, 24, 81
'E'-series tanks, 24, 81
East Prussia, 120, 123–4, 135
Eastern Front, 9, 41, 44, 56, 74, 96, 99, 118, 123, 125–6, 129, 132–5
Eberan, Prof.-Ing. von, 31, 44
Economic Warfare, Ministry of, 22
Eifel, 131, 136
Eisenach, 119
electric drive, 19
Elefant self-propelled tank destroyer, 32, 33, 34, 75, 83, 90, 131–3, *132*, 137
energy, chemical, 22; kinetic, 22
Enigma cipher, 99, 104
Ergste, 139
Ernst, Hptm Albert, 137, 139
Eschweiler, 136
Europe, NW, 18
Euskirchen, 131

face-hardening, 21
Faid, 107
Falaise, 129
Falaise Gap, 128
Fallingbostel, 45, 94, 96, 99, 102, 115, 118, 125, 131, 149
FAMO-Ursus, 42
Faun, 37
Feifel air pre-cleaners, *55*, 102
Ferdinand 8.8cm self-propelled tank destroyer, 32, 83, 90, 132
ferry, amphibious tracked, 63
Fichtner, 44
Field Post Number, *98*, 100
Fieseler Storch, 44
Fighting Vehicle Proving Establishment, 8, 141
firepower, 8–9, 21
Fischhausen, 124–5, 134
FlaK 36 8.8cm anti-aircraft gun, 7
flame-thrower, 65
Flammtiger, 65
Fliederblüte, Operation, 116
Flying Fortresses, 115
Foerster, Hptm.von, 120
Ford Motor Company, 19, 22
Forlimpopoli, 127
Forty, Lt.Col. George, 89–90
Fr. Garny, 76
France, Vichy, 102, 104
Frankfurt/Oder, 135
Freikorps Sauerland, 139
French North Africa, 7
Fu7 radio, 82
Fu8 radio, 82
Führer, 86, 98–9
Fuller, Maj Gen JFC, 10, 15
'funnies, 18, 63
FVPE, 8, 141

Gaeta, 126
Gafsa, 116
Garigliano, River, 126
GC & CS, 99
Gdansk, 124
Gdynia, 124
gearbox, Maybach Olvar, 43, 52, 76
Geilenkirchen, 136
'German Tanks of World War II', 89
Germany, Economic Survey of, 22
Gieselwerder, 134
Goering, Reichsmarschall Hermann, 99
Goldschmidt, Lt. Karl, 118, 126–7
Gollnick, General, 123
Gory, 118
Government Code and Cipher School, 99
Gratkorn im Muntal, 134
Graziani, Marshal, 127
grenades, anti-personnel, 77
Grevenbroich, 136
'Grossdeutschland' Panzer Grenadier Division, 125
Grosstraktor, 12, *14*, 26
Guderian, Colonel-General, 31, 44, 124
gun, AA, 139; assault, 14, 63; FlaK 36 (L/56) anti-aircraft, 7, 42; FlaK 36 (L/56) tank, 42; KwK 42 (L/70) tank, 42; KwK (L/24), 92; PaK 39 (L/48) anti-tank, 124; PaK 43 (L/71) anti-tank, 44; PaK 44 or PaK 80 (L/55) anti-tank, 83; self-propelled, 18, 63, 83; self-propelled anti-tank, 82; tank, 21-2; Type 0725, 44
Gustav LIne, 126

Hagen, 139
Hajmasker, 134
half-tracked tractors, 49, 63, 93, 96, 119, 127
Harkort, Lt., 126
Harpe, Generaloberst, 139
Hartmann, Oblt.W., 6, 102, 111
Harz, 134
Hasenfelde, 135
Hauptauschuss für Panzerwagen und Zugmaschinen, 23–4
Haustenbeck, 24, 41, 46, 149
HE, 22
HEAT, 22
heavy tank, 27
heavy tank battalion, 118–19, 126, 128, 133
Heavy Tank Battalions, 45
heavy tank hunter battalion, 137
heavy tank hunter unit, 137
heavy tractors, half-track, 63
Heeresgruppe Mitte, 125, 132
Heeresgruppe Sud, 125
Heerestechnische Verordnungsblätter, 11
Heereswaffenamt, 11, 13–15, 19, 23, 26–7, 35, 38, 74
Heiligenbeil, 135
Heim, Oblt. Herbert, 117, 126
helical spring, 21
Hemer, 139
Henschel und Sohn GmbH, 10–11, 13–15, 18–19, 21–2, 24, 26–7, 31–2, 34–5, 37–9, 41–6, 74–7, 81, 86, 96, 98, 131, 134, 149
Henschel proving ground, 24, 41, 46, 149
Hermann Goering Division, 116
Hetzer 7.5cm tank destroyer, *124*, 125
Heydekampf, Dr. Stieler von, 11, 19, 22–3, 26
high explosive, 22
Hill, 112, 128
Hitler, Adolf, 11, 13, 18–19, 24, 26–9, 32, 34–6, 41–2, 44, 65, 68, 75, 77, 85–6, 96, 98–100, 115, 118–19, 124, 127, 130
Hobo's 'Funnies', 63
Hohne training area, 149

Hollabrunn, 134
Holland, 136
hollow charge, 22
hollow-charge projectile, 21
Honey light tank, 104
HtV-Army, 11
Hummel, Oblt., 117, 136
Hungarian Artillery School, 134
Hungary, 90, 125, 133–4, 136–7
Hunting Tiger, 82–3, 85, 137
Hunt's Gap, 111
HWA, 13, 24, 31, 35–7, 42, 44, 75, 77
hyper-velocity gun Type 0725, 41

I Army Corps, 123
In.6, 13, 23
Independent, Vickers heavy tank, 11, 18
Infantry tank Mark II Matilda, 9
Intelligence, technical, 84–5, 90
IS-2 heavy tank, 120
IS-3 heavy tank, 35
Iserlohn, 139
ISU-122 heavy tank destroyer, 134
Italian Campaign, 126
Italian front, 90
Italy, 65, 102, 126–7, 133
IV SS Panzer Corps, 134

Jagdpanther 7.5cm medium tank destroyer, 23, 83, 89
Jagdpanzer 38 (Hetzer) 7.5cm light tank destroyer, 124, *124*
Jagdtiger 12.8cm heavy tank destroyer, 8, 11, 21, 23, 77, 82–6, *83–4*, *86*, *88*, 89–90, 92, 133–4, 136–7, *139*, *139*, *150*
Jägerregiment Hermann Goering, 116
Jahde, Major, 119
Japan, 46
Ju 52 transport aircraft, 98, 102
Jucava, 120
Jungenfeldt, Oberstleutnant (LtCol) von, 132

Kama, 12
Kampfgruppe Koch, 102
Kampfgruppe Lang, 111, 115
Kampftruppenschule, II, 82
Kaplitz, 134
Kassböhrer, 49
Kazan, 12
Kesselring, Commander-in-Chief, South, 107
Kielce, 134
King George VI, 7
King Tiger heavy tank, 77
Kniepkamp, Ministerialrat Dipl.-Ing. (Heinrich) Ernst, 11, 13, 36–7, 44
Koblenz, 68, 131
Königsberg, 124, 134
Königsgratz, 134
Königstiger heavy tank, 8, 11, 35, 74, 77
Korps Abteilung, 92
Krauss Maffei, 149
Krupp, Friedrich, AG, 11, 13–15, 18–19, 21–2, 24, 27–56, 75–6, 81
Krupp-Traktor, 15
Kuberle, 118
Kühn, Hauptmann, Friedrich, 126
Kühn, Major, 127
Kummel, Major, 100
Kummersdorf Proving Ground, 15, 24, 46
Kurland, 123–4
Kursk, 34, 129, 132
KV heavy tank, 22, 24
KwK43, 8.8cm (L/71) tank gun, 76

L.a.S., 10–11, 13–15, 17
L.a.S.100, 15, *18*
Laa, 134
Lake Ladoga, 119

Landsverk, 13
Landwirtschaftlicher Schlepper, 10–11, 13–15, *17*
Lange, Major, 136
Langschede, 139
launcher, anti-personnel grenade, 22
launcher, Gerät 562, naval 38cm, 65
launcher, rocket, 66
launcher, smoke grenade, 22, 56
leaf spring, 21
Leichte Kampfwagen A light tank, 14, *17*
leichter Traktor, 12, *12–13*
Lemberg, 125
Leningrad, 96, 98, 118–19
Leonhardt, Hauptmann, 120
Leopard medium tank, 26–7, 30
Leopard 2 main battle tank, 81
Libau, 123
Liddell Hart, Captain Sir Basil, 10, 15
Light Tank Mk, VI, 15
Ligurian Army, 127
LIII Panzer Corps, 139
Linz, 135
Litzen, 135
LKA, 13, *17*
loading gauge, rail, 30, 37, 49
Löwe heavy tank, 24, 81
Lüdenscheid, 139
Lueder, Major Hans-Georg, 94, 102, 111
Lugo, 127
LXXVI Panzer Armee Korps, 128

MAN, 11, 13–14, 22, 26, 37–9, 44, 74
Magdeburg, 134
Mailly le Camp, 125
Maknassy, 115
Maknassy Pass, 115
Malmédy, 136
Mammut, 35, 95
Manstein, FM von, 118
Maréchal Foch barracks, 102
Märker, Major Richard, 94, 96, 98–9
Maschinenfabrik Augsburg-Nürnberg, 13, 26
Maschinenfabrik Niedersachsen-Hannover, 22
Massa, 126
Massa Lombarda, 127
Massa Marittima, 127
Maus, 24, 32, 35–6, 75, 81
Maybach Motorenbau GmbH, 19, 32, 37, 39, 43, 52, 76, 81, 132
McCune, Major Boyd H., 139
Me-323 'Gigant' transport aircraft, 102
Medium tank Mk II, 12, *13*
Medjez-el-Bab, 102, 111, 116
Meinerzhagen, 139
Memel, 123
Memel bridgehead, 124
Menden, 139
Meppen proving ground, 24
Messina, 117
MG, auxiliary, 56
MG13, 15
MG34, 15, 17, 56, 76
MG34, auxiliary, 66
MG34, coaxial, 65
Mga, 119
Mga station, 96
MI 10, 8, 84
M.I.A.G., 15, 22
Military College of Science, 7
M.N.H., 22
mobility 8–9
Model, Feldmarschall, 139
Moldau, R., 134
Montepescali, 127
Morocco, 100
Münster, 136

Münsterlager, 82
muzzle brake, double baffle, *57*, 76

N. Africa, 7, 99–100, 102, 115, 117–18
Naples, 126
Narev bridgehead, 134–5
Narva bridgehead, 119
Nasielsk, 134
Nb.Fz. heavy tank, *16*, 18–19
Nettuno, 128
Neubaufahrzeuge heavy tanks, 18–19
Neuhausen, 124
Neuhauser Forst, 125
Neuruppin, 94
Nevel, 119
Nibelungenwerk, 11, 26–9, 32, 44, 77, 86, 132, 137
Nickelswalde, 125
Nikopol, 133
NITA gearbox, 35
Noak, Major, 132
nominal ground pressure, 9
Nordbau, 19
Normandy, 126, 128, 135
Norwegian campaign, 18
NW Europe, 84, 128

Oberkommando des Heeres, 13–15, 98–100, 132
Ohrdruf, 125, 128, 136
Ohrdruf/Thuringia training area, 125, 128, 136
OKH, 13–15, 98–100, 132
Oosterbeek, 136
Opel, Adam AG (General Motors), 19, 22
Operation Barbarossa, 128
Operation Béja, 111, *112*, *114*; Eilbote I, 107, *107–10*; Fliederblüte, 116; Frühlingswind, 107, 111, *111*; Market Garden, 136; Ochsenkopf, 111; Silberstreifen, 123; Sonnenblüme, 134; Totalize, 129; Vulcan, 116; Zitadelle, 34, 125, 133
Orel, 44
Ortelsburg, 135
Ortona, 126
Osterode, 134
Ostrov, 119–20
Outline Specifications: 12.8cm PaK 44 oder PaK 80 (L/55) auf Pz.Jäg.Tiger, Ausf.B (Jagdtiger) (Sd.Kfz.186), 90; 38cm RW61 auf Stu.Mrs.Tiger, 68; 8.8cm PaK 43/2 (L/71) auf Pz Jäg Tiger (P) (Sd.Kfz.184) (Elefant, früher Ferdinand), 36; Pz.Kpfw.Tiger, Ausf.B (Sd.Kfz.182) (Königstiger), 82; Pz.Kpfw.VI (H) Ausf H1 (Later Pz.Kpfw.Tiger Ausf.E) (Sd.Kfz.181), 56

Paderborn training area, 24, 39, 90–93, 118–19, 123, 125–6, 128, 134–5, 137, 139
PaK 43/3 8.8cm (L/71) anti-tank gun, 89; 44 12.8cm (L/55) anti-tank gun, 85; 80 12.8cm (L/55) anti-tank gun, 85
Palermo, 102
Panther medium tank, 7, 19, 21, 23, 26, 30–31, 44, 46, 56, 74–7, 81
Panther armoured recovery vehicle, 81, 119, *121*
Panther II (neu), 77
Panzer Kommission, 19, 23, 26
Panzer Regiment 'Grossdeutschland', 135
Panzerarmee, 99
Panzerbefehlswagen Tiger, Ausf.E., 65
Panzerkampfwagen, general, 10; I, 11, 15, 17; VI (H), 9
Panzerprogramm 41, 41
Paris, 128, 135–6

Parolla, 127
Parthenay, 126
People's Car, 11, 26
periscope, sighting, 22
Pillau, 124–5, 134
Piombino, 127
Pisa, 127
platoon, AA, 136; anti-aircraft, 93, 136; engineer, 93; light, 92–3; medical, 93; motorcycle reconnaissance, 93; reconnaissance, 134; recovery, 93, 119, 127; signals, 93; Stu.Mrs. 130; workshop, 104
Po, River, 127
Poland, 15, 133
Polish Armoured Division, 130
Polish campaign, 15
Pont du Fahs, 104, 107
Pontremoli, 126
Porsche, 19, 24, 26–32, 34–7, 39, 42, 44, 74–6, 81–2, 131–2
Porsche, Dr.-Ing.h.c.F., 11–12, 19, 21, 24, 26, 44
Porsche KG, 11, 26–7, 28–9, 38, 44
portable 10-tonne gantry crane, 93, *96*, *106*, *121–2*
power-to-weight ratio, 9
power traverse, 56
Praga, 22
Prague, 134, 136
Preekuln, 123
projector, smoke bomb, 76
Proletarskaya, 118
protection, 8–9, 21, 142
proving ground, Aberdeen, 46, 68, 82, 90, 131; Arys, 85; Döllersheim, 46; Haustenbeck, 39, 149; Kummersdorf, 36, 39; Meppen, 36; Ulm, 15
Putlos training area, 91, 94
Pz.Bergewagen Panther, 81, *121*
Pz.Ers.-u. Ausb.Abt.500, 125, 134, 137
Pz.Jäg. 38(t) (Hetzer), 23, *124*; Tiger, Ausf.B, 77, 82, 85, 137; Tiger für 8.8cm PaK 43/3 (Sf), *83–86*, *88*, 89, *139*, *150*; Tiger (P), 32, *33*, 75, 90, 132, *132*, 137
Pz.Kpfw., general, 10, 15; Panther, 18, 63; Tiger, Ausf.B, 11, 35, 74, 77; Tiger, Ausf.E, 26, 46, 68, 91, 130; I, 11, 15, *17*, *21*; II, III and IV, 63; II, 11, 15, *18*, 21; III, 7, 11, 15, 18–19, *21*, 37–9, 63, 65, *91*; 92–3, *95*, 96, 98–9, 104, 116–17, 119, 130; III Model N, 92–3, *95*, 100, *108*; III/IV, 19, 21; IV, 11, 15, 17 18, 21, 22, 25, 27, 37–8, 91, 111, 116–17, 125, 134, 139; V, 18; VI, 18, 41; VI, Ausf.B, 41; VI, Ausf.H, 45–6; VI (H), Ausf.H1, 34; VII, 37
Pz.Kw., 10
Pz.Sfl.V, 41
Pz.Stu.Mrs.Kp.Tiger, 130

R-35 medium tank, 9, 18
radio aerial, 'star', 65
radio, Fu 5, 65; Fu 7, 65; Fu 8, 65
Rapallo, Treaty of, 12
Rastenburg, 28, 31–2, 43
recovery, 49, 96, 127
recovery vehicles, armoured, 63, *121*
Reggio/Calabria, 102, 126
Regiments, SS Panzer, 92
Reichsbahn, 49
Remagen, 139
Remagen bridgehead, 90, 137
Rheinmetall Borsig, 11–12, 15, 18, 21–2, 39, 42–3, 66
Rhine, River, 131, 139
Riga, 120
Rimini, 127–8
road wheels, steel-tyred, 30; resilient, 76
Robaa, 104

rocket round, 66, *72*, *73*
Roer, River, 136
Rohland, Dr., 23
Rohrig, Officer Cadet, 127
Rome, 126–7
Rommel, Feldmarschall Erwin, 45, 99–100, 102, 107, 115, 118
Roskiskis, 120
Rostov, 118, 128
Royal Military College of Science, Shrivenham, 82
Royal Tiger, 11, 74, 77, 83, 85, 134, 136
Ruhr, 90
Rohr Gebeit, 131
Ruhr, River, 139
Rupierre, 135
Russia, 119
RW 61, naval rocket launcher, 66, *66–7*, *70*, 130–1

Saarpfalz, 133
Salerno, 126
Samland, 124–5
San Vicenzo, 127
Sangro, River, 126
Sarzana, 126
Saumur, 82
Scherf, Hptm (later Major), 137
Schleswig-Holstein, 135
Schlossberg, 123
Schmidt-Bonarius, Oblt., 111
Schönberg, 120
School of Tank Technology, 7–8
Schröter, Oblt., 117
Schwaner, Major (Dipl.Ing.) Hans-Joachim, 119
schwere Panzer Abteilung, 91
Schwerewagen, heavy tank, 37
Schwetzingen, 125
Scotland Yard, 84
Sd.Kfz., 10–11, 15
Seidensticker, Major August, 94, 115
Seine, River, 136
self-propelled tank destroyer, 132
Sennelager training area, 24, 125, 135–6, 139
SHAEF, 24
Sherman medium tank, 24, 89–90, 111, *112* *114*, 127, 130, 136, 139
Sicily, 115, 117–18, 126, 136
Sidi bou Zid, 107
Siebel ferry, *100–1*
Siegburg, 139
Siegen, 139
Siemens, 29
sight, periscopic, 22
sighting telescope, stationary-eyepiece, 56
Simmering-Graz-Pauker, 26
Sinsheim, Baden/Württemberg, 46
smoke grenade launchers, 46
snorkel tube, 48
Socherl, 136
Sonderfahrzeug I, 26
Sonderfahrzeug II, 28
Sonderfahrzeug III, 74
Sonderkraftfahrzeug Nummer, 10
Sorau, 134
Soviet Union, 27
SP anti-aircraft gun, 134
Spanish Civil War, 10, 15
Speer Ministry, 22–3
Speer, Reichsminister Albert, 32, 36, 42, 127
SS Pz.Korps, 92
Ssungar, 118
SSyms wagons, 49, *51*, *119*, *121*
St. Polten, 125, 134
Stalingrad, 34
steel-tyred resilient wheels, 46

Steinhöfel, 135
Steinwachs, Major, 132
Steuber, Lt., 126
Steyr Daimler Puch, 11, 22
Strait of Messina, 117, 126
STT, 7–8, 141, 144
Stuart light tank, 104
Sturmgeschütz, 15
Sturmmörser Tiger, 38cm Raketenwerfer 61 auf, 65–5, *66–70*, *72–3*, 90, 130–31, *131*
Sturmwagen heavy tank, 37
submersion, 48
Suostas, 120
super-heavy tank, 32
Supply Company, 136
suspension, Porsche, 86
suspension systems, tank, 19, 21
suspension, torsion bar, 132
SW heavy tank, 37–8
system, sighting, 22

T-26 medium tank, 9
T-34 medium tank, 9, 22, 24, 31, 35, 37, 44, 71
T-34(85) medium tank, 120, 123
Taksony, 136
tank, 16-tonner (Vickers), 12, *14*; anti-aircraft, 63; armoured OP, 63; Bataillonsführerwagen (BW), 11, 15, 25, 38; BT medium, 9, 37; Centurion MBT, 19, 147; Challenger MBT, 81; Char B heavy, 9, 18; Chieftain MBT, 81; Christie fast, 27; Churchill, 7, 99, 116–17; command, 63, 65, 134, 136; Crusader cruiser, 104–5 *105*; destroyer, 23, 32, 63; Durchbruchwagen (DW) 1, 37–8; DW 2, 38–9; E-5 light, 24; E-100 super-heavy, 24, 81; engines, diesel, 19; flame-thrower, 63, 65; heavy, 11, 18–19, 21–2, 26, 35; heavy (Infantry), 18; Honey light, 104; hunter regiment, 132; Independent heavy, 11, 19; Infantry, 18; Infantry, Mk II Matilda, 9, 19; IS-2 heavy, 120; IS-3 heavy, 35; KV heavy, 22, 24; Leopard medium, 26–7, 30; Leopard 2 MBT, 81; Light, Mk VI, 15; Löwe super-heavy, 24, 81, 82; M-3 medium, *105*; Mammut super-heavy, 35; Matilda (Infantry) Mk II, 9, 19; Maus super-heavy, 24, 32, 35–6, *36*, 75, 81; medium, 18, 21; medium (cruiser); 18; Medium Mk II, 12, *13*; museum, general, 68, 90, 117, 131; Bovington, 46, 82, 90; French, 82; US Army Ordnance Corps, 46, 68, 82; Neubaufahrzeuge (Nb.Fz.) heavy, *16*, 19; Panther medium, 7, 19, 21, 23, 26, 30–31, 44, 46, 56, 63, 74–7, 81; Panther II (neu) medium, 77; production, German annual, 22; R-35 medium, 9, 19; Schwerewagen (SW) heavy, 37–8; Sherman, 131; Sherman 'Firefly', 129; super-heavy, 19, 24; SW heavy, 37–8; T-26 medium, 9; T-34 medium, 44, 129; T-34 (85) medium, 120, 123; Tiger heavy tank; see 'Tiger 1', 'Tiger 2' & 'Tiger (Porsche)' below; Tiger-Maus, super-heavy, 24, *82*; Universal, 18; Valentine Infantry, 104, *105–6*; Zugführerwagen (ZW) medium, 11, 15, *21*, 38
Tebourba, 104
technical Intelligence, 8
telescope, 22
Teatour, 116
Thomale, Colonel, 31, 44
Tiger 1, *7*, 7–9, *9–10*, 11, 18, 21, 24, 30, *30*, 35, 37, 42, 44, *45–6*, 48, 48–9, *50–51*, *52–3*, 55, 56, *57–9*, 59–61, 63,

65–6, 68, 74–7, 81, 90–1, 93, 96, *97*, *99*, *100–1*, 99–100, *103*, *106–11*, *112–14*, *116–19*, *121–4*, 125–8, *129*, 130, 133–4, 136–7, *140*, *142–4*
Tiger 2, *2*, 11, 18–19, 23–4, 30–1, 35, 44, 46, 50–1, 74–5, *75–7*, 77, *79–80*, 81–3, 85, 90, 123, 125, 127–8, 130, *133*, 133–6, *135*, *137*, *145–6*, *149–50*
Tiger, command, 92
Tiger Grave, 115
Tiger-Maus, 24
Tiger (Porsche), 8, 21, 24, 27–8, *28*, 30, *30*, 32, *33–4*, 34–5, 125, 131–2
Tiger ARV, *63–4*
Tiger units, 63, 65
'Torch' landings, Allied, 100
torsion bar, general, 21–7, 49; longitudinal, 19, 27, 35–6, 74, 86; transverse, 37, 38, 76, 86
Tortona, 127
tractor, agricultural, 10, 12–13
trailer, low-loader, 49
training area, Arys, 65; Döllersheim, 89, 133, 137, 139; Mailly le Camp, 136; Milowicz, 134; Ohrdruf, 125, 128, 136, 149; Paderborn, 24, 39, 90–93, 118–19, 123, 125–6; Putlos, 18; Sennelager, 136, 139; Soltau, 149; Ulm, 14, 15, 126
transmission, electric, 35, 74
transportation, rail, 49; road, 49

Treaty of Versailles, 12
trials, submersed running, 46
Trier, 131
Tukkum, 120
Tula, 44
tungsten carbide, 41
Tunis, 7, 102, *103*, 104, 111, 115
Tunisia, 7, 46, 99, 102, 104, 115–17, 119, 125–6
turret ring, 9
Typ 100, 26–7; 101, 27–8; 102, 35; 103, 35; 130, 34; 180, 35–6; 180/181, 74; 181, 35; 200, 27; 205, 24, 35, *36*, 75
Type 0725 gun, 41–2

unit flash, 94, *95*, *98*
Unna, 139
US 1st Amored Division, 104; 6th Corps, 126; 9th Infantry Division, 116; Army Ordnance Corps, 90, 131; Fifth Army, 126
USSR, 48

Valentine infantry tank, 104, *105–6*
Variorex gearbox, 37, 39
vehicles, ammunition supply, 68; Command, 65; commander's, 65
Verona, 127
Versailles, Treaty of, 9, 12–13, 26

Vesprem, 134
Via Emilia, 128
Vickers, 11–12, 18
Vickers Medium Mark II, 12
Vienna, 127
Vienna/Modling, 125
Villers Bocage, 128–9
Vistula Lagoon, 124
Vitebsk, 125
VK 2001, 11, 15; 3001, 26–7, 37–9; 3001(H), 38–9, *38*, *40*, 41; 3001(P), 26–30, *29*, 32, 35; 3601, 41–3, *42*; 4501, 24, 26–8, 31–2, 35, 44, 74; 4501(H), 34, 42–4, *43*; 4501(P), 27–9, *28*, *30*, 30–2, 34–5, 44, 75, 131; 4502, 35; 4502(P), *74*, 74–5; 4503, 35, 74–7, 81; 6501, 37–9, *39*; 7001, 24, 81, *82*
Voith, 27, 35
Volkswagen, 11, 26–7
Vollkettenfahrzeug, 11, 15
volute spring, 21
VOMAG, 22
Vulcan, 116

WaPrüf.6, 11, 13–15, 23, 26, 37–9, 42, 44, 74
Waffen-SS heavy tank battalions, 126, 128
Waffenprüfungsamt 6, 11
War Office, 84

Warsaw, 130
waterproofing, 48
Weber, General, 107
Wehrtechnische Studiensammlung, 131
Wesel, 136
Weser, River, 134
West Wall, 136
Western Front, 125, 133, 136
Wezep bei Zwolle, 118, 126, 128
Wittmann, Sturmbannführer Michael, 128–30
Woll, Balthasar (Bobby), 129–30
workshop company, 93, 96, 99, 127, 134, 136

X Army Corps, 120
XXIV Pz.Korps, 134
XXVIII Army Corps, 123
XXXXI Corps, 132
XXXXVI Army Corps, 127

Zaghouan, 107
Zahnradfabrik, 19
ZF electric gearbox, 46
Zimmerit, 2
Zugführerwagen (ZW), 11, 15, 38
Zutphen, 136